TRUE

Feelings

TRUE
Feelings

Perspectives on emotions
in Christian life and ministry

Edited by **Michael P. Jensen**

APOLLOS (an imprint of Inter-Varsity Press)
Norton Street, Nottingham NG7 3HR, England
Email: ivp@ivpbooks.com
Website: www.ivpbooks.com

First published 2012

British Library Cataloguing in Publication Data
A catalogue record for this book is available from the British Library.

UK ISBN: 978-1-84474-593-7

Set in Monotype Garamond 11/13pt
Typeset in Great Britain by CRB Associates, Potterhanworth, Lincolnshire
Printed and bound in Great Britain by Ashford Colour Press Ltd, Gosport, Hampshire

Inter-Varsity Press publishes Christian books that are true to the Bible and that communicate the gospel, develop discipleship and strengthen the church for its mission in the world.

Inter-Varsity Press is closely linked with the Universities and Colleges Christian Fellowship, a student movement connecting Christian Unions in universities and colleges throughout Great Britain, and a member movement of the International Fellowship of Evangelical Students. Website: www.uccf.org.uk.

CONTENTS

List of tables   7

List of contributors   9

List of abbreviations   11

Introduction   15
Michael P. Jensen

PART 1: SERMON

1. The affections of Christ: Philippians 1:8   21
   Richard J. Gibson

PART 2: SETTING THE SCENE

2. What is at stake? A cultural overview of the emotions 37
   Andrew J. B. Cameron

3. The Puritans, theological anthropology and emotions   65
   Keith Condie

PART 3: EMOTIONS DIVINE AND HUMAN

4. Does God have feelings?   95
   Gerald Bray

5. Whose tears? The emotional life of Jesus   113
   Richard J. Gibson

6. The Spirit's perfecting work on the emotions   141
   David A. Höhne

7. On being moved: a theological anthropology
   of the emotions   165
   Michael P. Jensen

   PART 4: EMOTIONS IN THE CHRISTIAN LIFE

8. From sad and mad to glad: the pilgrim's passions   185
   Rhys S. Bezzant

9. Touching the emotions: preaching the Gospels
   for divine effects   206
   Peter G. Bolt

10. Together, with feeling: corporate worship and
    the emotions   235
    David G. Peterson

11. Music, singing and the emotions: exploring the
    connections   254
    Robert S. Smith

    Index of Scripture references   279

TABLES

2.1	Emotion-related words with a wide 'moral' range	64
5.1	Jesus' emotions in Mark's Gospel	116
5.2	Luke's parallels to Mark	126
5.3	The seven contexts where Luke attributes emotion to Jesus	132
9.1	Emotional terms in Luke 24	224

CONTRIBUTORS

Rhys S. Bezzant teaches Church History, Theology and Christian Worship at Ridley College, Melbourne. He previously worked as Anglican Chaplain at Latrobe and Melbourne University. His doctoral work focused on the ecclesiology of Jonathan Edwards, and he leads the Jonathan Edwards Center at Ridley, a satellite of the Jonathan Edwards Center at Yale. He has published on the thought of Archbishop Rowan Williams, the history of Ridley College, contributed to a volume on Edwards and justification, and awaits the publication of his thesis in 2013.

Peter G. Bolt is the Head of New Testament and Greek, Moore College, Sydney. He has recently published (with Sharon Beekman) *Silencing Satan: A Handbook of Biblical Demonology* (Wipf & Stock, 2012). His previous publications include *Jesus' Defeat of Death: Persuading Mark's Early Readers* (Cambridge University Press, 2003) and *The Cross from a Distance: Atonement in Mark's Gospel* (Apollos, 2005). He has also edited *Christ's Victory Over Evil: Biblical Theology and Pastoral Ministry* (Apollos, 2009) and (with Mark Thompson) *The Gospel to the Nations* (Apollos, 2000).

Gerald Bray is Research Director of the Latimer Trust, editor of Churchman, Research Professor at Beeson Divinity School and author of *God is Love: A Biblical and Systematic Theology* (Crossway, 2012). He is currently writing a historical theology, a commentary on the Pastoral Epistles and a full-length study of Augustine of Hippo.

Andrew J. B. Cameron is Senior Lecturer in Ethics and Social Ethics at Moore Theological College, and author of *Joined-up Life:*

A Christian Account of How Ethics Works (IVP, 2011). He is director of the Sydney-based Centre for Christian Living and chairman of the Social Issues Executive of the Anglican Diocese of Sydney.

Keith Condie is Dean of Students and teaches Ministry and Church History at Moore College. His PhD examined meditation in the thought of Richard Baxter. His research interests include Puritan spirituality and theological, psychological and pastoral perspectives on marriage.

Richard J. Gibson has been a member of the faculty at Moore College since 1994. His doctoral research focused on the relationship between divine and human emotion. He teaches Introductory Greek, New Testament, Early Church History and a course on the History of Preaching. At the moment his main research interest is the literary structure of Romans.

David A. Höhne is Senior Lecturer in Theology and Philosophy and the Dean of Part-Time Studies at Moore College. His previous publications include *Spirit and Sonship* (Ashgate, 2010) as well as chapters in *Jürgen Moltmann and Evangelical Theology* (Wipf & Stock, 2012) and *Engaging with Calvin* (Apollos, 2009).

Michael P. Jensen lectures in Theology and Church History at Moore College. He is the author of *Martyrdom and Identity: The Self on Trial* (T. & T. Clark, 2010) and (with Tom Frame) *Decisive Commitments and Defining Convictions* (Barton, 2010).

David G. Peterson served as Principal of Oak Hill College London and is now an Emeritus Faculty Member at Moore College. His most recent books are *The Acts of the Apostles*, PNTC (Eerdmans/Apollos, 2009) and *Transformed by God* (Inter-Varsity Press, 2012).

Robert S. Smith lectures in Systematic Theology and Music Ministry at Sydney Missionary and Bible College. He is the author of *Justification and Eschatology: A Dialogue with the New Perspective on Paul* (Reformed Theological Review, 2001) and a number of other articles and reviews.

ABBREVIATIONS

ABD	*Anchor Bible Dictionary*, ed. D. N. Freedman, 6 vols. (New York: Doubleday, 1992)
Add.	addendum
AV	Authorized (King James) Version
BAGD	W. Bauer, W. F. Arndt, F. W. Gingrich, F. W. Danker, *A Greek–English Lexicon of the New Testament and Other Early Christian Literature*, rev. F. W. Gingrich and F. W. Danker, 2nd ed. (Chicago: University of Chicago Press, 1979)
BDAG	W. Bauer, F. W. Danker, W. F. Arndt and F. W. Gingrich, *A Greek–English Lexicon of the New Testament and Other Early Christian Literature*, rev. and ed. F. W. Danker, 3rd ed. (Chicago: University of Chicago Press, 2000)
BECNT	Baker Exegetical Commentary on the New Testament
Bib	*Biblica*
CASE	*Centre for Apologetic Scholarship and Education*
Chm	*Churchman*
Clem.	*De clementia* (Seneca)
diss.	dissertation
Ep.	*Epistulae morales* (Seneca)
ESCT	Edinburgh Studies in Constructive Theology
ESV	English Standard Version
Eth. nic.	*Ethica nichomachea* (Aristotle)
fol.	folio
GBSNTS	Guides to Biblical Scholarship, New Testament Series

Gk.	Greek
HCSB	Holman Christian Standard Bible
Her.	*Quis rerum divinarum heres sit* (Philo)
ICC	International Critical Commentary
Ios.	*De Iosepho* (Philo)
ISBE	*The International Standard Bible Encyclopedia*, ed. G. W. Bromiley et al., *The International Standard Bible Encyclopedia*, 4 vols. (Grand Rapids: Eerdmans, 1979–86)
JBL	*Journal of Biblical Literature*
JETS	*Journal of the Evangelical Theological Society*
JPTSup	Journal of Pentecostal Theology, Supplement Series
JR	*Journal of Religion*
JRE	*Journal of Religious Ethics*
JSNT	*Journal for the Study of the New Testament*
JSNTSup	Journal for the Study of the New Testament, Supplement Series
LCC	Library of Christian Classics
ll.	lines
LXX	Septuagint
Marc.	*Ad Marciam de consolatione* (Seneca)
Mos.	*De vita Mosis* (Philo)
MS	manuscript
NET	New English Translation
NICNT	New International Commentary on the New Testament
NIDNTT	*New International Dictionary of New Testament Theology*, ed. C. Brown, 3 vols. (Exeter: Paternoster, 1975, 1976, 1978)
NIGTC	New International Greek Testament Commentary
NIV	New International Version
NJB	New Jerusalem Bible
NovT	*Novum Testamentum*
NT	New Testament
NTS	*New Testament Studies*
OT	Old Testament
Pneuma	*Journal for the Society of Pentecostal Studies*
PNTC	Pillar New Testament Commentary

Polyb.	*Ad Polybium de consolatione* (Seneca)
Prob.	*Quod omnis probus liber sit* (Philo)
RTR	*Reformed Theological Review*
SCHT	Studies in Christian History and Thought
sig.	signature
SNTSMS	Society for New Testament Studies Monograph Series
TDNT	*Theological Dictionary of the New Testament*, ed. G. Kittel and G. Friedrich, tr. G. W. Bromiley, 10 vols. (Grand Rapids: Eerdmans, 1964–76)
tr.	translated (by), translation
TynB	*Tyndale Bulletin*
Virt.	*De virtutibus* (Philo)
WBC	Word Biblical Commentary

INTRODUCTION

Michael P. Jensen

There is no place, it seems, in which feelings do not run high about feelings. The whole of western civilization is still caught between adoration of the emotions as sublime and denigration of them as merely animal. Can we trust our feelings? Should we suppress them or should we indulge them? In what part of our persons do feelings occur?

Contemporary Christianity is no less vexed about emotions. The rise of the charismatic movement in the late twentieth century, with its emphasis (many would say overemphasis) on experiential Christianity, has led to an equally strong reaction of suspicion against talk of the emotions as significant for the Christian life. Though these questions have an everyday, practical importance, they also point to profound theological questions about the nature of the triune God and the ascription of emotions to him in the Bible. Does God himself have feelings?

The chapters in this volume were prepared for a conference held at Moore Theological College, Sydney, in September 2011 under the same title. Like the conference, the book opens with a sermon by Richard Gibson that meditates on the text 'I yearn for you all with the affection of Christ Jesus' (ESV) from Philippians 1:8. Gibson points us to the desire of Paul for compassion and mercy to fill him to overflowing.

The chapters that comprise the rest of the book are divided into three parts. The first two, by Andrew Cameron and Keith Condie, serve to orient us to the subject. Cameron gives us a masterful introduction to contemporary culture's wrestling with human emotions. Condie takes a somewhat different tack, reminding today's evangelical Christians of the rich heritage to be found in Puritan thinkers like Baxter and Edwards – though it is to be critically received. Both these chapters herald one of the recurring themes of the book: that emotions are integral to human life in the created world.

The third part contains a group of theological chapters. What can be said about the divine emotions in the light of the gospel of Jesus Christ, and how are human beings to understand their emotional selves theologically? Gerald Bray gives a persuasive account of the doctrine of impassibility, but carefully nuances it to show how we can still meaningfully speak of the love of God (for example) in a personal way. The distance between divine and human emotions must be preserved if God is to remain as God. Richard Gibson, differing from Bray on the value of the term 'impassibility', shows from his reading of the Gospels that Jesus' emotions are actually meant to echo the emotions of Yahweh as they are on display in the pages of the Old Testament.

David Höhne's chapter on the perfecting work of the Spirit on the emotions builds a bridge from theology proper to a theological account of the human. In conversation with John Owen and John Calvin and in the context of contemporary Pentecostal accounts of the Spirit's work, Höhne argues that the Spirit's role is to bring human creatures to fulfil God's purposes for them, which must include their emotional lives. Patient endurance rather than ecstatic rapture is more often the emotional mark of this perfecting work. Michael Jensen's piece considers the human person as an emotional being and argues that an unnecessary dualism with a preference for reason has marred orthodox considerations of the feelings.

The final part of the book includes a number of chapters that address the emotions from the perspective of pastoral theology. Rhys Bezzant considers the emotions in the Christian life, with

Jonathan Edwards as his guide and help. Emotional maturity is surely part of authentic Christian discipleship, just as discipline of mind and body are. Peter Bolt's chapter is designed to show preachers how the gospel narratives themselves produce in their implied readers an astonishing array of emotions – without which it is impossible to read them rightly, or preach them well. David Peterson addresses the often hotly debated matter of the place of the emotions in the worship of the gathered community of Christ. Scriptural faithfulness demands that the corporate life of God's people be designed in all its facets to move our hearts in love to one another and to God, without resorting to a manufactured emotionalism. In the final chapter in this volume Rob Smith, himself a fine composer and musician, addresses the place of music and singing in both personal and congregational life. Singing the words of God, as Scripture amply shows, is a God-ordained means by which human creatures can respond to God in their full humanity.

A number of people have been instrumental in bringing this collection together. The Principal and faculty of Moore Theological College are to be thanked for their courage in agreeing to address such a potentially controversial topic at their annual School of the Theology. The contributors are to be thanked for their diligence and their willingness to bring fresh perspectives to bear on often well-travelled paths. Andrew Judd deserves a vote of thanks for his perseverance with the manuscript over his summer break. Of particular importance was the patience and assistance of Philip Duce and the team at IVP, who once again have proved themselves dedicated to supporting evangelical scholarship.

PART 1

SERMON

1. THE AFFECTIONS OF CHRIST:
PHILIPPIANS 1:8

Richard J. Gibson

Emotional Intelligence: paradigm shift or fad?

In the mid-1990s Daniel Goleman published his book *Emotional Intelligence*.[1] It was a clever synthesis of a revival of Aristotle's cognitive approach to the emotions, a decade of research in the fields of psychology and brain science, and lots of accessible anecdotes, all communicated with reforming zeal. It raced to the top of the *New York Times* bestseller list and stayed there for over a year.

The idea of Emotional Intelligence (EI) was hailed as a paradigm shift from the traditional 'far too narrow' view of human intelligence. As *Good Housekeeping* declared on the back cover of the paperback edition, 'Forget IQ. Brains may come in useful, as may social class and luck, but as a predictor of who will succeed in any area of life, EQ is the thing to worry about.' Goleman insisted that

---

1. Daniel Goleman, *Emotional Intelligence: Why It Can Matter More Than IQ* (New York: Bantam, 1995).

Emotional Quotient (EQ) was a much better indicator of which people had the potential to excel in the workplace and to have flourishing relationships.

The Emotional Intelligence phenomenon

The book tapped into the *zeitgeist*. It was a self-help book that claimed scientific support and promised renewed relationships and personal success. An industry was born. Goleman and others followed with books applying EI to the workplace[2] and leadership.[3] You can buy books that test your EQ to 'find out how emotionally intelligent you really are'.[4] The movement has spawned coaches and consultants offering EI training and administering EQ tests. Goleman himself participated in a dialogue between leading emotion scientists and the Dalai Lama, published as *Destructive Emotions: How We Can Overcome Them?*[5]

Defining Emotional Intelligence

So what is all the fuss about? One of the earliest definitions of what makes for EI was offered by Mayer and Salovey.[6] They identified four building blocks:

---

2. Daniel Goleman, *Working with Emotional Intelligence* (New York: Bantam, 1998); H. Weisinger, *Emotional Intelligence at Work: The Untapped Edge for Success* (San Francisco: Jossey-Bass, 1998); C. Cherniss and D. Goleman (eds.), *The Emotionally Intelligent Workplace* (San Francisco: Jossey-Bass, 2001).

3. Daniel Goleman, R. Boyatzis and A. McKee, *Primal Leadership: Realizing the Power of Emotional Intelligence* (Boston: Harvard Business School, 2002).

4. M. Davis, *Test Your EQ: Find out How Emotionally Intelligent You Really Are* (London: Piatkus, 2004).

5. New York: Bantam, 2003.

6. Weisinger, *Emotional Intelligence at Work*, pp. xvii–xviii.

1. The ability to accurately perceive, appraise, and express emotion.
2. The ability to access or generate feelings on demand when they can facilitate understanding of yourself or another person.
3. The ability to understand emotions and the knowledge that derives from them.
4. The ability to regulate emotions to promote emotional and intellectual growth.

To this skills-based approach have been added other trait-based definitions, and Mayer and Salovey have since then offered modified versions of these building blocks. Goleman proposes four broad domains: 'self-awareness, social awareness, self-management and relationship management', broken down further into twenty specific competencies.[7] These are the kinds of qualities that set people apart in relationships and the workplace. Are they also then the key to effective congregational life and pastoral ministry?

As Christians, what are we to make of this phenomenon? How are we to evaluate the movement from a biblical perspective? Could we have neglected the significance of emotional awareness and expression at a cost to ourselves, our families, our congregations, our evangelism, even our relationship to God? Should we crave emotional intelligence?

Paul and emotion

As a starting point for reflecting on these questions, we shall consider Paul's assurance in Philippians 1:8 to the congregation: 'For God is my witness, how I yearn [Gk. *epipothō*] for you all with the affection [Gk. *en splanchnois*] of Christ Jesus.'[8]

This is a verse where Paul expresses strong emotion. In this case it is a deep longing for his brothers and sisters in Philippi. The verb

---

7. Davis, *Test Your EQ*, p. 10.
8. Unless stated otherwise, Bible quotations in this chapter are from the ESV.

translated 'I yearn' (*epipothō*) by the ESV is rendered 'I long' by most
other versions. The Holman's more insipid 'I deeply miss' does not
quite capture the depth of feeling. The lexicon defines it as 'to have
a strong desire for someth., with the implication of need'.[9] Peter
O'Brien speaks of an 'intense yearning to be reunited with the
congregation that meant so much to him'.[10] In 2 Corinthians 5:2 it
is the word Paul uses for his aching for the resurrection body.
This is how Paul feels about Timothy when he remembers his tears
(2 Tim. 1:4). Peter likens this kind of desire to a baby's craving for
mother's milk (1 Pet. 2:2).

This is how Paul feels for the Philippians. The first eleven verses
of the letter offer insight into why Paul feels this way. From the first
day of their relationship they have been his partners in the gospel.
They stood by him while he suffered in prison. Just as importantly,
their support has been tangible through the routine times, as he has
defended and confirmed the gospel. As a result, they are lodged
securely in his heart. His deep feeling is a measure of how he values
them, cherishes their fellowship, longs to be in their presence again.

We know that Paul felt this way only because he communicated
the fact to them. This in itself is striking. People do not express this
kind of sentiment to me very often. I am secure in the fact that a
variety of people love me and value me, but only rarely is this
expressed in a manner comparable to Paul's language here. Perhaps
the closest I hear is, 'I can't wait to see you,' after a period of separation
from an old friend. Yet Paul spoke this way. Apparently, Paul
was convinced this was a way of serving them, of strengthening and
encouraging their faith, by reminding them of their place in his heart
and his intense yearning to be with them again.

I take it that Paul is genuine in sharing this deep longing. There
are some who would put this kind of expression down to rhetorical
convention or calculated persuasion. They point to the ancient
handbooks that trained people in how to manipulate people to win
a court case or a popular vote. But this is a letter, and in the ancient

9. BDAG, p. 377.
10. Peter T. O'Brien, *The Epistle to the Philippians: A Commentary on the Greek
Text*, NIGTC (Grand Rapids: Eerdmans, 1991), p. 71.

world people generally wrote letters to share themselves with their readers.[11]

More importantly, this is the man who insists elsewhere, 'We refuse to practise cunning or to tamper with God's word, but by the open statement of the truth we would commend ourselves to everyone's conscience in the sight of God' (2 Cor. 4:2b).

To the Philippians Paul vouches for his sincerity by introducing his expression of his longing with an oath, 'God is my witness.' It is very important for Paul that they know his feelings for them. As something arising from Paul's innermost parts, there is no way of authenticating his love for them. Only God can do that.[12]

Most striking of all about this remarkable expression of emotion is what follows. Paul's intense yearning springs from Jesus in some sense. His longing for them is derived from the character of Jesus' love. Paul uses an expression best understood instrumentally: he yearns for them 'with the affection of Christ Jesus'. As O'Brien puts it, Paul yearns 'with nothing less than the love of Christ himself'.[13] 'Affection' translates the plural Greek noun for the viscera or entrails (Gk. *splanchna*), rendered by the AV as 'bowels'. Paul has in mind the heart, liver and lungs as the seat of the most strongly felt emotions, such as anger and love.[14]

This noun, always in the plural, is used only once for literal entrails (Acts 1:18). Otherwise, the ESV construes it as a reference to the seat of emotion, so 'heart' (Phlm. 7, 12, 20; 1 John 3:17) or as 'affection(s)' (2 Cor. 6:12; 7:15; Phil. 2:1), and once as 'compassion' (Col. 3:12). The only instance in a Gospel refers to the 'tender mercy' of God (Luke 1:78). The cognate verb (Gk. *splanchnizomai*), which is used only in the Synoptic Gospels, is usually rendered by 'have compassion' or 'pity' (e.g. Matt. 9:36; 14:14; 15:32; 18:27; 20:34). In Philippians 1:8 most English versions opt for 'the compassion of Christ Jesus' or 'the affection of Christ Jesus'.

---

11. See Abraham J. Malherbe, *Ancient Epistolary Theorists* (Atlanta: Scholars Press, 1988), pp. 2–5.

12. O'Brien, *Philippians*, p. 71.

13. Ibid.

14. Gerald F. Hawthorne, *Philippians*, WBC 43 (Waco: Word, 1983), p. 25.

This connection between the verb, confined to the Synoptic Gospels, and its cognate noun, almost exclusively confined to the epistles, is surely significant. The evidence in the Gospels is even more noteworthy. There, of twelve uses of the verb, nine are attributed to Jesus. The other four are predicated of characters in parables: the forgiving master (Matt. 18:27), the prodigal's father (Luke 15:20) and the good Samaritan (Luke 10:33). In other words, Jesus is the only 'real' character who exhibits this quality, which is otherwise associated with God.

This is foundational for any distinctively Christian approach to the emotions. Paul claims that Jesus has profoundly shaped his capacity for loving people. The emotional intensity of Paul's longing for the Philippians is driven by the impact on Paul of Jesus' tender heart. Some would attribute Paul's emotional effusiveness to his own personality, or his native, Mediterranean culture. Paul anchors his longing for the Philippians in Jesus' compassion. The self-confessed former 'blasphemer, persecutor, and insolent opponent' (1 Tim. 1:13) now craves the company of his Christian brothers and sisters. 'The grace of our Lord overflowed . . . with the faith and love that are in Christ Jesus' (1 Tim. 1:14).

Philippians is not the only possible starting point for reflecting on the sources of Paul's emotional experience. The phrase 'with the affection of Christ Jesus' recalls another remarkable construction in 2 Corinthians 11:2. In his much more fractured relationship with the Corinthians he claims to be jealous for them 'with the jealousy of God' (my tr.). Again, Paul is motivated by an intense emotion, which galvanizes him to keep on struggling for their loyalty to him and to God. As he does so, he claims to channel the jealousy of Yahweh. In some ways this makes an even more promising starting point for integrating Paul's various emotions, in the same way that Yahweh's jealousy integrates the emotions attributed to him in the Old Testament.[15] The tender heart of Jesus, however, will suffice for this brief reflection.

---

15. Richard J. Gibson, 'Name Above All Names: Preaching Exodus', in
      Brian S. Rosner and Paul R. Williamson (eds.), *Exploring Exodus: Literary,
      Theological and Contemporary Approaches* (Nottingham: Apollos, 2008),
      pp. 208–211.

Paul's feelings for other congregations

This depth of feeling and freedom of expression is not confined to the Philippians. We could multiply examples of Paul's extravagance in exposing his inner person.

Longing for the Thessalonians (1 Thess. 2:17 – 3:9)
Take for instance Paul's longing for the Thessalonians in his first epistle to them. Listen to the way the apostle pours out his eager desire, joy, anxiety, fear, relief:

> But since we were torn away from you . . . in person not in heart, we endeavoured the more eagerly and with great desire to see you face to face . . . For what is our hope or joy or crown of boasting before our Lord Jesus at his coming? . . . For you are our glory and joy. . . .
>
> For this reason, when I could bear it no longer, I sent to learn about your faith, for fear that somehow the tempter had tempted you and our labour would be in vain.
>
> But now that Timothy has come . . . you always remember us kindly and long to see us, as we long to see you . . . For now we live, if you are standing fast in the Lord. For what thanksgiving can we return to God for you, for all the joy that we feel for your sake before our God.
> (1 Thess. 2:17 – 3:9)

Grieving over the Corinthians (2 Cor. 1:23 – 2:11)
Paul's relationship with the Corinthians has a very different emotional tenor, but no less intense. Again, he calls 'God to witness against' him should his expressions of affection prove insincere (2 Cor. 1:23). In a fragile and fraught pastoral situation, in which his own relationship with the congregation is severely tested, Paul reveals an impressive emotional awareness of his own feelings, those of the Corinthian Christians and those of the brother who has been disciplined.

Paul appears convinced that the goals of faith, obedience and reconciliation will be secured only if the strong emotions of each party are navigated openly, patiently and sensitively. Not to do so would be to remain vulnerable to being 'outwitted by Satan' (2 Cor. 2:11). This is a relationship that ought to be a source of mutual joy

(2 Cor. 1:24; 2:3). Instead, it has proven to be intensely painful for all parties. He freely admits his own 'affliction and anguish of heart' and the 'many tears' that accompanied his letter to them (2 Cor. 2:4). He insists that his aim was to communicate his love to them (2 Cor. 2:4).

At the same time he is acutely aware that he has been a source of sadness to them. Paul has acted to minimize the grief, even cancelling a visit to the Corinthians for a time, so as not to exacerbate their suffering (2 Cor. 2:1–2). Finally, he urges them to extend forgiveness to a brother who has sinned and been disciplined. Now it is time to comfort him lest he 'be overwhelmed by excessive sorrow'. They should reaffirm their love, comforting him, just as Paul has done to them (2 Cor. 2:7).

Anxious for all the churches (2 Cor. 11:28–29)
In the same letter Paul makes clear that this level of emotional engagement is not confined just to a few of the churches, those congregations at either end of the spectrum between healthy and dysfunctional. In the midst of a catalogue of his trials Paul writes:

> And, apart from other things, there is the daily pressure on me of my anxiety [Gk. *merimna*] for all the churches. Who is weak, and I am not weak? Who is made to fall, and I am not indignant? (2 Cor. 11:28–29)

The burden of responsibility is a constant source of worry or care for Paul. It comes at a cost that he recognizes but does not shirk. Such is his engagement and identification with the people in his care that news of anyone's fall causes him to burn with indignation.

Anguished by the unbelief of his kinsmen (Rom. 9:1–5)
It would be remiss to omit from this brief survey Paul's sadness over the failure of his fellow Jews to embrace their Christ. Romans 9:1–5 is yet another context where Paul solemnly underlines the depth of his feeling: 'I am speaking the truth in Christ – I am not lying; my conscience bears me witness in the Holy Spirit' (Rom. 9:1). On this occasion the Spirit corroborates the 'great sorrow and unceasing anguish' (v. 2) that Paul has in his heart for his 'kinsmen according to the flesh' (v. 3).

In a number of ways Paul emerges from these contexts as something of an ancient embodiment of EI. Here is someone able to reflect on his own experience of intense emotion and prepared to express these emotions candidly in pastoral situations, ranging from secure and settled relationships to conflict situations. As he does, he demonstrates an acute awareness of the other parties: whether it is the affectionate support of the Philippians, the reciprocated longing of the Thessalonians or the hostility and grief of the Corinthians. Yet he is not so immersed in Christian communities as to have become insensitive to the tragedy of those who reject Christ. Sorrow and anguish are never entirely absent from his heart as he goes about his mission.

Paul's expectations of other believers

The fact that Paul identifies the source of his yearning for the Philippians in the compassionate heart of Jesus raises the question of whether he expected others to be impacted in a similar way. The rest of the epistle to the Philippians suggests as much. Philippians 4:9 makes explicit that Paul offers himself as a model of the Christian life. The scope of his instructions makes it difficult to exclude the things we have heard from him at the beginning of the letter: 'What you have learned and received and heard and seen in me – practise these things, and the God of peace will be with you.'

This comprehensiveness seems to imply that Paul's own emotional responses and expression of longing constitute an aspect of this modelling process. On this reading, Paul expects the Philippians to follow him in feeling strongly for one another. This also seems to be the case in 1 Thessalonians, where their 'joy of the Holy Spirit' in the midst of suffering imitates Paul's (1 Thess. 1:6). Significantly, the Corinthian correspondence also urges imitation of Paul, as he imitates Christ (1 Cor. 4:16; 11:1).

Appealing to Jesus' tender heart (Phil. 2:1–2)
Importantly, Jesus is their resource as well. Paul can appeal to the same tender heart of Jesus that has determinatively shaped his capacity for longing, passionate affection for his brothers and sisters.

In calling them to unity and love, Paul invokes the tenderness of
Jesus again. This is the basis of Paul's appeal in Philippians 2:1–2:

> So if there is any encouragement in Christ, any comfort from love, any
> participation in the Spirit, any affection [Gk. *splanchna*] and sympathy
> [Gk. *oiktirmoi*], complete my joy by being of the same mind, having the
> same love, being in full accord and of one mind.

Though the term 'affection' is not qualified, Paul's use of the same
noun (Gk. *splanchna*) as in 1:8 suggests that he has Jesus' compassion
in mind. The word rendered 'sympathy', *oiktirmoi*, is used by Paul
elsewhere for God's mercies (Rom. 12:1; 2 Cor. 1:3; cf. Rom. 9:15).
Luke uses the related adjective twice in Luke 6:36: 'Be merciful, even
as your Father is merciful'.

Apparently, Paul invokes the compassion of Jesus as the basis for
loving, unified congregational life because he is convinced this is a
resource available to all believers as they relate to their brothers and
sisters. For this reason I wonder if the remarkable passage that
follows in 2:5–11 should be read as a hymn to Jesus' *splanchna*, his
gut-wrenching, tenderhearted compassion for sinful humanity. The
passage is understandably read as an exposition of Jesus' humility
(Phil. 2:3, 8). However, the journey would never have begun if Jesus
had not been moved by compassion for our desperate need.

The tender compassion of Christ in other congregations

Paul's concern that Jesus' tender compassion should shape Christian
relationships is found not only in Philippians. The Ephesians are
exhorted, 'Be kind to one another, tender-hearted [Gk. *eusplanchnoi*],
forgiving one another, as God in Christ forgave you. Therefore be
imitators of God, as beloved children' (Eph. 4:32 – 5:1). As God's
'chosen ones' the Colossians are urged to put on 'heartfelt compassion' (Gk. *splanchna*) and 'kindness' (Gk. *oiktirmou*, Col. 3:12 HCSB).
The apostle Peter shares the same vision, calling on the scattered
believers, 'all of you, have unity of mind, sympathy, brotherly love,
a tender heart [Gk. *eusplanchnoi*], and a humble mind' (1 Pet. 3:8).
For John, the absence in a person of this response in the face of
material need raises serious questions about the reality of God's
presence in their life (1 John 3:17).

Should we crave Emotional Intelligence?

So should we crave Emotional Intelligence? Is this a vital ingredient
missing from our lives, our churches, our pastoral relationships, our
training of leaders? More than one person has told me that one of
the biggest deficiencies amongst graduates of my own theological
college is a lack of emotional intelligence. They point to clumsiness
in pastoral situations, an inability to read what is going on for other
people and insensitivity to the responses they arouse. Does the EI
movement offer resources we are foolish to neglect?

It is fair to say that the jury is still out on the validity and value
of the EI movement. In recent years it has been subjected to increasing, critical assessment. In 2009 Zeidner, Matthews and Roberts
published *What We Know About Emotional Intelligence*, the most com-
prehensive review of the status of EI to date. They aim to 'present
the state of an emerging science of emotional intelligence', drawing
on both their own and a growing body of research.[16]

Their findings are mixed. The book laments the way popular
literature on the subject has 'far outpaced scientific research'.[17] EI
is difficult to define and even harder to measure. The theoretical
basis of EI is not yet secure. EI does not prove to be the predictor
of happiness and effectiveness that its advocates have claimed. It
has the hallmarks of a fad: 'fast growth trajectory', 'promise of a
great deal more than can be delivered' and the 'evocation of intense
reactions, both positive and negative'. In answer to the question 'Will
EI stay or will it go?' Zeidner, Matthews and Roberts answer, 'Only
time will tell.' They also insist that the 'spirit of "letting a hundred
flowers bloom"' should not excuse 'poor science' and unsubstanti-
ated claims.[18]

So I remain unconvinced that EI is the paradigm shift that will
transform our Christian lives, families, small groups, congregations

---

16. M. Zeidner, G. Matthews and R. D. Roberts, *What We Know About
    Emotional Intelligence: How It Affects Learning, Work, Relationships, and Our
    Mental Health* (Cambridge, Mass.: MIT Press, 2009), p. xi.

17. Ibid., p. x.

18. Ibid., p. 371.

and ministry training. That does not mean there is nothing for which
we should be grateful. Goleman and others have popularized a vast
body of serious research that has forced us to rethink the place of
emotions. They have crafted ways of talking about our anger, fear,
compassion, amazement, anxiety, disappointment and joy that allow
our generation to reflect on the information and motivation these
emotions bring to our lives. In turn, this has forced us to reflect on
what place these are given in the Bible without the assumption that
they are peripheral to life and faith.

I long to be more like Paul

What I do know is that I want to be more like Paul. Paul passed
through a paradigm shift far greater than the EI movement can offer.
Jesus took hold of his life, his goals, his relationships, his priorities.
But I do not want to lose sight of the fact that this paradigm shift
profoundly impacted Paul emotionally.

I want to be more like Paul in the way he genuinely loved and
longed for people, the way he rejoiced over them constantly in
prayer. I want to burn with indignation when my brothers and sisters
are caused to stumble, and to grieve over our sin and broken relationships. I want his tender heart, and I want to communicate that
more clearly and fully to people other than my children and dearest
friends. I do not want to do so in order to draw attention to myself.
Rather, I want to serve and strengthen them the way Paul did. I want
to learn how to enter into the most demanding pastoral situations
aware of the responses being triggered in me and in those I seek to
care for and nurture.

Philippians reinforces the rightness of my desire to be more like
Paul in this area of life. More importantly, Paul directs me to the
one who brought about the transformation in him and who supplies
the resources for each one of us to grow in our love for our brothers
and sisters and those outside Christ. It is Christ's compassion that
I really long for. It is Christ's tender-heartedness that can transform
our fellowship, our friendships and our families.

At the same time, Paul's letters come with a warning. Conformity
to Christ will not always see me winning in the workplace or

influencing people for my own benefit. Paul is emphatic that you cannot have the 'affections of Christ' without the 'afflictions of Christ'. I am not sure any recipe for EI would advocate a lifestyle that is 'afflicted in every way ... perplexed ... persecuted ... struck down' (2 Cor. 4:8–9). But Paul did. The affections of Christ brought him the afflictions of Christ. He was prepared to be 'always carrying in the body the death of Jesus, so that the life of Jesus may also be manifested in our bodies ... always being given over to death for Jesus' sake, so that the life of Jesus also may be manifested in our mortal flesh' (2 Cor. 4:10–11). Paul was content for death to be 'at work in us, but life in you' (2 Cor. 4:12). Paul was not expecting to be a star. Few would have regarded him a 'success' in human terms and it is clear his personal dreams did not all come true.

Conformed to the image of his Son

Philippians 1:8 teaches me that what I should really yearn for is to be conformed to the image of the Son in the area of my emotions. I cannot imagine any formula for EI coming up with the incarnation. But the tender-hearted mercies of the Father and compassion of the Son did. I want him to live in me so that I love with the affection of Christ. I want to feel with his tender heart, be moved by his compassion, long for people and their welfare with his gut-wrenching commitment. I want to weep over sin and unbelief because that is what he did. And I want to know the joy of living for the Father's will. Like Paul's experience of apostolic responsibility, Jesus' incarnate life also reminds me that I cannot expect to have his affections without his afflictions.

PART 2

SETTING THE SCENE

2. WHAT IS AT STAKE? A CULTURAL OVERVIEW OF THE EMOTIONS

Andrew J. B. Cameron

So you're browsing a book on the emotions. What drew you here? Was it, perhaps, some *emotion*?

- *Curiosity* perhaps – a dawning intrigue about something worth knowing?
- Was it *frustration*, that sense of having missed out on something for far too long?
- Do you take *delight* at the prospect of reading about something so interesting?
- Were you somehow *envious*, wanting and needing what others have?
- Was it the *hope* of finding more about something dear to you?

'Well,' you might say, 'it was one of those things . . . but those are thoughts, aren't they? How are they emotions?' Welcome to a surprisingly complex scene!

My daughter was about a month old. We were in a park at dusk. A few minutes before, my wife and I had been on some rocks near the sea where we'd had a slightly scary moment near the pounding surf. So we were already in a heightened emotional state, and by now the light was dimming to the point where I could hardly see. Across the park I saw a smudge – a shadow coming towards me – and heard a deep, throaty bark. As it loomed closer, I thought, *Large dog*. My veins ran cold and I remember the icy clarity of the thought that formed next, with diamantine precision: *If that dog comes near this baby, I will rip it to pieces.* I've never killed a dog, yet I knew exactly how I would kill it.

The dog came to within about 10 metres where there was light enough for me to see that it was actually two dogs – a middle-sized one and a little one. The bigger one stopped barking. Both came to a dead stop and took a careful look at me emerging from *their* dusk. Something about my demeanour was amply apparent to them, and immediately both turned and fled. I'd never seen anything like it before and haven't since.

Rarely have I had such a primal experience. Were there thoughts? Yes. Was it an emotion? Definitely. What was it? Anger, although the coolest, clearest anger I've ever had. Was it voluntary? No. Was it good? Was it Christian? We shall have to wait and see.

This deceptively simple word *emotion* turns out to encompass many areas of human experience, and many disputes about the nature of that experience. A few simple questions help us to glimpse the difficulties involved:

- How much are emotions related to thoughts?
- Are there good and bad emotions?
- Are there 'Christian' emotions?
- Are emotions involuntary? Can you command an emotion?

There are no simple answers to any of these questions, partly because the concept of emotion has a complicated cultural history. If we are naive about that history, we restrict the options available to us for reflecting on emotion.

In this chapter I shall attempt to orient us to some of the issues at stake in reflecting on the experiences we call 'emotions'. I've called it 'a cultural overview of the emotions'. Even that title may be too extravagant, but I want to orient us to some relevant twists and turns in western thought about it. I shall do that in six sections:

1. *How to get our bearings?* A quick look at science and philosophy.
2. *Recent history*: some twentieth-century thinking.
3. *Evaluative judgments, but no less than a feeling*: what the 'cognitive' view offers.
4. *'Emotion', passion or affection?* The way nomenclature misleads us.
5. *Elliott's proposal*: a biblical scholar on emotion.
6. *Augustine versus the Stoics*: a theologian on emotion.

Although I take the Bible as our authority in matters of life, I haven't dealt head-on with what it says about emotion because this is an area where our reading of Scripture is *especially* misled if we fail to notice our environment and interrogate our assumptions. Therefore throughout this 'cultural overview' I shall reflect on some aspects of Scripture and on our attempts to use Scripture in relation to emotion.

How to get our bearings

Definitions for 'emotion' vary widely. Some argue that emotions are a kind of experience that is primarily 'feelingful', while for others they are a complex kind of judging thought that is not a feeling, and a spectrum of views prevails between these poles. The difficulties of definition are summarized by Robert C. Solomon:

> It would be a mistake . . . to put too much emphasis on the term 'emotion', for its range and meaning have altered significantly over the years, due in part to changes in theories about emotion. So too, the word 'passion' has a long and varied history, and we should beware of the misleading assumption that there is a single, orderly, natural class of phenomena that is simply designated by different labels in different languages at different times. The language of 'passion' and 'emotion' has a history in which various feelings, desires, sentiments, moods, attitudes and more explosive responses enter and from which they exit, depending not on arbitrary philosophical stipulation but on an extensive network of social, moral, cultural and psychological factors. Thus we will often find that the focus is not an emotion as such, but rather

some particular class of emotion and its role in the manners or morals of the time.[1]

How might we untangle this complexity? In his excellent summary of recent scientific research into emotion, Dylan Evans begins by listing a set of *basic emotions* found in all the people of the world: disgust, joy, surprise, anger, fear and distress.[2] These are based on the ground-breaking ethnological work of Paul Ekman, who found that people in widely differing cultures facially express and identify the same basic emotions.

Citing philosopher Paul E. Griffiths, Evans also points to *higher cognitive emotions* such as romantic love (which was not, *pace* C. S. Lewis, 'invented' in medieval times). These include love, guilt, shame, embarrassment, pride, envy and jealousy, and are fundamentally social. Some basic emotions can be co-opted for social purposes (e.g. disgust). Higher cognitive emotions can include experiences that are recognizable to us but are better described in another language; for example, Japanese *amae* (a pervasive feeling of social well-being and belonging).[3] Finally, there are *culturally specific emotions* – emotions specific to certain cultures, such as 'being a wild pig' in New Guinea. This emotion is specific to newly married and indebted young men, who are viewed with pity as they tear up the camp and lightly attack random others. Their debts are usually forgiven.[4]

Griffiths uses a slightly different taxonomy:

- autonomic bodily reflexes (e.g. 'fear', 'aggression');
- strongly expressed personal concerns (e.g. 'lust', 'longing', 'ambition', 'outrage'); and

---

1. Robert C. Solomon, 'The Philosophy of Emotions', in Michael Lewis and Jeannette M. Haviland-Jones (eds.), *Handbook of Emotions*, 2nd ed. (New York: Guilford, 2000), p. 4.
2. Dylan Evans, *Emotion: The Science of Sentiment* (Oxford: Oxford University Press, 2001), p. 7.
3. Ibid., pp. 1–3, 27–30.
4. Ibid., pp. 17–20.

- social performances (e.g. 'patriotism', 'indignance', 'revenge').[5]

If we presume to map each range onto the other, we arrive at three broad domains, which may be summarized as follows:

- basic emotions (Evans) and autonomic bodily reflexes (Griffiths);
- higher cognitive emotions (Evans) and strongly expressed personal concerns (Griffiths); and
- culturally specific emotions (Evans) and social performances (Griffiths).

These three domains begin at what is more innate, and proceed to the less innate. They range from emotions that are fastest to appear to those that 'gestate' for much longer before they appear.[6] The first domain encompasses responses to many stimuli; the last expressly relates to social functioning.

Given this range, Griffiths argues that 'emotion' is merely a false categorization, an obsolete and inappropriate word for three quite different arenas of experience. To denote them all as 'emotion' is as false a grouping as the 'superlunary objects' of ancient astronomy, where everything beyond the orbit of the moon was held to be of the same kind.[7] When discourse about 'emotion' suffers under its unhelpfully large semantic range, we often find ourselves referring to different things and equivocating in our utterances. In many discussions of emotion, we simply talk past one another.

So, rather than simply discussing 'biblical emotions', we might heuristically experiment with domains of thought such as those above. It seems fair to assume that biblical authors are familiar with basic emotions. And it seems very clear that higher cognitive

---

5. Paul E. Griffiths, *What Emotions Really Are: The Problem of Psychological Categories* (Chicago: University of Chicago Press, 1997), pp. 14–17 and *passim*. (The examples are my own.)

6. Evans, *Emotion*, p. 30.

7. Griffiths, *What Emotions Really Are*, pp. 14–17.

emotions, with their social emphasis, are amply expressed in Scripture (e.g. in the language of the NT virtue- and vice-lists). We might also need to keep an eye out for emotions like *amae* or 'being like a wild pig' that are specific to the culture of a biblical author, although I cannot yet think of a possible candidate.

Recent history

Emotions are now Balkanized among many disciplines:

> in primacy of interest, disciplinary seemliness, and volume of empirical work, psychologists 'own' the topic of emotions. Yet, given the scope, span, and ramifications of emotion phenomena, many other disciplines are also legitimately concerned with affective life. Physiologists link emotions to anatomical structures and processes; anthropologists tie emotions to particular cultural logics and practices; historians trace emotions of today to emotions of the past; ethnologists seek what is phylogenetically given as well as distinctively human in emotions; and sociologists examine how emotions are triggered, interpreted, and expressed by virtue of human membership in groups.[8]

Ten years after this assessment neurobiologists might now also claim to 'own' emotion. Psychology's 'ownership' of emotion was actually a sprawling century-long tussle among various competitors. This landscape is surveyed by William Lyons[9] and Robert C. Solomon.[10] Lyons rightly observes the inestimable effect of Descartes upon modern psychology: 'From the seventeenth century to roughly the end of the nineteenth century, the Cartesian theory

8. Theodore D. Kemper, 'Social Models in the Explanation of Emotions', in Lewis and Haviland-Jones, *Handbook of Emotions*, p. 45.

9. William Lyons, *Emotion* (Aldershot: Gregg Revivals, 1993; originally published Cambridge: Cambridge University Press, 1980), pp. 1–52.

10. Robert C. Solomon, *The Passions: Emotions and the Meaning of Life*, 2nd ed. (Indianapolis: Hackett, 1993).

was the orthodox theory,'[11] according to which the 'emotions' were 'hidden' in an immaterial soul.

Eventually, psychologists and philosophers rejected the private and 'mentalist' nature of the Cartesian view,[12] but retained an essential hiddenness to emotion in a nineteenth-century 'hydraulic model', which emerged under the influence of Freud. On this view, each emotion is a wild, alien force that presses up against rational thought, like steam against a valve that contains it. The model generates words such as 'repression', 'energy', 'overwhelmed', and so on. (Brain structure reveals a kernel of truth to the 'hydraulic model': the frontal parts of our brain prevent the impulsivity associated with emotion. If we damage this region of the brain, we become impulsive and antisocial, and lack insight.) Christians may misread the Bible under the influence of the 'hydraulic model'. For example 1 Peter 2:11, the exhortation to 'abstain from the desires of the flesh that wage war against the soul' (NRSV), could be taken as a condemnation of emotion as such.

At the end of the nineteenth century William James shifted attention from the hiddenness of emotion to the body's physiological disturbances. Lyons cites the 'core' of James's theory:

> bodily changes follow directly the perception of the exciting fact, and . . . that our feeling of the same changes as they occur is the emotion. Common-sense says, we lose our fortune, are sorry and weep . . . The hypothesis here to be defended says . . . we feel sorry because we cry.[13]

After being independently propounded by Carl Lange, this position came to be known as the James–Lange thesis. According to it, emotions arise from their physiological correlates. (Interestingly, some modern research may support it. Our feelings of empathy, for example, may be heightened or even triggered when our own facial expressions faintly mimic another's.)

---

11. Lyons, *Emotion*, p. 2.
12. See further Anthony Kenny, *Action, Emotion and Will* (London: Routledge & Kegan Paul, 1963), pp. 13–16.
13. Lyons, *Emotion*, p. 13, citing William James (dated 1884).

It is only a short step to twentieth-century behaviourism, where emotions are *only* the observable behaviours they generate. Behaviourism was interested solely in physiological changes, and forbade reference to inner states. The behaviourists exclusively measured physiological and behavioural responses, and behavioural psychology was at best agnostic and at worst hostile to the feelingful inner world of what it disparagingly called 'folk psychology'. 'The "emotions" are excellent examples of the fictional causes to which we commonly attribute behaviour,' declared eminent behaviourist B. F. Skinner.[14] Such unrealistic behaviourist scepticism led in turn to a 'cognitive revolution' in psychology, which I shall outline in the following section.

It is worth acknowledging that these twentieth-century developments were largely motivated by properly scientific aims. Human motivation and behaviour, like any other aspect of the material order, can be observed for regular patterns, and theories can then be formed. The best aspects of psychology arise from observations and analyses of thoughts, feelings and acts that fall into regular bounds. People use behaviours to increase well-being or reduce anxiety. Those behaviours may be illicit and harmful or helpful and constructive, but such evaluations are not relevant to psychology's scientific aims. The cultural upshot of the practice of science was more troubling: any moral analysis of emotion effectively became impossible in twentieth-century emotion discourse.

Evaluative judgments, but no less than a feeling

To anyone who cares about the feelingful aspect of emotion, the label 'cognitive' in psychology's 'cognitive revolution' does not sound very promising. But this label simply refers to the view that each emotion is *a complex and feelingful judgment about affairs in the world*. Thoughts and feelings are interwoven into complex sets that we call

---

14. B. F. Skinner (1953); cited in Jaak Panksepp, *Affective Neuroscience: The Foundations of Human and Animal Emotions* (New York: Oxford University Press, 1998), p. 9.

'emotions'. As Matthew Elliott puts it, 'Rightly understood, our emotions are connected to what we focus on, what we know, what we value, and what we believe. What we *think* and how we *feel* work together to point us to the truth.'[15]

Cognitive theories of emotion have a very useful central feature that behaviourism could not offer: that something about an 'emotion' can usually be thought and articulated. ('My anger towards that dog arises from my precious estimate of my daughter and my fear that it will hurt her.') In other words, emotions have their own logic. Contrary to the 'hydraulic model' (which imagined an emotion to be the opposite of a thought) each emotion is an interwoven package of thought and feeling. This observation is now amply supported by what is known of the brain's structure, where neuronal bundles join regions associated with basic emotions to regions that govern cognition.

One such cognitive approach is offered by Lyons.[16] He takes each specific occurrence of emotion as the paradigmatic unit of consideration. (He avoids considering emotions dispositionally to sidestep semantic debate over whether an 'emotion' differs from a 'mood'.) Each occurrence involves an evaluation *and* a significant physiological change. These two facets of an emotion are necessarily constitutive to it; and the evaluations usually have a 'personal twist' – that is, they relate specifically to the person doing the evaluating. That an evaluation is involved distinguishes emotional experiences from other physiological experiences. That a physiological change is involved distinguishes emotional thought from other forms of thought. Different emotions can be discerned by their different evaluative aspects. An emotion's central evaluative aspect brings about emotional behaviour, because the evaluation rationally expresses some desire. (Therefore on the cognitive view, denunciations of emotion as 'irrational' are simply fanciful. The detractor does not share or understand the rationality of the one who emotes.)

---

15. Matthew Elliott, *Feel: The Power of Listening to Your Heart* (Carol Stream, Ill.: Tyndale House, 2008), p. 117, emphases original.

16. Lyons, *Emotion*, pp. 52–69.

Scripture seems to assume something like this cognitive approach. For example, when the apostle James mentions two kinds of wisdom (Jas 3:13 – 4:12), he focuses upon *zēlos* (envy/jealousy) and *eritheia* (rivalry/ambition, v. 14). Both are arguably 'higher cognitive emotions'. The subsequent analysis (3:16 – 4:1) observes that where these emotions exist, there arises disorder, war and discord. Hence when *hēdonē* (v. 1) is mentioned – variously translated as 'cravings' (HCSB, NRSV), 'desires' (NIV, NJB), 'passions' (ESV NET) or 'lusts' (AV) – the point is not to condemn all desire. Rather, the author brings to our awareness the way our most powerfully held construals of what matters most – our desires – make intelligible our jealousy and rivalry.[17] The higher cognitive evaluations in this passage are expressly social, and drive 'emotional' behaviour via desire. Unlike our modern morally neutral emotion discourse, James's analysis enables us to proceed to a moral evaluation of the emotions mentioned in verse 1.

So far I have been complimentary about cognitive theories of emotion. However, there is great variance among cognitive theorists in the degree to which they admit emotions as 'feelingful'. The matter is a storm centre of dispute. Cognitive approaches can become fallaciously reductive. Michael Stocker tells of his corres-pondence with 'a respected philosopher who has done considerable work on emotions', who insisted that he played with children, made love and engaged in community activities – all without feelings. This philosopher thought that feelings were not necessary for a good life, and are unnecessary to an account of emotion. He did not mean that he had no momentous feelings, but that he had no feelings at all. Yet on meeting the philosopher, Stocker found him to be friendly, outgoing and personable.[18]

---

17. The five NT occurrences of *hēdonē* are generally negative (Luke 8:14; Titus 3:3; Jas 4:1, 3; 2 Pet. 2:13), although it is more positively regarded in OT literature (LXX Num. 11:8; Prov. 17:1; Wisdom 7.2; 16.20). It is evaluated from various perspectives in 4 Maccabees (1.20, 24, 28, 33; 5.23; 6.35; 9.31), although with quite different conclusions than are implied by the Protestant canonical references.

18. Michael Stocker, *Valuing Emotions* (Cambridge: Cambridge University Press, 1996), p. xvii.

We saw a moment ago in the Bible that feelingful longing can make us bad. But Stocker's story reminds us to wonder whether the absence of feeling can also be bad. It was not obviously so in the case of the respected philosopher, but the psychopath is someone who reports no feelings about others.

Some 'feelingless' discourse in cognitive emotion theory trades upon feelings that are not emotions (such as itchiness) to assert that other feelings, which may be emotions (such as affection), also are not emotions. I recounted Lyons's view above because I think it is an elegant cognitive theory that excludes 'feelingless' cognitive theories. Other trenchant rebuttals exist against views that emotion is essentially feelingless,[19] and I am persuaded by these. As anthropologist R. Shweder puts it, 'Three-year-olds, Ifaluk islanders, and psychoanalysts (in other words, almost everyone, except perhaps the staunchest of positivists) recognize that emotions are *feelings*.'[20]

This dispute between 'feelingless' and 'feelingful' cognitivists is reflected in Christian discourse, when it is sometimes claimed that biblical 'love', 'joy' and 'hope' are thoughts that need not be feelingful. Matthew Elliott offers a compendium of quotations from various Christian preachers and thinkers who think these words are not primarily feelingful, but are basically thoughts.[21]

I believe this kind of strategy represents a well-motivated, but ultimately misguided, strategy among preachers. (Elliott is less sanguine!) Thinking that our emotional state is basically beyond our control (perhaps on a 'hydraulic' view), they seek not to create a load too great to bear. So they address what they take to be within our control: our cognition and rationality. It *seems* kinder to speak of 'love' or 'kindness' as sets of actions and choices, because we think we have control over actions and choices. A feeling cannot be commanded; but love is commanded; the Bible is never erroneous

---

19. Ibid., pp. xvii, xix, 17–18, 25–26, and *passim*; and David Pugmire, *Rediscovering Emotion* (Edinburgh: Edinburgh University Press, 1998), p. 104 and *passim*. See Justin Oakley, *Morality and the Emotions* (London: Routledge, 1992), for a thorough survey.

20. Cited in Stocker, *Valuing Emotions*, pp. 17–18, emphasis original.

21. Elliott, *Feel*, pp. 15–17.

in what it commands; therefore love is not a feeling. (Three of the four statements in the syllogism are profoundly indebted to the German philosopher of the Enlightenment, Immanuel Kant.) Conversely, it seems cruel to speak of love and kindness as including affection towards someone, because we think we cannot switch our feelingful selves on and off.

But these preachers and thinkers believe that our feelingful aspect *can* be altered through preaching and persuasion. What follows, they hope, is a kind of 'trickle-down' effect. Theology offers the kind of cognitive reframing that can result in an altered emotional profile. Yet there is no guarantee that such an altered profile will result in the present: it may prove only to be God's gift to each of us in the eschaton.

Although well intended, this kind of approach can become effectively Pelagian if changes to the emotions are made finally to rely upon the power of mind and will. The approach also begs the question of whether God commands what he alone can give: in this case, a reordering of the affections. Elliott is utterly hostile to what I call the 'trickle-down' view. He describes 'a knot in the pit of my stomach' during a typical 'bait and switch' sermon, where a promise of joy to sustain us in hard times was finally interpreted as another kind of thinking and an effort of mental will.[22]

When lust, jealousy, anger and envy are contrasted with love, joy, peace, kindness and faithfulness (Gal. 5:19–22), and when the first three are so overtly emotional, surely it breaks the text to try to claim that these last are free of affection. Since these are fruits of the Spirit, preachers may rightly hold out the hope that the Spirit works a kind of affection that we cannot easily work in ourselves.

'Emotion', passion or affection?

By introducing the term 'affection' I allude to another complaint that has been made against the term 'emotion'. Thomas Dixon argues that until the eighteenth century the word 'emotion' simply

---

22. Ibid, p. 100.

referred to 'disturbances' in our bodies. The semantic 'heavy lifting' was done by words such as 'passion', 'affection' and 'virtue'.[23]

In the eighteenth century a profound and lively Christian 'soul science' was steeped in Christian theology and anthropology, as espoused (among others) by Jonathan Edwards and Isaac Watts. Just as the apostle James located passion and affection in a social and moral context, eighteenth-century theological psychology did so by means of four distinctive characteristics:

1. The absence of a reason–passion dichotomy.
2. A distinction between 'passion' and 'affection'.
3. A moral (and social) contextualization of the passions and affections.
4. The importance of the 'soul'.[24]

The passions in traditional Christian psychology form only a subset of those phenomena that move us. The affections – the movements of our 'souls' towards what is good – are the crucial second half of the traditional Christian picture. Our 'affections' motivate us towards whatever was good, while our 'passions' propel us towards bad ends. So 'passions' often had an overtone of whatever drove antisocial acts, while 'affections' were the kinds of sympathies

---

23. For Thomas Dixon on 'passion' and 'affection', see n. 26 below. The addition of 'virtue' to this account is indebted to Gertrude Himmelfarb, *The De-moralization of Society: From Victorian Virtues to Modern Values* (New York: Knopf, 1995).

24. It is beyond our scope to consider the role of the 'soul' in a Christian account of emotion. I believe that body–soul monism is biblically defensible (so that the soul is the emergent property of a human body that is preserved by God for the resurrection body). If so, we may provisionally treat older references to the soul as similar to what is now known of the central nervous system and its consciousness. See further Hans Walter Wolff, *Anthropology of the Old Testament*, tr. Margaret Kohl (London: SCM, 1974); and John W. Cooper, *Body, Soul, and Life Everlasting: Biblical Anthropology and the Monism–Dualism Debate*, 2nd ed. (Grand Rapids: Eerdmans; Leicester: Apollos, 2000).

that promoted care for others. In this way, our feelingful aspect was understood within a wider moral and social framework.

The eighteenth-century discourse Dixon describes had its roots in a much earlier century, and arose from a trinitarian and soteriological framework. It constituted a way of thinking for much Christian pastoral practice. It did however lead to its own problems. Our language of 'emotion' is deliberately amoral: emotions are neither bad nor good. We may observe them simply as phenomena, postponing any moral evaluation of resultant behaviours and antecedent desires. But the language of passion and affection carries morality already embedded. In such discourse it becomes difficult simply to accept and work with a person in a state of brokenness or in a heightened emotional state. (In this volume Keith Condie examines the related problem of Puritan introspection.)

The nineteenth century saw the discourse on emotion effectively secularized; and, as we have seen, twentieth-century thinkers observed and analysed emotion as a set of phenomena in its own right without much reference to moral implications.[25] This modern development replaced a rainbow of 'involuntary appetites', 'passions', 'commotions of animal nature', 'moral sentiments' and 'voluntary affections' with the undifferentiated concept of 'emotions'. So, not only do 'emotions' come to be considered as morally neutral phenomena (twentieth-century thought made 'emotion' a single and

---

25. We can see how the term 'passion' also now spans the moral spectrum. The ten senses for 'passions' supplied by the *Oxford English Dictionary*, 2nd ed. (1989) on CD-ROM (v. 4.0.0.3) (Oxford: Oxford University Press, 2009), include 'an eager outreaching of the mind towards something; an overmastering zeal or enthusiasm for a special object; a vehement predilection'. This would seem to describe what we have when our awe is inspired. But 'passion' is also 'an outburst of anger or bad temper' – sometimes, then, it is a form of unmitigated evil. Yet 'passion' can sometimes be used value-neutrally, to describe 'any kind of feeling in which the mind is affected or moved; a vehement, commanding, or overpowering emotion', which is simply a broad initial description of experience full of feelings. None of these definitions enables us to settle whether or not 'passion' is a moral category.

self-referential word, stripped of theological or moral reference and devoid of the previous centuries' finer distinctions), but they have become the kind of false categorization outlined above.[26]

Today, then, most people (whether Christian or not) find it odd to ask whether a given emotion is 'good' or 'bad', and make such judgments only about actions. We tend also to be what psychologist Diane Tice calls 'mood purists . . . people who [say] they would never try to change a mood since, in their view, all emotions are "natural" and should be experienced just as they present themselves'.[27] Conversely, an older generation of Christians with a 'hydraulic' view will be suspicious of nearly all emotions, depending on rationality to force emotions down so as to act well.

So what should Christians do? Should we continue with the broad modern category 'emotion', or try to return to those older concepts of 'passion' and 'affection'? I am attracted to some advantages in the concepts of 'passion' and 'affection', for these words reintroduce the evaluative nature of emotion that has been stripped out of modern emotion terminology. But they risk oversimplistic use (an artefact of our repristinating the terms, not necessarily a feature of the earlier centuries' usage). The Bible contains another nuanced language of emotional experience, and there is no short cut to a careful inductive assessment of this biblical language. For example, in the New Testament vice- and virtue-lists each term is a fascinating specific package of a thought, an emotion and an action, all characterized as an ongoing and settled pattern. This is an incredibly efficient way of describing complex human experiences in a morally ordered way.[28]

---

26. For the details of this account, see these works by Thomas Dixon: 'Theology, Anti-Theology and Atheology: From Christian Passions to Secular Emotions', *Modern Theology* 15.3 (1999), pp. 297–330; *From Passions to Emotions: The Creation of a Secular Psychological Category* (Cambridge: Cambridge University Press 2003), pp. 45–61 and *passim*; and 'Revolting Passions', *Modern Theology* 27.2 (2011), pp. 298–312.

27. Cited in Daniel Goleman, *Emotional Intelligence: Why It Can Matter More Than IQ* (London: Bloomsbury, 1996), p. 58.

28. Andrew J. B. Cameron, *Joined-up Life: A Christian Account of How Ethics Works* (Nottingham: Inter-Varsity Press, 2011), pp. 194–202.

I also examine *epithymia*, 'strong desire', in the appendix below. There are more terms for 'strong desire' than *epithymia*, with one team of lexicographers finding over twenty words inhabiting the conceptual field of 'strong desire'. But in *epithymia* we begin to see the complexity of feelingful human phenomena in Scripture. Misreadings of Scripture have produced a distorted and sub-Christian account of desire. This distortion is a 'demonizing' of desire, because it presumes that all desire is represented and described by the dark side of desire.

In the New Testament *epithymia* is often guilty by association or through collocation with some negative adjective or verb (see Appendix, §§b–c). It is a word that attracts several negative quali-fiers: 'deceitful', 'lustful', 'worldly', 'corrupt', 'debauched', 'ungodly'. But, looking more closely, in the LXX *epithymia* is used across the moral spectrum (Appendix, §a), more often positively than nega-tively. We also find several New Testament texts where strong desire is morally unobjectionable, and even reflects moral excellence (Appendix, §§d–e). Disciples, prophets and angels long to see divine truth; apostles long to see Christ, or to see their people, or for their people to progress in faith; and young men rightly long to care for God's people. Also, a most surprising twist becomes apparent when in Luke 22:15 Jesus alludes to the LXX translation of Numbers 11:4 by using *epithymia* twice in a double-barrelled phrase (an emphatic conjoining of the noun and cognate verb) to tell of how ardently he longs to eat the Passover with his disciples. He takes a phrase associated with the illicit craving for meat in the desert and eclipses it with his most righteous craving that is every bit as intense. Jesus reverses desire in its most negative form to make desire as good as it can be.[29]

But our task needs to go even beyond this kind of biblical lexi-cography. The following sections set out both a recent and an ancient attempt to go further. They may also help us to understand our emotions.

---

29. I am indebted to Richard Gibson for this insight.

Elliott's proposal

Matthew Elliott builds on his scholarly treatment of New Testament emotion language[30] with a popular work, *Feel* (mentioned above), which challenges Reformed Christian thought on emotion.[31] I have already outlined some of Elliott's concerns. There is much to appreciate in his work. He shows how our modern views of emotion have little in common with the views of the biblical authors, who show God's wanting people to experience deep affection for him and for each other (i.e. 'love'), woven through with joy, hope and the right kinds of hate (for evil, not finally for people). There is an infectious style and tone in *Feel* that achieves Elliott's goal to help us feel differently. The book is laced with stories, exhortations and examples that enable us to visualize and imagine new emotions. Elliott describes such an experience in the company of the quadriplegic Christian Joni Earickson-Tada, whose words he could not quite remember, but whose hopeful presence filled him with hope.[32] In turn, his own description of her 'rubs off' a little on the reader.

Elliott's strategy in this respect is reminiscent of Augustine's comments in a sermon delivered in Carthage. Drawing vividly upon

---

30. Matthew Elliott, *Faithful Feelings: Emotion in the New Testament* (Leicester: Inter-Varsity Press, 2005).

31. Elliott does not address Pentecostal views. It seems to me that a major difference, if not a defining difference, between recent Reformed and Pentecostal Christianity is in precisely this arena. My impression is that for some Pentecostal and charismatic Christians, the presence or absence of good feelings in a Christian directly results from the presence or absence of the Holy Spirit in her, so that emotions are not even finally a function of being human. Good emotions arrive when the Holy Spirit arrives, whereas bad emotions arise from elsewhere – from evil spirits perhaps. In contrast, Reformed Christians have sometimes sounded as if we believe that the Holy Spirit primarily affects only a person's thoughts and actions, and that our emotional state bears no relationship at all to the work of the Spirit. Both views are, I think, mistaken.

32. Elliott, *Feel*, pp. 182–183.

the experience of the stadium, Augustine reminds the (apparently young male) listeners of what comes over them there. Simply by watching their friends and attending to the action, a deep love for the sportsmen and the sport grows. Though mysterious, this kind of change to how we feel is nevertheless quite accessible.[33]

But Elliott is on less sure ground when he offers a fourfold strategy for altering our emotional profile, which he explains as 'focus, know, value, believe'. I risk ruining it through brief description; but briefly, it is as follows:

- We *focus* upon the contours of our current emotional state: what drives it, and what thoughts characterize it.
- We then set out to *know* the actual state of the reality that confronts us.
- We (re)*value* the goods that are before our eyeballs according to their proper worth.
- We evaluate what we truly *believe* about how the world works, and if necessary, believe differently.

I am sympathetic to some of what Elliott offers here, and to why he offers it. In this schema he shows that we need not accept emotional 'purism' as the last word about our emotions. That is, our emotions *are* susceptible to change, although not by a direct form of control. (In this respect Kant was half-right: emotions are not directly commandable.) We are able to exert some indirect influences over our emotional state.

Elliott expresses respectful agreement with cognitivist philosophers of emotion William Lyons and Robert C. Solomon. His fourfold 'toolbox' for altering our emotional profile follows from his adopting a cognitivist position on emotion. The reason I think he is on less sure ground is not because I doubt the cognitivist view. It has some merits. The problem is rather that Elliott has perhaps looked too quickly to these cognitive accounts as his authoritative source on emotional change, and, in so doing, has

---

33. Peter Brown, *Augustine of Hippo: A Biography*, new ed. with epilogue (London: Faber & Faber, 2000), pp. 448–449.

inadvertently looked past a deeper theological account of the human condition.

For humans are sometimes completely helpless. Our emotional state can seem to us so beyond rational control, and our frame of reference so completely imprisoned by it, that we resemble the psalmist in 'the Pit' of Psalm 88. Similar comments apply to otherwise helpful suggestions peppered throughout Elliott's work. He suggests small and significant practices that can alter our emotional state. These have the advantage of offering ways forward that involve bodily, not just mental, action; and bodily action is often a more reliable means than thought for altering how we feel. (In this respect, James and Lange were on to something.) Yet human helplessness is such that even these baby steps can seem impossible.

Thankfully, God does not leave humanity squirming on the pin of helpless culpability. He 'proves His own love for us in that while we were still sinners, Christ died for us!' (Rom. 5:8 HCSB). In the same passage, 'God's love has been poured out in our hearts through the Holy Spirit who was given to us' (Rom. 5:5 HCSB). Augustine rejoiced in this text, and looked forward to God's Spirit giving a kind of love within that we cannot create ourselves. Whether or not this is the thought of Romans 5:5, it is amply attested elsewhere in Scripture (e.g. Ps. 36:7–10 [where God's love, vv. 7 and 10, attracts metaphors of refuge, abundant feasting and a life-giving fountain]; Rom. 15:30; Gal. 5:22; Col. 1:8; 2 Tim. 1:7). In other words, the gospel reveals God's accepting us at our most unfeeling, and setting about redeeming not only our reprobate state but also our emotional bankruptcy.

Hence I think Elliott moves too quickly to his 'focus–know–value–believe' stratagem. He resents preachers and thinkers who require mental exercises that trickle down into changed feelings. Yet his fourfold stratagem also requires a degree of ratiocination that I suspect is beyond many of us. A thicker theological account of the emotional Christian life might return to something like Elliott's conclusions, but by a route that inserts some missing pieces into his account. It is a route that may be schooled by the Psalms, in practices of lament, thanksgiving and corporate song. It may reflect on the helplessness of despondent Christians, and the mysterious work of the Spirit to reorder our affections. It may look to the epistles' quiet optimism about a maturity on offer before death, and wonder about the emotional constituents of that maturity. It will always rely upon security in Christ, even when the Christian feels nothing, or worse.

Augustine versus the Stoics

Augustine of Hippo, arguably Christianity's first and most significant theoretician of human emotion, also offers some clues as to how we might proceed. But before we can understand him, we need to notice a fundamental difference between the way ancient and modern thinkers regard our future.

For late modern people like ourselves, it has become easy to believe that in order to find 'who we are' we must 'follow our heart' and 'find our destiny'. 'Following our heart' consists in responding to whatever our emotions seem to signal that we need next (the same procedure, incidentally, that the apostle James thought resulted in envy and rivalry, then discord and war). Without that, we think we have no other way to orient ourselves towards the future. Our forward path then becomes a series of acts of will that are bound to our emotional longings. Our lives become an adventure story of our own making, where we hope to arrive at a personally constructed version of our authentic self. Many modern people expect that even God should respect these 'authentic' choices.

But for biblical and ancient authors our deepest longings are properly understood as a function of a goal, end or future that is stitched into our very being and is not of our own making. The Greek word for this aspect of ourselves was our *telos*. Augustine believed that our deepest loves are related to our proper *telos*, and that our emotions are connected to what we love. Just as a stone is 'carried by its weight wherever it is carried', so also 'the soul is carried by its love'. If humanity were simply cattle, 'we should love the carnal and sensual life, and this would be our sufficient good', says Augustine. If the self was proper 'gravity' for this 'weight', then people would be 'blessed' when their love terminated upon themselves, and all would be well. But such 'blessing' is *so often tried and found wanting* that Augustine suspects the proper 'gravity' of our love to have lain elsewhere all along.[34]

We moderns find it odd to be likened to a stone carried by its weight. According to Augustine's biographer, Peter Brown, the ancients meant by this 'weight' 'a momentum by which each part of the universe sought out its place of rest, with the mute insistence of a homing pigeon seeking to regain its nest'.[35] It is an Aristotelian idea that we no longer apply to inanimate objects, but it retains some traction as a description of how each person has a divinely given purpose, which is meant to be discovered and is meant to carry us forward through life. Brown describes how this is the same 'weight' of 'glory' that God places into hearts (2 Cor. 4:17), making Christians 'the *heavy people*, held on course, despite the high winds of the world, by the gathering momentum of a "gravity of love"'.[36] In other words, the New Testament contributes to this ancient thought world by showing that eschatology discloses our true destiny, that our identity follows from our destiny, and that our behaviour arises from our identity.[37]

In this volume David Höhne considers how the perfecting work of the Spirit reorients us to our proper *telos*. This proper *telos* becomes the proper criterion for evaluating our various loves, and the emotions that arise from them. It follows that Augustine has no interest in demonizing emotion:

> In our ethics, we do not so much inquire whether a pious soul is angry, as why he is angry; not whether he is sad, but what is the cause of his sadness; not whether he fears, but what he fears. For I am not aware that any right thinking person would find fault with anger at a wrongdoer which seeks his amendment, or with sadness which intends relief to the suffering, or with fear lest one in danger be destroyed.[38]

---

34. Augustine, *The City of God Against the Pagans*, tr. R. W. Dyson (Cambridge: Cambridge University Press, 1998), p. 487 (11.28).

35. Brown, *Augustine of Hippo*, p. 512.

36. Ibid., emphasis original.

37. I am indebted to Brian Rosner for this way of putting it.

38. Brown, *Augustine of Hippo*, p. 365 (9.5).

Whether an emotion is 'good' or 'bad' depends upon how it is directed. An emotion is functioning properly when it takes us towards our proper *telos* (sometimes called an 'affection'), whereas it functions poorly when it takes us away from our proper *telos* (sometimes called a 'passion').

On this basis Augustine spares no quarter in his attacks upon the Stoics, who declared emotion itself an evil. They held to what was arguably an early version of the 'hydraulic model', insisting that 'virtue' consisted in repressing all and every emotional impulse. In this the Stoics paralleled other ancient received wisdom, where an uncontroversial consensus held that 'the mind is master of all [emotional] disturbances, and, by withholding its consent from them and resisting them, exercises a reign of virtue'.[39] Therefore, according to Augustine, Stoics even screened out compassion from the disturbance-free-zone of their mind – and therefore became emotionally and ethically perverse:

> The Stoics, indeed, are wont to reproach even compassion. But how much more honourable it would have been if the Stoic . . . had been disturbed by compassion for a fellow man . . . And what is compassion but a kind of fellow feeling in our hearts for the misery of another which compels us to help him if we can? This impulse is the servant of right reason when compassion is displayed in such a way as to preserve righteousness, as when alms are distributed to the needy or forgiveness extended to the penitent. . . . [But] the Stoics are not ashamed to number [compassion] among the vices . . .[40]

The Stoic denies the proper 'weight' of the soul's love. By deploying strategies to eliminate 'disturbance' – that is, by seeking to be free from all emotions, as if that were a virtue – the Stoic curtails proper love. In a scouring *ad hominem* attack Augustine amusingly describes a Stoic on a boat in a storm, white-faced and facing shipwreck. Later, the man boasted of how he was free from any 'disturbance' about the fate of his fellow-passengers. But a large and jolly

39. Ibid., p. 365 (9.4).
40. Ibid., pp. 365–366 (9.5).

fellow-traveller took some delight in recalling the Stoic's white-faced fear, pointing out that the Stoic remained highly 'disturbed' – out of love for his own precious self![41]

Some thinkers have challenged Augustine's portrayal of the Stoics. But he uses them as a foil to offer a deeply Christian beginning to our analysis of emotion. Emotions are a good gift of creation, and should not be denigrated or demonized. But they can be expressed in various directions, depending on the primary orientation of what we love most – on what the biblical authors called our 'heart'. In the following quotation 'will' does not refer to modern 'will-power' but to the shape of what we want, based as it is on what we love:

> good and bad men alike will, are cautious, and contented; or, to say the
> same thing in other words, good and bad men alike desire, fear, rejoice,
> but the former in a good, the latter in a bad fashion, according as the
> will is right or wrong.[42]

Conclusion

What, then, about me? Was it Christian, was it good, to be ready to kill a dog in ice-cold rage? To make that evaluation, we would have to consider my *telos*, my baby's *telos* and even the dog's *telos*. We'd have to have a way to evaluate the universe morally before we could know. I think that at the end of that kind of enquiry the Stoic would say that I shouldn't have been in the grip of such a force – that I'd lost my calm, my cool, my *apatheia*. In our context the modern evolutionary neurobiologist might shrug and say, it is what it is. You've evolved to propagate your genes, and you have the circuitry to do it. It isn't good or bad. It's an emotion; that's all. (This assessment owes more to our amoral habits of emotion discourse than the speaker may realize.)

---

41. Ibid., pp. 362–363 (9.4).
42. Augustine, *The City of God*, ed. Philip Schaff, tr. Marcus Dods (Grand Rapids: Eerdmans, 1988; originally published 1886), p. 268 (14.8). For this quotation, the older translation is preferred.

Augustine might say, your passions and affections are too mixed to declare them unambiguously good. But you were acting for the good of another, whose *telos* trumps the dog's. You may equally have fled in fear and hid with her. You may courageously have taken the bites for her. But one thing we do know: that the wrong would have been to stand by, feel nothing and do nothing. For 'good and bad men alike desire, fear, rejoice, but the former in a good, the latter in a bad fashion, according as the will is right or wrong'.[43]

It is probably not too much to claim that the best Christian pastoral theology that followed drew deeply from the well that Augustine dug into Scripture. We hope that this volume digs similarly, and rediscovers this well.

Appendix: *epithymia* in biblical thought

(a) *Epithymia* spans a range of objects and moral connotations in the LXX OT:

- Gen. 31:30; 49:6: Jacob longs for home in an illicit circumstance, and Simeon and Rueben illicitly desire to hamstring oxen.
- Num. 11:34–35, 'the tombs of craving'; cf. Ps. 78:23–31, esp. vv. 29–30 (LXX Ps. 77); and Ps. 106:14 (LXX Ps. 105). This episode becomes the archetypal example of a desire expressed in hostility against God. Desire here is a form of disastrous craving. They were those in 1 Cor. 10:6 who 'desire evil'.
- In Deut. 12:15, 20–21 God states that the people may eat all the meat they desire.
- In 2 Chr. 8:6 Solomon builds whatever he desires.
- The boastful cravings of the wicked are observed in Pss 10:3 (LXX 9:24); 112:10 (LXX 111:10); and 140:8 (LXX 139:9); but the poor and afflicted also have desires in Ps. 10:17 (LXX 9:38).

---

43. Ibid.

- The king's desires are given by God in Ps. 21:2 (LXX 20:3).
- God is the one who satisfies desires in Ps. 103:5 (LXX 102).
- The man 'whose quiver is full' (Ps. 127:5) becomes the man 'whose desire is filled' in LXX (Ps. 126).
- Everyone craves in Proverbs: the wicked, the righteous, the sluggard, young men after beautiful women – with 'desire fulfilled', or 'a good desire' (LXX) being a 'tree of life' (Prov. 13:12).

(b) *Epithymia* (as noun, adjective and verb) can be made 'guilty by association' in the NT:

- The adulterous-hearted man looks 'to desire' a woman (Matt. 5:28).
- Desires contribute to choke the Word (Mark 4:19).
- Jesus' opponents follow desire, like their father the devil (John 8:44).
- Paul has not desired others' money (Acts 20:33; cf. Rom. 7:7; 13:9).
- God gives people over in judgment to the desires of their hearts (Rom. 1:24).
- Desire is that aspect of mortal bodies that sin makes us 'obey' (Rom. 6:12).
- 'Every' desire is produced when sin meets the tenth commandment (Rom. 7:7–8).
- Desire is crucified with flesh (Gk. *sarx*) along with passions (Gk. *pathēma*, Gal. 5:24).
- Those pursuing riches fall into 'many foolish and harmful' desires (1 Tim. 6:9).
- Desire leads weak women (2 Tim. 3:6) and motivates others to gather false teachers (2 Tim. 4:3).
- Desire motivates people in their pre-Christian ignorance (1 Pet. 1:14) and governs the vices of unconverted Gentiles (1 Pet. 4:3).
- 'Fleshly' desire wars against the soul (1 Pet. 2:11).
- Scoffers and malcontent false teachers follow their desires (2 Pet. 3:3; Jude 16).
- The whore of Babylon desires fruit (Rev. 18:14).

(c) *Epithymia* is made 'guilty' by grammatical pairing with some adjectival or verbal form of the following:

- flesh (*sarx*, Eph. 2:3; Gal. 5:16; Rom. 13:14);
- deceit (*apatē*, Eph. 4:22);
- evil (*kakos*, Col. 3:5);
- passion (*pathos*, 1 Thess. 4:5);
- youth (*neōterikos*, 2 Tim. 2:22);
- world (*kosmos*, Titus 2:12);
- enslavement (*douleuō*, Titus 3:3);
- decadence and corruption (*phthora* and *miasmos*, 2 Pet. 1:4; 2:10);
- debauchery (*aselgeia*, 2 Pet. 2:18);
- ungodliness (*asebeia*, Jude 18).

(d) *Epithymia* (verbal form) can be morally neutral:

- The son longs for the pods (Luke 15:16).
- Lazarus longs for scraps (Luke 16:21).
- The Spirit and the flesh desire in contrary directions (Gal. 5:17).
- People long for death (Rev. 9:6).

(e) *Epithymia* (as both noun and verb) can be very morally positive:

- Prophets 'longed to see' and angels 'long to look' (Matt. 13:17; 1 Pet. 1:12).
- Disciples long to see the days of the Son of Man (Luke 17:22).
- Jesus 'ardently longs' to eat the Passover with the disciples (*epithymia epethymesa*, Luke 22:15).
- Paul desires to depart and be with Christ (Phil. 1:23).
- Paul wishes to see the Thessalonians 'with much desire' (1 Thess. 2:17).
- The desire to oversee a church is noble (1 Tim. 3:1).
- The author desires the Hebrew Christians to show earnestness (Heb. 6:11).

(f) Texts that offer particular analysis of *epithymia*:

- 1 John 2:16–17; Jas 1:14–15; 4:1–2.

(g) Lexicographers' conclusions on *epithymia*:

- BDAG for *epithymia* lists neutral uses (Mark 4:19; Rev. 18:14), positive uses (LXX Prov. 10:24; Phil. 1:23; Luke 22:15; 1 Thess. 2:17) and many negative uses (similar to §§b–c of this appendix).[44]
- Friberg, Friberg and Miller list a neutral sense of *strong impulse* (e.g. Mark 4:19); a good sense of natural and legitimate desire – *(eager) longing, (earnest) desire* (e.g. 1 Thess. 2:17); and a bad sense of unrestrained desire for something forbidden – *lust, craving, evil desire* (e.g. 1 Tim. 6:9).[45]
- Louw shows *epithymia* both as appropriate strong desire (§25.12) and as illicit desire (§25.20).[46] Eighteen other entries treat twenty-three other words pertaining to strong desire. Such work illustrates that in order to arrive at an account of the NT language of emotion, we would need to repeat this appendix for at least those twenty-three other words.

(h) The table overleaf lists examples of other emotion-related words with a wide 'moral' range.

---

44. BDAG, p. 372.
45. Timothy Friberg, Barbara Friberg and Neva F. Miller, *Analytical Lexicon to the Greek New Testament* (Grand Rapids: Baker, 2000), p. 164.
46. Johannes P. Louw and Eugene A. Nida (eds.), *Greek–English Lexicon of the New Testament, Based on Semantic Domains*, 2nd ed. (New York: United Bible Societies, 1989).

Table 2.1 Emotion-related words with a wide 'moral' range

	Morally bad	*Morally neutral*
peirasmos	Temptation: Matt. 26:41; Mark 14:38; Luke 4:13; 22:40, 46; 1 Cor. 10:13; 1 Tim. 6:9; Heb. 3:9.	Trial: Matt 6:13; Luke 8:13; 11:4; 22:28; Acts 20:19; Gal. 4:14; Jas 1:2, 12; 1 Pet. 1:6; 4:12; 2 Pet. 2:9; Rev. 3:10.
pathēma	Strong desire: Rom. 7:5; Gal. 5:24.	Suffering: Rom. 8:18; 2 Cor. 1:5, 7; Phil. 3:10; Col. 1:24; 2 Tim. 3:11; Heb. 2:9–10; 10:32; 1 Pet. 1:11; 4:13; 5:1, 9.
hēdonē	Pleasures: Luke 8:14; Titus 3:3; Jas 4:1, 3; 2 Pet. 2:13.	Pleasant: LXX Num. 11:8; Prov. 17:1; Wisdom 7.2; 16.20 (Apocrypha).
pathos	Strong desire: Rom. 1:26; Col. 3:5; 1 Thess. 4:5.	Deep interest: (Other Hellenistic literature)

3. THE PURITANS, THEOLOGICAL ANTHROPOLOGY AND EMOTIONS

Keith Condie

The love of a friend hath its sweetness and delight: and when we love them, we feel such pleasure in our love, that we love to love them. How pleasant then would it be to love thy God! – O blessed, joyful life, if I could but love him as much as I desire to love him! How freely could I leave the ambitious, and the covetous, and the sensual, and voluptuous, to their doting, delusory, swinish love! How easily could I spare all earthly pleasures! How near should I come to the angelical life! Could I love God as I would love him, it would fill me with continual pleasure, and be the sweetest feast that a soul can have.

(Richard Baxter)[1]

So wrote Richard Baxter, Puritan pastor and author, in his massive treatise on practical theology, *A Christian Directory*. The emotionally laden nature of Baxter's language is immediately apparent, but what

1. *A Christian Directory* (Morgan, Pa.: Soli Deo Gloria, [1673] 1996), pp. 132–133.

is more significant is what the quote reveals of his understanding of authentic spiritual life. Baxter consistently challenged believers to fulfil their responsibilities before God – the language of 'duty' and clear directions for Christian practice pervade *A Christian Directory* and many of his other works. Yet he perceived that more was needed than stoic obedience or disciplined activism; the godly life should also be marked by warm affection towards God and delight in his service. His comment even suggests that such affections provide the means to turn from worldly habits. For Baxter, therefore, emotional states played a central role in Christian experience.

What Baxter captured in these few lines is typical of other Puritan writers. They too held that true piety involved more than intellectual assent to a creed or formal adherence to a set of practices. In the words of the influential Cambridge Puritan William Perkins, theology is best described as 'the science of living blessedly forever'.[2] There was a liveliness to true faith, borne of a heart that had been softened by God's grace to pursue his ways with eagerness and joy. Thus the common caricature that Puritans were austere and miserable, captured in the witty but cutting comment that this was a movement that had 'the haunting fear that someone, somewhere, may be happy', does not ring true.[3] Negative emotions had their place – for example, sorrow for one's sin was entirely fitting. But so too was the positive; hence the gladness and elation that attends so much Puritan literature, where authors have grasped what it means to be forgiven and welcomed home by God.[4] The reality is that Puritan spirituality featured a broad range of emotional

---

2. William Perkins, *A Golden Chaine* (London: 1612), p. 4. Cf. Richard Baxter's statement 'the doctrine of christianity is *scientia affectiva practica*; a doctrine for head, heart, and life'. Richard Baxter, *The Reasons of the Christian Religion*, in *The Practical Works of Richard Baxter*, 4 vols. (Morgan, Pa.: Soli Deo Gloria, [1667] 2000), vol. 2, p. 162.

3. H. L. Mencken, *A Mencken Chrestomathy* (New York: Alfred A. Knopf, 1949), p. 624.

4. See e.g. Jean Williams, 'Puritanism: a Piety of Joy', *Kategoria* 10 (1998), pp. 11–35.

responses, and these responses were by no means peripheral to a life lived in faithfulness before God.

Who were the Puritans?

While historians have wrestled with how best to define 'Puritanism', the vigorous form of piety just described was an essential mark of this movement.[5] Within the fluidity that characterized the English religious landscape of the sixteenth and seventeenth centuries, Puritans were the 'hotter sort of Protestants',[6] distinguishable from the general religious temper by their lively and active faith. Their agenda ranged beyond concern for the state of individual souls and encompassed a vision for the entire nation and beyond. Dissatisfied with the extent of reform within the Church of England following the Elizabethan settlement of 1559, for the next century they laboured to see the work of reformation completed and godliness promoted in the land. For much of the Elizabethan and early Stuart period, Puritans were ridiculed and marginalized and made little progress in pursuit of their goals. By 1620 many thought that their cause was lost in England. Some fled to Holland, then New England, to try to create a 'holy commonwealth' in what they thought would be a more favourable context. By the 1630s Puritan ideals were under even more severe challenge due to the policies of King Charles I and Archbishop William Laud. Although fortunes revived following the victory of the Parliamentary forces during the Civil Wars, this

---

5. For helpful brief overviews of the nature of Puritanism, see John Coffey and Paul C. H. Lim, 'Introduction', in John Coffey and Paul C. H. Lim (eds.), *The Cambridge Companion to Puritanism* (Cambridge: Cambridge University Press, 2008), pp. 1–15; J. I. Packer, *A Quest for Godliness: The Puritan Vision of the Christian Life* (Wheaton: Crossway, 1990), chs. 2–3.

6. The expression was used by the pamphleteer Percival Wilburn, *A Checke or Reproofe of M. Howlet's Untimely Screeching*, cited by Patrick Collinson, *The Elizabethan Puritan Movement* (London: Jonathan Cape, [1581] 1967), p. 27.

was quickly reversed when the monarchy was restored in 1660 and those of Puritan sympathy were driven into dissenting groups and entrenched nonconformity. While some Puritan emphases lived on in these new contexts and had spilled out beyond the geographical confines of England and its national Church, the movement itself was over.

Why are we talking about the Puritans?

The Puritans are worthy of consideration in this discussion on the place of emotions in Christian life and ministry for a number of reasons. First, the Puritans share a similar theological pedigree to that of the contributors to this volume. They affirmed key Reformation and Protestant doctrines such as justification by grace through faith alone, and the necessity of the work of the Holy Spirit in the process of sanctification. Most were Calvinist in their theological convictions, insisting upon the sovereignty of God in the work of salvation. Here, then, is a theologically and psychologically informed group of believers that provide a helpful point of comparison for contemporary evangelicals to consider what place emotions should be granted in Christian experience.

Secondly, due to the influence of writers such as J. I. Packer and Martyn Lloyd-Jones, there has been a revival of interest in Puritan spirituality in recent decades. Various publishing houses have reprinted many Puritan works and this particular expression of Christian faith continues to shape evangelical leaders such as John Piper and Timothy Keller. Features of Puritanism, therefore, remain a continuing force and there is merit in gaining a deeper understanding of just what that influence might be.

Finally, it is worth asking why this centuries-old religious movement has gained such traction in recent times. Perhaps the answer in part lies in the fact that Puritans were so attentive to the place of emotions in the life of faith. While they did not specifically use the word 'emotion' (a term introduced at a later date, as the previous chapter has indicated), when they spoke of 'affections' and 'passions' it is clear that it is emotional states they had in mind. Puritans took seriously what it meant to live for the glory of God with one's whole life and being. Christian living involved more than simply informing the mind and commanding the will; it was necessary to keep Christ foremost in the believer's affections while other emotional responses needed to be kept in check. Due to their sophisticated understanding of human motivation and behaviour, Puritan pastors were adept at applying Scriptural truth wisely into an individual's life circumstances, becoming known as 'physicians of the soul'. The attractiveness of such a perspective to those of conservative theological disposition in our present experiential age is apparent – this was an approach to the life of faith that was warm-hearted without slipping into emotionalism, and that offered ready assistance to believers who sought day by day to live faithfully for God.

This chapter will provide an overview of Puritan theological anthropology, then consider the place of emotions within Puritan thought in more detail, and finish with some of the pastoral implications that flow from the Puritan perspective on the emotional life.

Puritan theological anthropology

The place of emotions within Puritan thought needs to be considered in the light of their overall theological anthropology. While Puritanism was deeply rooted in the convictions of the Protestant Reformation, much of the movement's understanding of the nature and functioning of human persons derived from a rich intellectual heritage that traced its origins to Greek philosophy. In effect what Puritan writers did was to take the common 'scientific' understanding of their times about the workings of the body and soul and combine this with their reading of what the Bible taught about how we function as human beings. While Scripture was normative in their analysis, a debt to Aristotelian faculty psychology and Hippocrates' theory that bodily fluids (or 'humours') influenced human behaviour must also be acknowledged. Such an approach was not without its dangers – one could easily read contemporary meanings into biblical texts rather than engaging in careful exegesis of those texts in their historical and literary contexts. But it should be noted that the same problem is evident today. For example, the biblical words for 'heart' and 'mind' are often understood in the light of current discourse that tends to draw a sharp division between thought and emotion, something that careful exegesis of these terms does not bear out.

The place of faculty psychology in Puritan theological anthropology

Aristotle maintained that a fundamental distinction existed in the natural world between things that were inanimate and those that were alive. What distinguished the two was the fact that animate beings possessed a *psychē*, usually translated as 'soul'. It was the *psychē* that gave life to living things by means of certain powers and capacities (or 'faculties'), and from this understanding arose the concept of 'faculty psychology'.[7] Some of these capacities were common to all living things, such as the ability to take in nutrients in order to stay alive. Other faculties, such as the capacity to gather information through the senses, distinguished animals and humans from plant life. But a third set of powers separated human life from the animals. For example, only human beings were able to use rational thought to govern the choices they made, had a sense of right and wrong, and were able to remember things not immediately accessible to the senses. The two key faculties that distinguished humanity from animals were the intellect (or 'understanding') and the will. From the time of Aristotle through to the era of the Puritans there was much debate about the workings of the faculties within the human soul, but there was general consensus that this was a useful conceptual tool. Faculty psychology, therefore, arose from an attempt to make sense of how living beings functioned.

Recognizing that the New Testament emphasized the eternal significance of the human soul, Puritan divines wrote at length about the soul and how the faculties should operate in pursuit of the godly life. Most of these discussions did not include systematic expositions of how the faculties were structured within the soul. Some authors,

---

7. For a brief exposition of Aristotle's psychological understanding, see Jonathan Barnes, *Aristotle* (Oxford: Oxford University Press, 1982), pp. 65–68.

however, such as Richard Baxter, did provide fuller accounts.[8] Baxter held that three 'general faculties' could be distinguished within the one indivisible soul of a person:

- the *mental (or rational) soul* that was unique to humans;
- the *sensitive soul* that was also found in animals; and
- the *vegetative (or igneous) soul* that was common to all living beings, including plants.

For Baxter, the rational soul further comprised three 'distinct faculties':

- the *intellect* (or understanding), which was the power to know;
- the *will*, which was a free ability to act or not act, and which had a natural inclination towards that which it held to be good; and
- *vital active power*, which was the ability to do things and achieve purposes, both by exciting the intellect and will into action and also by carrying out the directions of the intellect and will.[9]

All Puritan writers acknowledged the significant role of the intellect and will in enabling believers to live holy lives, but Baxter was somewhat idiosyncratic in including this third faculty of vital active power.

The location in the soul of passions and affections

Where did the Puritans locate the emotions within their understanding of the workings of the human soul? The answer is not

---

8. Other more complete Puritan descriptions of the workings of the soul can be found in Edward Reynolds, *A Treatise of the Passions and Faculties of the Soule of Man* (London, 1640), and John Flavel, *Pneumatologia, a Treatise of the Soul of Man* (London, 1685).

9. Richard Baxter, *The Catechising of Families* (1683), in *Practical Works of Richard Baxter*, vol. 4, pp. 69, 86; Richard Baxter, *A Treatise of Knowledge and Love Compared* (1689), in ibid., p. 613; Richard Baxter, *The End of Doctrinal Controversies* (London, 1691), pp. x–xvi.

straightforward, due to the diversity of terminology that they employed and the fact that writers sometimes attributed different meanings to the same terms or used different terms interchangeably.

Generally speaking, the passions were considered to be part of the sensitive soul. There was something animal-like about these emotionally charged reactions to persons and things, and therefore many Puritan writings display some wariness about the passions due to their ability to distort human functioning away from God-ordained ends. Despite this caution, the passions did have a part to play in fulfilling the Creator's intentions for humankind. For example, Baxter saw particular significance in the two related emotions of love and delight; he considered love to be 'the master passion of the soul' and delight to be 'the most powerful, commanding affection, and the end of all the other passions'.[10] Thus he granted a legitimate and dignified place to these emotional states when they were aligned with divine purposes. This combination of guardedness and appreciation of emotional responses led some Puritans to draw a clear distinction between passions and affections, suggesting that the latter were responses within the highest level of human functioning, the rational soul.[11] William Fenner is a case in point, and here he describes how affections draw one towards what is good but repel one from what is perceived to be evil:

> The affections are the forcible and sensible motions of the heart, or the will, to a thing, or from a thing, according as it is apprehended to bee good or to bee evill. . . . I know Aristotle and most of our Divines too,

---

10. Baxter, *Christian Directory*, pp. 139, 275.
11. J. Stephen Yuille, 'Puritan Moderation: The Pursuit of Self-Mastery', *Chm* 121 (2007), p. 224, n. 3, identifies three different perspectives on the relationship between passions and affections within Puritan thought. Some equated passions and affections and located both in the sensitive appetite; some distinguished the two, locating the passions in the sensitive appetite and the affections in the rational appetite; a third group equated passions and affections and believed they belonged both to the rational and sensitive appetites.

doe place the affections in the sensitive part of the Soule, and not in the will, because they are to be seene in the beasts. But this cannot bee so, for a mans affections doe most stirre at a shame or disgrace.[12]

Similarly with the last great Puritan writer, Jonathan Edwards: 'The affections are no other than the more vigorous and sensible exercises of the inclination and will of the soul.'[13]

As will become apparent later, this perspective within Puritan thought that recognized that emotional responses exist at the highest level of human functioning challenges any viewpoint that would marginalize their role in the Christian life.

The corruption of the soul's workings due to sin

The Puritans believed that God made the soul with a hierarchy in functioning. The intended order was that the body, including the vegetative and sensitive souls, should be subordinate to the workings of the rational soul. Baxter described the process in these terms:

> God hath made every man a governor of himself. For God made him with some faculties which must be ruled, (as the appetite, senses, and tongue, and other bodily members, yea, and passions too,) and with some which must rule the rest, as the understanding by guidance and the will by command.[14]

This self-government is the nub of what it means to be human – what separates us from the animals as creatures made in God's image. But within fallen human beings this intended order has been subverted. Too often sinful passions take control and distort our true human nature. The idea is captured well in Milton's great poem *Paradise Lost*:

---

12. William Fenner, *A Treatise of the Affections; or, The Soules Pulse* (London, 1642), sigs. B^r–B2^v.

13. Jonathan Edwards, *The Religious Affections* (Edinburgh: Banner of Truth, [1746] 1961), p. 24.

14. Baxter, *Catechising of Families*, p. 72.

Reason in man obscured, or not obeyed,
Immediately inordinate desires
And upstart passions catch the government
From reason, and to servitude reduce
Man till then free . . .[15]

The divine work of sanctification involves a redressing of this situation by enabling the intellect and will to keep unruly faculties in check so that the body might be appropriately governed. Many works of Puritan practical divinity provide suggestions to aid in this process. For example, within *A Christian Directory* Baxter has chapters giving directions for the government of the thoughts, the passions, the senses, the tongue and the body.

The soul's relationship to the body

As well as appropriating the common psychological understanding of the day, the Puritans also adopted the common medical or physiological understanding of their times. The received wisdom was that the soul is contained within the body and the different faculties are located in particular parts of the body. The intellect, for example, is found in the brain, and the will within the heart. Communication between the faculties takes place by means of animal spirits (fine particles in the nerves) that carry images (phantasms) from faculty to faculty.[16] This means that there literally could be a blockage between the head and heart, if for some reason the animal spirits were unable to convey information from one to the other.

Also significant from a physiological point of view was the place of bodily humours in understanding how people function. Hippocrates in the fourth century BC proposed that human emotions and behaviours were influenced by four key body fluids or 'humours': blood, yellow bile, black bile and phlegm. Several centuries later Galen developed this theory further and defined different

---

15. John Milton, *Paradise Lost*, in John Leonard (ed.), *The Complete Poems* (London: Penguin, [1667] 1998), bk. 12, ll. 86–90.
16. Charles L. Cohen, *God's Caress: The Psychology of Puritan Religious Experience* (New York: Oxford University Press, 1986), p. 28.

temperaments on the basis of the relative distribution of these humours within the body. Ideally, there should be a balance between the four humours, but when one became dominant, it would issue in one of four temperamental categories, depending upon which of the humours was most prevalent. These four temperaments were the *sanguine* (cheerful, hopeful and extraverted), the *melancholic* (thoughtful, considerate and sad), the *choleric* (active, passionate and dominating) and the *phlegmatic* (self-content, kind and consistent).

During the period of the Puritan movement, this ancient under-standing was still in vogue. Due to their belief in the connection between soul and body, Puritan divines held that bodily humours could affect the soul:

> And as men naturally differ in quickness and dulness of wit, so they do in the temperature of all their humours and bodies, which accidentally will cause great difference in their minds. A sanguine man hath usually other thoughts and perceptions than a phlegmatic man, and phlegmatic man hath other thoughts and sense of things than the choleric have; and the melancholy man differeth from them all, and often from himself. As these tempers variously affect the phantasy and the passions, so consequently they do usually the intellect and the will.[17]

For Puritans, therefore, bodily states could affect one's emotional life and vice versa.

This recognition of a connection between the body and emotions was a contributing factor to the sophistication of Puritan pastoral practice. Puritan pastors paid careful attention to the root causes of human problems, making fine distinctions that enabled them to avoid simplistic solutions. Consider, for example, Richard Baxter's treatise on the management of 'melancholy', the seventeenth-century term to describe depression.[18] While it is spiritual causes and their resolution that occupy most of Baxter's discussion, he also

---

17. Richard Baxter, *The True and Only Way of Concord* (1680), in *Practical Works of Richard Baxter*, vol. 4, p. 716.
18. Richard Baxter, *The Cure of Melancholy and Overmuch Sorrow by Faith*, in ibid., pp. 920–935.

gives attention to the impact of physiology and temperamental factors, since he believes that melancholy is a 'perfect complication of the maladies of mind and body'.[19] In considering the role of temperament, he writes that it is those 'whose natural temper is timorous and passionate, and apt to discontent and grief, who fall into crazedness and melancholy'.[20] His suggestions for managing the condition include, amongst other things, disciplined control of one's thoughts (in a manner similar to contemporary cognitive behavioural therapy), spending time in the company of others, and utilizing the medical treatments available at the time. In short, the Puritans were attuned to connections between soul and body, including emotional responses, in a way that shaped their approach to pastoral care.

The Puritans and 'emotions'

The discussion above about theological anthropology has provided some insight into where emotions fit within Puritan thought and practice. It has, however, raised some issues worthy of further consideration.

A breadth of terminology

Andrew Cameron's chapter has already made mention of Thomas Dixon's work on the emergence of 'the emotions' as a psychological category.[21] Dixon argues that after the eighteenth century, the word 'emotion' became a catch-all term that failed to distinguish between a variety of states that had been described in an earlier intellectual

---

19. Ibid., p. 934.
20. Ibid., p. 923. A link between certain temperaments and some forms of depression continues to be acknowledged in the medical profession. See e.g. <http://breeze.blackdoginstitute.org.au/ nonmelancholicdepression>, accessed 2 Mar. 2012.
21. Thomas Dixon, *From Passions to Emotions: The Creation of a Secular Psychological Category* (Cambridge: Cambridge University Press, 2003).

climate. Subtle distinctions encompassed in terms such as 'passions', 'affections', 'sentiments' and 'appetites' were lost. Emotions came to be viewed by some as mere disturbances in the body and any moral evaluation of them was deemed inappropriate.

The Puritans wrote prior to this terminological shift and, as noted above, employed a range of terms to describe emotional states of one form or another. In particular, many Puritans found profit in distinguishing between 'passions' and 'affections', with the latter being viewed in a more positive light than the former.[22] But is this distinction a helpful one?

On first appearance the terms employed by the Puritans might seem to discriminate between emotional states in a fairly arbitrary manner. Why should one emotional response be deemed a 'passion' while another is considered to be an 'affection'? Is this an inappropriate bundling of emotions into categories that results in a derogation of a central part of what we are as human beings? For example, Jonathan Edwards paints a negative picture of passions relative to affections, claiming that passions produce actions 'that are more sudden, and whose effects on the animal spirits are more violent, and the mind more overpowered, and less in its own command'.[23] The problem appears to be compounded by the close link between body and soul in Puritan thought, and the desire of some writers to detach the affections entirely from the body and situate them in the mind:

> Such seems to be our nature, and such the laws of the union of soul and body, that there never is in any case whatsoever, any lively and vigorous exercise of the will or inclination of the soul without some effect upon the body, in some alteration of the motion of its fluids, and especially of the animal spirits. And, on the other hand, from the same laws of the union of the soul and body, the constitution of the body and the motion of its fluids may promote the exercise of the affections. But yet it is not the body, but the mind only, that is the proper seat of the affections. . . .

22. But note the sometimes inconsistent use of terminology – see n. 11 above.

23. Edwards, *Religious Affections*, p. 27.

an unbodied spirit may be as capable of love and hatred, joy or sorrow, hope or fear, or other affections, as one that is united to a body.[24]

One can understand why Edwards would argue this way. As John Piper states, the Scriptures attribute affections to God even though he is not embodied, and the New Testament suggests that believers after death will be with the Lord in a state of joy while waiting for the resurrection of their bodies.[25] Yet, even taking account of the truth affirmed in the doctrine of total depravity that every aspect of human nature has been tainted by sin, many strong emotions seem to be marginalized within Edwards's framework.

Closer examination, however, suggests that the Puritans had grasped an important truth with their use of the category of 'affections'. In essence they were following in the tradition of Augustine, who believed the core issue was not the nature of the emotion itself, but its object. To hate God was culpable; but to hate sin was entirely appropriate. For Augustine, all was determined by the state of the will:

> the character of the human will is of moment; because, if it is wrong, these motions of the soul will be wrong, but if it is right, they be not merely blameless, but even praiseworthy ... And generally in respect of all that we seek or shun, as a man's will is attracted or repelled, so it is changed and turned into these different affections.[26]

Augustine's point is that when the human will is aligned with God's intentions and purposes, one's love will be 'well directed' and the affections that issue will also be good. These believers will experience a breadth of emotions – they will 'both fear and desire, and grieve and rejoice' – but 'because their love is rightly placed, all these affections of theirs are right'.[27]

---

24. Ibid., p. 26.

25. John Piper, *Desiring God* (Leicester: Inter-Varsity Press, 1986), p. 85.

26. Augustine, *The City of God*, tr. Marcus Dods (New York: Modern Library, 2000), 14.6 (pp. 447–448).

27. Ibid. 14.7, 9 (pp. 449, 452).

The same understanding is found in Puritan thought. For example, Edward Reynolds affirms that human nature has been created by God to be drawn towards what is perceived to be good and repelled by objects that stand in the way of that good. He writes:

> Passions are nothing else, but those natural, perfective, and unstrained
> motions of the Creatures unto that advancement of their Natures,
> which they are by the Wisdome, Power, and Providence of their
> Creator, in their owne severall Spheares, and according to the
> proportion of their Capacities, ordained to receive, by a regular
> inclination to those objects, whose goodnesse beareth a naturall
> conveniencie or virtue of satisfaction unto them; or by an antipathie
> and aversation from those, which bearing a contrarietie to the good
> they desire, must needs be noxious and destructive, and by consequent,
> odious to their natures.[28]

At this point he uses the term 'passions' as a general category, inclusive of both 'passions' and 'affections' within the schema of other writers. But elsewhere in his treatise it is apparent that at the conceptual level, by his using the language of both passion and affection, his thinking is consistent with that of other Puritans. Of critical importance, however, is the fact that within Reynolds's treatise he echoes Augustine in recognizing that these 'motions' or 'inclinations' can be well directed or misdirected.

Puritan divines, therefore, were willing to ascribe moral evaluations to emotional states, not as a function of the felt emotion, but in response to the object towards which the emotion is directed. In the words of Stephen Charnock:

> The Passions and Affections are the same, as to the Substance and
> Nature of the Acts; but the difference lies in the object. . . . The acts of a
> renewed man, and the acts of a natural man, are the same in the Nature
> of acts; as when a man loves God, and fears God; or loves man, or fears

---

28. Edward Reynolds, *A Treatise of the Passions and Faculties of the Soule of Man* (London, 1640), pp. 31–32.

man, 'tis the same act of love, and the same act of fear; there are the
same motions of the soul . . . the difference lies in the Objects.[29]

According to the Puritans, regeneration brought a change in perception regarding certain 'objects'. Whereas formerly God may have
been treated with disdain or indifference and the individual might
have found delight in pursuing selfish ends, the converted person
comes to love God and sin loses its attractiveness. The objects
remain the same but the heart has changed, resulting in changed
affections towards these objects. Facilitating this shift in affections
was central to Puritan pastoral work. By means of the ministry of
the word, Puritan pastors sought the conversion of souls and then
to see the regenerate strengthened in the faith so that the continuing
effects of indwelling sin would not draw believers' affections away
from their Lord and Saviour.

Affections central to authentic spiritual life
Within Puritan thought, therefore, affections were an indicator of
the genuineness or otherwise of a person's faith. A speculative or
notional understanding of God meant nothing. The true believer
was marked by a love for divine things and a delight in them, alongside
a diminished interest in the ways of worldliness. As Richard Sibbes
affirmed, 'Our affections show us what we are in religion.'[30]

---

29. Stephen Charnock, *A Discourse of the Nature of Regeneration*, in *The Works of
    the Late Learned Divine Stephen Charnock*, vol. 2, rev. ed. (London, 1699),
    p. 44. The same thought is expressed by John Bunyan, *The Greatness of the
    Soul* (London, 1683), p. 29: 'these passions of the Soul are not therefore
    good, nor therefore evil, because they are passions of the Soul: but are
    made so by two things, to wit, Principle and Object. The Principle I count
    that from whence they flow, and Object that upon which they are pitched.'
    See the helpful discussion in J. Stephen Yuille, *Puritan Spirituality: The Fear of
    God in the Affective Theology of George Swinnock*, SCHT (Milton Keynes:
    Paternoster, 2007), pp. 72–75, which drew my attention to these references.
30. Richard Sibbes, *A Glance of Heaven*, in Alexander B. Grosart (ed.),
    Works of Richard Sibbes, 7 vols. (Edinburgh: Banner of Truth, [1638]
    1983), vol. 4, p. 182.

This is not to claim, however, that every emotional response that arose within religious contexts was indicative of a divine work. This issue was critical in the genesis of Jonathan Edwards's treatise *The Religious Affections*, the most thorough treatment of the place of emotions in Christian life within the Puritan corpus. The work emerged in the context of the controversies associated with the spiritual revival, or 'Great Awakening', that arose in Northampton, Massachusetts, in 1734–5. A group that came to be known as the 'Old Lights' were alarmed at the excesses that attended the revival, such as laughing, screaming and shrieking within church services.[31] Others were much more positive in their assessment of the revival (the 'New Lights'), but some within this group were undiscerning in their assessment of the various manifestations of religious fervour and failed to acknowledge that in spiritual matters the spurious can coexist alongside the genuine.[32] Edwards's contribution is a finely nuanced piece of theological argument. He believed that the revival was a genuine work of God and, counter to the Old Lights, demonstrated that holy affections were pivotal to true religion. Yet the burden of his treatise was to correct the extreme New Lights. Heightened states of emotion proved nothing; they must be tested to see whether they were truly of God. Edwards provided twelve signs by which to conduct such an assessment, but it is the final one that is decisive: 'Gracious and holy affections have their exercise and fruit in Christian practice.' In other words, while real Christian faith will be marked by affections, 'the way to gauge the genuineness of one's faith was not to look at one's feeling, but at one's practice'.[33]

A second factor further reveals the centrality of the affections within the Puritan conception of the Christian life. They held that the affections were not only markers of genuine faith, but were also a means to godly living. These divines believed that individuals

31. George M. Marsden, *Jonathan Edwards: A Life* (New Haven: Yale University Press, 2003), pp. 268–270.

32. John E. Smith, 'Religious Affections and the "Sense of the Heart"', in Sang Hyun Lee (ed.), *The Princeton Companion to Jonathan Edwards* (Princeton: Princeton University Press, 2005), p. 113.

33. Marsden, *Jonathan Edwards*, p. 288.

always do what they really want to do. That is, whatever has captured the heart and affections directs a person's choices and actions. Without affections, claims Edwards, 'there would be no such thing as activity amongst mankind'.[34] God has given affections to humankind 'to be the springs that set men a-going'.[35] Other Puritans asserted the same. 'The affections are the Soules horses', wrote William Fenner, 'that draw her as it were in a Coach to the thing that shee affects: a man is moved by his affections.'[36] Similarly, Richard Sibbes reckoned that 'Christian affections are as the wind, to carry us on in holy life,'[37] and John Owen maintained that 'affections are in the soul as the helm in the ship'.[38] Within Puritan thought, therefore, affections function to stir up and direct human action.[39] With such a central role in motivating godly living, it is once more apparent why so much attention was given to the affections within the Puritan pastoral agenda.

The pastoral implications of the Puritan perspective on the emotional life

Preaching and other pastoral work
Due to the God-ordained role of the affections in directing human behaviour, Puritan pastors believed that simply informing people of what is right and commanding them to pursue the same was an

---

34. Edwards, *Religious Affections*, p. 29.

35. Ibid.

36. Fenner, *Treatise of the Affections*, sig. B2ᵛ.

37. Richard Sibbes, *The Life of Faith*, in Grosart, *Works of Richard Sibbes*, vol. 5, p. 368.

38. John Owen, *The Grace and Duty of Being Spiritually Minded*, in William H. Goold (ed.), *The Works of John Owen*, 16 vols. (Edinburgh: Banner of Truth, [1681] 1965), vol. 7, p. 397.

39. Brad Walton, *Jonathan Edwards, Religious Affections and the Puritan Analysis of True Piety, Spiritual Sensation and Heart Religion* (Lewiston, N. Y.: Edwin Mellen, 2002), p. 193. For this paragraph, see Walton's discussion pp. 191–194.

inadequate means to promote godly living. What was required was that the affections be won over to the cause of Christ. Consider, for example, an individual caught in a besetting sin. At the intellectual level he might know that the behaviour is wrong and its consequences harmful. But he still finds himself entrapped in the behaviour, because his affections have been captured by this particular sin. At the core of his being he still loves doing what his mind is telling him is wrong. Puritan pastoral practice maintains that the only way out of this trap is by means of a shift in affections. The individual concerned needs a clearer vision of the beauty of God in all his holiness and love, and a new appreciation of the vileness of sin. This is the only means to turn the heart from its attachment to what is evil and to reorient it to pursue the ways of God in obedience and joy.

This brings into consideration another faculty of the soul recognized by the Puritans, that of the 'fancy' or 'imagination'. This faculty mediated information from the senses to the intellect and the memory. As was the case with the passions, Puritans believed the imagination had the capacity to sway human behaviour in inappropriate directions. The apprehensions of the imagination are 'shallow'; they are 'taken from the senses' and operate 'before the use of reason', and thereby can influence action without recourse to the appropriate governing role that the Puritans believed was assigned to the intellect.[40] The imagination has great power over the soul 'because it stirs up the affections'; 'for as the imagination conceiveth, so usually the judgment concludeth, the will chooseth, the affections are carried, and the members execute'.[41] This is how Sibbes describes the relationship between the imagination, the affections and human action:

> Things work upon the soul in this order: 1. Some object is presented.
> 2. Then it is apprehended by imagination as good and pleasing, or as evil and hurtful. 3. If good, the desire is carried to it with delight; if evil, it is rejected with distaste, and so our affections are stirred up suitably to our

---

40. Richard Sibbes, *The Soul's Conflict with Itself*, in Grosart, *Works of Richard Sibbes*, vol. 1, p. 178.

41. Ibid., pp. 179, 182.

apprehension of the object. 4. Affections stir up the spirits. 5. The spirits raise the humours, and so the whole man becomes moved, and oftentimes distempered; this falleth out by reason of the sympathy between the soul and body, whereby what offendeth one redoundeth to the hurt of the other.[42]

Yet the capacity of the imagination to exert such influence over the soul can be used for good. 'We should make our fancy service-able to us in spiritual things,' urged Sibbes.[43] If the mind is kept replete with Scriptural truth, the imagination will have no place to wander and will in fact be taken hold of by material that can direct the soul in a godly course. Pastors should utilize this strategy, especially in their preaching. As Sibbes notes:

> The putting of lively colours upon common truths hath oft a strong working upon the fancy and our will and affections. The spirit is refreshed with fresh things, or old truths refreshed. . . . and our Saviour Christ's manner of teaching was by a lively representation to men's fancies, to teach them heavenly truths in an earthly, sensible manner; and indeed, what do we see or hear but will yield matter to a holy heart to raise itself higher?[44]

This is why many Puritan sermons and treatises contain long and vivid descriptions that appeal to the imagination. The goal was to fill the mind's eye with a picture of a wonderful and majestic God and of the horror of sin so that affections would be moved in a fitting direction.[45]

---

42. Ibid., pp. 179–180.
43. Ibid., p. 185.
44. Ibid., pp. 184–185.
45. For a very helpful analysis of the interrelationships between the workings of the various faculties of the soul within Puritan thought, including the role of the imagination, see Timothy J. Keller, 'Puritan Resources for Biblical Counselling', *Journal of Pastoral Practice* 9 (1988), pp. 11–44. Also available online at <http://www.ccef.org/puritan-resources-biblical-counseling>, accessed 1 Mar. 2012.

Emotional states and spiritual health

It has been argued that certain affections – love for God, finding joy and delight in him, a hatred of sin, and so on – were marks of authentic spirituality within Puritan thought. What does it mean, however, if believers find these emotional states wanting in their own experience? Is this necessarily a sign of spiritual insufficiency?

The fact is that some who fell under the sway of the Puritan movement did judge the quality of their spiritual life by the yardstick of their emotions. One example of this tendency is Mary Rich, countess of Warwick, who left a record of her vigorous piety in a range of spiritual and autobiographical writings penned during the 1670s and 1680s. Two consecutive diary entries reveal the significance of her feelings in her assessment of her spiritual condition. On 25 August 1675 Rich was meditating and rejoicing in her 'hapy and blessed condition of one that was reconsiled to God by Christ', experiencing 'very lively afectiones In the duty, In which my heart make strong sallies, and egress after God'.[46] The next day, however, she meditated upon 'the danger of backslideing ... which I was doing'. She had read earlier entries in her diary 'of the lively affections I had formerly in holy dutyes'. But this was not the case now: 'how dull I was too often of late grown In them, which had this effect upon me to make me selfe-condemned and with many teares to bemone my backslideings'.[47]

It is possible that Mary Rich may have been misreading her emotions. Perhaps in her heart of hearts she possessed a deep love for God but her bodily state or some other factor influenced her in such a way that she believed that what she was feeling was evidence of defective affections towards God. Nonetheless, what appears to be lacking in her perceptions is a robust confidence in the work of God *outside* her own soul – the atoning work of Christ on the cross.

Puritan pastors were aware that emotions were not a foolproof measure of spiritual health. When Katherine Gell, a member of a prominent Derbyshire family, sought counsel from Richard Baxter

---

46. *Countess of Warwick's Diary*, British Library, London, Add. MS 27354, Diary entry 25 Aug. 1675.
47. Ibid., Add. MS 27354, Diary entry 26 Aug. 1675.

on the lack of 'liveliness' in her faith, Baxter knew that labile emotional states could be misleading. While 'lively affections and sensibility be very desirable', wrote Baxter, 'yet are they not the evidences by which the truth of Grace may so well be tried'.[48] Baxter was able to offer such advice in the context of one-to-one pastoring. But it must be remembered that much Puritan guidance was transmitted via printed treatises, a medium through which it was much more difficult to provide directions for specific cases and circumstances. Much of this literature affirmed the importance of cultivating godly affections and set forth a range of duties to facilitate that end – reading the Bible, prayer, listening to sermons, engaging in holy conversation, meditation, hymn singing, and the like. It appears, however, that many lay people became so overwhelmed with the precise nature of what was asked of them in pursuing godliness of life that the end goal of a deepened love for God was lost.[49] It would seem, therefore, that there was a certain paradox in the relationship between emotions and spiritual health within Puritan thought. While godly affections were of the *esse* of saving faith, and thus could not be ignored or overlooked, the pathway to achieve them sometimes produced a state of spiritual despair or insecurity.

In the light of this discussion, what, then, can be said about the relationship between emotional states and spiritual health? Maybe the Puritans would acknowledge the value in being attuned to what one is feeling and what this might indicate. Are there signals or alarms that alert us to what we are concerned about or what we are valuing? Might these emotions be a means of exposing the idols of

---

48. *Baxter Correspondence*, Dr Williams's Library, London, MS 59 vol. 5, fol. 217, accessed by microfilm.

49. For discussions of the demands and disciplines of the Puritan paradigm of the Christian life, see Theodore Dwight Bozeman, *The Precisianist Strain: Disciplinary Religion and Antinomian Backlash in Puritanism to 1638* (Chapel Hill: University of North Carolina Press, 2004), and David R. Como, *Blown by the Spirit: Puritanism and the Emergence of an Antinomian Underground in Pre-Civil-War England* (Stanford: Stanford University Press, 2004).

our hearts, providing information about areas of life in need of repentance and thereby enabling growth in our Christian life? Furthermore, if there is truth in the cognitive theory of emotions,[50] such an awareness enables us to rethink our circumstances in the light of Scriptural truth, which might lead to a change in our emotional state, or, to use the language of the Puritans, to subdue sinful passions and arouse godly affections.

Yet perhaps it could also be said that there was something lacking in the overall tenor of how the Puritans perceived the relationship between emotions and spiritual well-being. For while the Spirit is at work to reorder our affections and other aspects of our emotional life, we must also recognize that we stand under the gospel of Christ. This truth means that our brokenness and failings, even in our emotional lives, are never the final word in the context of a relationship with God that is grounded in grace. The paltry nature of our love for God, our despair in the midst of life's hardships, moments of delighting in sin – for those of living faith, the truth that 'no condemnation now exists for those in Christ Jesus' (Rom. 8:1 HCSB) remains. One wonders whether Puritan pastors would have been able to sit comfortably with such an understanding. Even if they would have acknowledged this truth at the level of their theological position, perhaps their concern about the nominalism within their churches would have led to some disconnect between the glorious message of free grace in Christ and the duties of faithful Christian living that was a dominant motif in what their parishioners heard preached to them week by week.

A division between head and heart?

Within everyday parlance it is common to speak of a disjunction between head and heart, but the Puritans, following the Bible, believed that both intellect and emotion were critical to healthy human functioning and the life of godliness. As Thomas Dixon has argued, it was later nineteenth-century writers who moved away from the Christian tradition and drove a wedge between intellect

---

50. See e.g. the discussion in Matthew Elliott, *Faithful Feelings: Emotion in the New Testament* (Leicester: Inter-Varsity Press, 2005), ch. 1.

and feeling.[51] Also of interest is the fact that recent research in the fields of neuroscience and experimental psychology challenges any sharp dislocation between reason and emotion.[52] At the level of neural pathways, 'emotion seems to be in some sense intrinsic to effective rational functioning'.[53] When it comes to the relationship between thinking and feeling, therefore, what the Puritans articulated seems to be endorsed by the findings of modern science.

The Puritans avoided the extremes of both emotionalism and rationalism. During the seventeenth century, the Puritans opposed another manifestation of Protestant Christianity, those often termed 'Enthusiasts' or 'Fanatics'. The moniker referred to various sects, such as the Quakers, that emerged during the time of the English Civil Wars. These groups broke from the traditional Reformed view that affirmed a conjunction of Word and Spirit. Furthermore, they granted the Spirit an immediacy of operation in human life that bypassed the usual constraints of the natural workings of the faculties of the soul. The Puritans held otherwise – the divine work of the Spirit normally occurred through the agency of means, including the usual processes of psychological functioning.[54] Baxter captures the standard Puritan approach:

> God's way to persuade their wills, and to excite and actuate their affections, is by the discourse, reasoning or consideration of their understandings, upon the nature and qualifications of the objects which are presented to them.[55]

Affections are not random emotional responses, nor do they normally issue from a direct supernatural intervention of the Spirit.

---

51. Thomas Dixon, 'Revolting Passions', *Modern Theology* 27 (2011), p. 304.

52. Sarah Coakley, 'Introduction: Faith, Rationality and the Passions', *Modern Theology* 27 (2011), p. 219.

53. Ibid., p. 223.

54. See Geoffrey F. Nuttall, *The Holy Spirit in Puritan Faith and Experience*, 2nd ed. (Chicago: University of Chicago Press, 1947).

55. Richard Baxter, *The Saints' Everlasting Rest* (1650), in *Practical Works of Richard Baxter*, vol. 3, p. 249.

Rather, they are closely connected with the reasoning of the intellect. The standard Puritan approach, therefore, was that one feels because of what one believes. Similarly, the Puritans gave no credence to a rationalist approach to religion. As has been argued, they gave short shrift to any form of spirituality that was cold and sterile and was bereft of liveliness towards God.

Returning to Jonathan Edwards, we find the Puritan ability to avoid the Scylla of emotionalism and the Charybdis of rationalism best exemplified in *The Religious Affections*. As already noted, Edwards argued that intense emotional states were no sure indicator of a genuine work of God. Yet the solution was not to treat the affections as irrelevant to the life of faith. Charles Chauncy, a key proponent of the 'Old Lights', pushed in this direction: 'an *enlightened mind*, and not *raised affections*, ought always be the guide of those who call themselves men; and this, in the affairs of religion, as well as other things'.[56] But Edwards, following in the tradition of other Puritans, stressed the conjunction between reason and affections: 'Holy affections are not heat without light; but evermore arise from the information of the understanding, some spiritual instruction that the mind receives, some light or actual knowledge.'[57] For Edwards, the rational soul was a unity, with the various faculties being powers of the whole person. His concept of the 'heart' encompassed cognitive, volitional and affective aspects of the personality.[58] As Walton recognizes, his integrative approach enabled him to be a mediating figure in the polemical context of the Great Awakening: the 'volitional-affective dimension' of Edwards's construal of the heart 'counteracts the excessively speculative character of rationalist religion, while the 'cognitive-percipient aspect counteracts the indiscriminate emotionalism of the enthusiasts'.[59]

---

56. Charles Chauncy, *Seasonable Thoughts on the State of Religion in New-England* (Boston, 1743), p. 327, cited from Marsden, *Jonathan Edwards*, p. 281, emphasis original.

57. Edwards, *Religious Affections*, p. 192.

58. Ibid., p. 160.

59. Walton, *Jonathan Edwards*, p. 161.

This conjunction between head and heart accords with scriptural teaching. While the Bible distinguishes between the mind (*nous*) and the heart (*kardia*), the terms remain closely connected. For example, note the parallelism in 2 Corinthians 3:14–15 (HCSB), where Paul writes, 'But their minds were closed. For to this day, at the reading of the old covenant, the same veil remains . . . Even to this day, whenever Moses is read, a veil lies over their hearts.' The heart is the term that expresses the core of what we are as human beings, 'the concept that preeminently denotes the human ego in its thinking, affections, aspirations, decisions, both in man's relationship to God and to the world surrounding him'.[60] The Bible, therefore, upholds the psychic unity of human personhood; feelings are neither distanced from thinking nor from the core of what it is to be created in God's image. To respond to God with single-mindedness is not much different to responding to him with whole-heartedness, since both terms capture the biblical sense of having the totality of our being aligned with God and his purposes.[61]

Conclusion

We inhabit an age where experiences and feelings count for so much. Yet within many churches today, there is widespread suspicion about the place of feelings in the pursuit of godly living. Do the Puritans have anything to offer us?

The Puritans need to be read in the context of their times and it is important to recognize that they will not have all the answers to contemporary concerns. The movement had its inadequacies: it lacked an integrated biblical theology; Puritans had some problems with their understanding of the place of the law in the Christian life;

---

60. Herman Ridderbos, *Paul: An Outline of His Theology*, tr. John Richard De Witt (Grand Rapids: Eerdmans, 1975), p. 119. See also Hans Walter Wolff, *Anthropology of the Old Testament* (London: SCM, 1974), ch. 5.

61. Ben Johnson, 'The Head, the Heart and Christian Experience', in *1st Century Answers to 21st Century Questions* (Croydon, NSW: Sydney Missionary and Bible College, 2002), p. 130.

their particular construction of the nature of the Christian life and its duties proved very challenging for some people. Moreover, scientific understanding has progressed and we now know more about the neuroscience of emotion and how the body works.

Yet the Puritans assist us in their willingness to place their discussion of emotional states within a moral framework that recognizes that some are good and some bad. They may have erred in some aspects of their anthropological understanding, and thereby marginalized the bodily nature of our emotional states. But the overall thrust of their analysis recognizes that our feelings are not peripheral to Christian discipleship. Furthermore, the Puritans also provide us with a helpful corrective to certain expressions of Christian faith. They remind us that our great need is to know God, and that such knowledge is beyond the notional and is not mere acquaintance with him. The Puritans wanted people to see God with the eyes of faith as he really is – to grasp his majesty and holiness and goodness and love – and in so doing, to be drawn to worship him with their whole beings and find in him their joy and delight. Their vision of the Christian faith was deeply emotional. They wanted to help people 'Taste and see that the LORD is good' (Ps. 34:8 HCSB) and to live as if that were true.

PART 3

EMOTIONS DIVINE AND HUMAN

4. DOES GOD HAVE FEELINGS?

Gerald Bray

The problem stated

'There is but one living and true God, everlasting, without body, parts, or passions; of infinite power, wisdom, and goodness; the Maker and Preserver of all things both visible and invisible.' The opening sentence of the first of the *Thirty-Nine Articles of Religion* states the classical doctrine of God with admirable succinctness. It is taken almost word for word from the Augsburg Confession of 1530, in which the followers of Martin Luther defined their evangelical faith. I say almost word for word, because Thomas Cranmer, after reducing the lengthy Lutheran article to a couple of sentences, made a small but significant addition to it. The Augsburg article says that 'there is only one living and true God, everlasting, without body or parts'. Cranmer reworked this by interpreting 'everlasting' as the third attribute of the one living and true God, and creating a new triad of 'body, parts and passions'. He did not intend to highlight any theological difference between the churches of England and Wittenberg, which were agreed on this point, but what to him was probably no more than a cosmetic addition has since become the most prominent and controversial aspect of what is now known as 'classical theism'.

In the sixteenth century, and for most (if not all) of Christian history before that, it was taken for granted that God has no body, and that since parts and passions are properties of a body, it follows logically that he does not have them either. This belief was inherited from Judaism. The well-known anthropomorphisms of the Old Testament, according to which God was said to have an eye, a hand, and so on, were regarded as figures of speech rather than as literal descriptions of a finite heavenly being. In a world where almost everyone else portrayed their deities in human terms, the Mosaic prohibition against idolatry was enough to prove that the God of Israel could not be reduced to bodily dimensions. Whether he had parts or not became something of an issue when the doctrine of the Trinity was first elaborated, because there were some naive individuals who thought that the Logos, or mind of God and the Spirit were detachable parts of the divine being, but this notion was easily refuted. Everyone realized that God did not lose his mind when the Son became a man, nor did he cease to be a spirit on the day of Pentecost, so it was not difficult to conclude that whatever the members of the Trinity were, they were not parts of a finite divine body.

The question of divine passions, however, caused much greater difficulty. It may be true that theological discussion in the early church reflected the concerns of men formed in the schools of ancient Greek philosophy, but that is not the only reason they had a problem. To the ancients, passion was a sensation inflicted by an external power and not a self-generated feeling. Three attributes of God, each of them amply attested in the Hebrew Bible, made it seem incompatible with his being and forced the early Christians to conclude that God must be impassible.

The first, and in some ways most important of these, was his transcendence. As the Creator, God dwelt above and beyond his creation. His being was unlike anything he had made and suffering was therefore just as inapplicable to him as anything else in the created order was. The second divine attribute that stood in the way was his perfection, which implied immutability. Suffering would involve some form of change and was therefore ruled out as impossible in God's case, because for a perfect being to change would necessarily involve a loss of that perfection. The third attribute that suffering called into question was God's sovereignty. If he could be attacked and harmed by an external force, that force would be more powerful than he is and would compromise his sovereignty over his creation, something the early church could never have accepted.

All these things argued in favour of a doctrine of divine impassibility, but there was another side to the Old Testament witness that also has to be accounted for. On many occasions God is portrayed as loving his people, as being angry with their disobedience, and even as hating people or things he rejected (see Deut. 1:27; Hos. 9:15; Mal. 1:3). From our modern point of view there is some ambiguity in these verses, because it is often not clear whether the mention of God's love or hate is a revelation of his inner feelings or just the human perception of God's actions, which vary according to our obedience or disobedience but do not reflect any real change in him. However, there are also several places where he is described as a God of compassion, whose love for his people overrides their disobedience and encourages him to show them mercy and forgiveness, even though they clearly do not deserve it (2 Kgs 13:23; 2 Chr. 36:15; Pss 78:38; 86:15; 111:4; 112:4; 145:8; Jer. 12:15; Lam. 3:32; Mic. 7:19). Some of these texts emphasize that God shows compassion because of the covenant he established with Abraham, Isaac and Jacob, which makes it clear that the Bible is not simply using human language to explain divine actions that in themselves have nothing to do with feelings. God is portrayed throughout the Old Testament as a God who has established what we would call a personal relationship with his creatures, and especially with the nation with which he has entered into covenant. We have to recognize that underlying all talk about divine emotions there lies this deeper question of how an infinite, transcendent God can have a meaningful relationship with beings that are finite and have been created by him.

It is also important to note that suffering and feeling are not identical. Even if we confine ourselves to external sensation, it is clear that the suffering I would get from being shot by an arrow is not the same as the feeling I would have if I were simply to touch it. This distinction was recognized by the ancients, who used different

words to describe the two things. Suffering was *pathos* and feeling
was *aisthēsis*, a word that could be applied to any form of sense
perception. Today we think of it primarily in relation to sight or
sound, as when we say that a work of art or music is aesthetically
pleasing. The more material meaning survives, but mainly in the
negative, so that when our bodily feelings are numbed we say we
have been anaesthetized, probably in order to avoid the pain of
suffering! In the New Testament *aisthēsis* plays a role in the healing
touch of Jesus, as it also does in the case of the woman who touched
his garment and was cured of her illness (Matt. 8:15; 9:20). In at least
one case, the healing of the two blind men at Jericho, we are told
that Jesus took pity on them, so it is clear that his emotions sometimes
played a part in his healing ministry, although it was his physical
touch and not his inner feelings that produced the cure (Matt. 20:34).

Did Jesus suffer on our behalf because of his compassion for us?
Hebrews 4:15 says that 'we do not have a high priest who is unable
to sympathize with our weaknesses' (ESV), but this is a mistranslation.
The Greek word is *sympathēsai*, which implies physical suffering in a
way that the English word derived from it does not. The high priest
could not be 'sympathetic', not because he was emotionally challenged, but because he did not suffer for the sins of the people. The
modern reader is liable to think primarily in terms of an emotional
bond and wonder how the Jewish high priest could have been so
hard-hearted! Perhaps he was not. Given that he was sacrificing for
his own sins as well as for those of the people, he may have been
extremely sympathetic to them in our sense of the word, but because
he could not be their substitute, the writer to the Hebrews argued
that he could not feel their pain. That is what Hebrews 4:15 means,
and the verse does not suggest that the temple priests lacked normal
human feelings. This is a good example of how changing perceptions of what *pathos* and *sympatheia* are can affect the way in which
we read and interpret ancient texts, and in turn modify our theological understanding based on them.

The importance of this change in perception must not be under-
estimated. To give a modern example, if a boy cuts his finger, what
should a compassionate father do? Should he cut his own finger in
order to show that he is not a father who cannot be touched by the
feeling of his son's infirmities? If he did that, the gesture would not

be appreciated by the son, and the boy's mother would probably tell him that he is completely useless, no good with children and even heartless for not taking the boy's pain seriously. In other words, her understanding of compassion would be practically the opposite of what it is in the Bible.

This does not mean that the writer to the Hebrews would not have done what any modern father would do in such circumstances; only that he would have expressed his reaction in different terms. Rather than talk about sympathy, he would most probably have used the word 'mercy'. Nowadays this concept has gone out of general use except in the context of a law court, where a judge can still show mercy on the accused by mitigating the severity of his punishment. A modern father who responded to his son's need by binding up his wound would probably not explain his behaviour as an act of mercy, but that is what it would be, and what he felt about it would hardly matter.

Pursuing this analogy further, it is interesting to observe that the Jesuit theologian Jean Galot (1919–2008) used two Old Testament examples of a father–son relationship as evidence that God the Father must also have felt for the suffering of his Son.[1] The first example he chose was that of Abraham, who was called to sacrifice his son Isaac, and the second was that of David and his son Absalom (Gen. 22:1–18; 2 Sam. 18:31 – 19:7). Unfortunately, there are difficulties with both of these cases if we try to use them as models for God's behaviour. How Abraham felt when he was told to sacrifice Isaac we do not know. The order came from God, but Isaac was the child of God's promise and Abraham's reaction must be understood in that light. Faced with the choice between obeying God or saving his son, Abraham obeyed God and was rewarded by seeing his son unexpectedly being spared at the last minute. If his personal feelings came into it, we are not told, and it is hard to know what they would have been. Abraham put his duty to God before any feelings he may have had for his son, and the Bible implies that this was the right thing for him to do. Consider the alternative. If Abraham had refused God's command, he would have lost the covenant promises,

---

1. Jean Galot, *Dieu souffre-t-il?* (Paris: Lethielleux, 1976), pp. 92–97, 114–118.

and would have ended up feeling far worse than he did. Instead, Abraham trusted God and told Isaac to do the same, and the whole emphasis of the story is on the triumph of faith over natural feeling. It therefore seems inappropriate to use it in the way Galot did.

As for the case of David and Absalom, David's grief over his son's death was an unmistakable display of fatherly feeling, but it was also inappropriate. As Joab had to remind the king, Absalom deserved what he got and David's reaction would be taken as a sign of his weakness, not admired as the proper reaction of a caring father. It should also be said that Absalom's death does not parallel that of Jesus. Jesus died voluntarily in obedience to his Father. The New Testament says nothing about the Father's reaction to his Son's death, but tells us that on the third day he raised him from the dead in confirmation of his perfect obedience. We also know that Jesus never asked the Father to pity him. On the contrary, when his hour came, Jesus asked the Father to glorify himself in his Son's sufferings, which is a rather different thing (John 17:4–5).

A large part of the problem we have with the idea of divine impassibility is that when we ask whether God has feelings, we want an answer to a question that would not have been put that way in the past and we find it hard to grasp the kind of response that would most likely have been given. People have not changed of course, and neither has God, but we must adjust our perceptions and our vocabulary if we are going to discover what the Bible and the theological tradition have to say about this, or else we shall end up talking at cross purposes. To sum it up, what to them was primarily an issue of how God acts, to us is primarily an issue of how God relates to his creatures and especially to his own people, whether that involves action or not.

The impact of the Son's incarnation

For Christians, discussion about feelings in God must also consider the incarnation of the Son. No one doubts that Jesus of Nazareth was fully human, with all the senses and emotions that any man would have. The Gospels tell us of his reactions to different events, and especially to the news that Lazarus had died before he arrived to heal him. The shortest verse of the Bible says it all: 'Jesus wept' (John 11:35 ESV). He shared fully in the joys of the wedding feast at Cana and in the sorrows of those who sought him out for healing and restoration. What he felt about Judas's betrayal or Peter's denial is not recorded, but we can imagine that he reacted in much the same way as any of us would. It is not the humanity of Jesus that raises difficulties, but his divinity, and it is on that aspect of the matter that the Christian theological tradition has always focused its attention.

Explaining how the impassible and immortal God could suffer and die was the greatest single challenge the early Christians faced, and we should not be surprised to discover that the problem of divine suffering lies at the heart of the two great Christological heresies that appeared in the fourth and fifth centuries. On the one hand there was Arianism, the belief that Jesus could not have been God because he suffered and died for us. Given the reality of that suffering, he must have been a creature – greater than any other creature no doubt, but a creature nonetheless. On the other hand there was Nestorianism, the belief that Jesus was a true man to whom the Son of God had been conjoined in the womb of his mother Mary. The union of the divine and human in him in no way compromised the integrity of each nature, and the man who died on the cross cried out that God had deserted him in the hour of trial. This, said Nestorius, was inevitable because God cannot suffer and die, and so the Son of God went away and left Jesus of Nazareth to die without him.

The remarkable thing is that the church refused to succumb to either of these distortions. It would not accept that Jesus was less than fully God, nor would it agree that the union of God and man was superficial and potentially dissoluble. Instead, the Council of Chalcedon in 451 decided that Jesus must be a single divine Person in two natures, one divine and therefore impassible, and the other human. On the cross the divine Person of the Son of God suffered and died in his human nature, because that was the only way that an impassible and immortal being could experience suffering and death. Biblical support for this can be found in the prologue to John's Gospel, and also in Philippians 2:5–11, where we are told that he who did not think equality with God was something to be grasped at humbled himself, took the place of a servant and became a man. Note that the servanthood preceded the incarnation. It was because the Son accepted the servant role that he became a man, and not the other way round. A man would have had no choice but to be (or refuse to be) a servant of God, but the Son chose the role freely and then did what was necessary for it to be accomplished.

To explain how the divine Son of God could become a man without ceasing to be God, the early church developed the concept of personhood, which had not existed before. When the creeds state that Jesus Christ was 'fully God and fully man' what they mean is that he was fully divine and fully human; words that we automatically interpret in personal terms were to them markers of his being, or nature. As a person, Jesus was fully divine but not human at all. Some theologians have objected to this, claiming that if Jesus was not a human person he could not have been a human being, but that is a misunderstanding. According to the Bible, human persons are also in a sense divine, because we are created in the image and likeness of God (Gen. 1:26–27). Human beings are set apart from the rest of creation by this inbuilt relationship to God, and it is that which the term 'person' tries to capture.

It is often claimed that the modern concept of 'person' is different from the ancient one, but that is only partly true and it is misleading to put too much weight on this supposed difference. What really distinguishes our approach from that of the early church is that we have developed the implications of what they said to a degree that they did not. They worked out that the relationship between God and man could be properly expressed only in personal terms, because categories of being and nature emphasize our mutual incompatibility. In the modern world these things have been pushed aside in favour of the all-importance of personal relationships, which unite us with him and bind us to one another. To put it a different way, as a modern person I am more interested in knowing that the Son of God loves me and died for me than that he had a human mind and soul just as I have, because I am more concerned with the quality of our mutual relationship than with the compatibility of our respective beings.

Personhood is what separates us from any other living creature, including chimpanzees and orang-utans, to which we are closely related in genetic terms. Animals can certainly suffer and die, but do they have feelings? This is a controversial subject and the question probably cannot be answered in objective terms. Suffice it to say that most people who think that animals – or at least some animals, like dogs – have feelings think this because they believe that feelings are part and parcel of relationships. Dogs establish relationships with their owners, and so it is possible to think that a rejected dog will feel hurt, just as a rejected human being would. But whether kennels are bulging with emotionally challenged canines may reasonably be questioned, and experience suggests that when one dog meets another, whatever feelings they may have for their human owners take a back seat.

You may think that this is taking us a long way from the incarnate Son of God, but actually it is helping us to clarify the issue. Dogs are not persons and cannot have relationships in the human or divine sense of the word. If feelings spring from relationships, then dogs do not have them, at least not in any way that we can understand. The real question is whether feelings are intrinsic to personhood, making it inevitable that a divine person will have them just as much as human ones do. As a man, Jesus could suffer and die, which is what he came to do and why he took on a human nature in the first place. But did the *kenōsis* of the Son of God include taking on the ability to have feelings, or was that ability already present in him before he became a man? If he acquired it in his mother's womb, then of course his feelings, like his ability to suffer and die, would belong exclusively to his humanity. But if he had feelings before his incarnation, then they would belong to his divinity and presumably would be shared with the other members of the Trinity. What is certain is that it is in and through our persons that we express our feelings. Assuming that Jesus had feelings like ours, he must have expressed them in and through his divine person, whether he possessed them before his incarnation or not. It therefore seems reasonable to conclude that his divine person must have feelings, and that these feelings are shared with the other divine persons, as well as with us.

That sounds logical, but if post-Chalcedonian theologians had been asked about it, they would have come up with a different answer. Few people are aware of it, but for two centuries and more

after Chalcedon the Eastern church was rocked by divisions that led
it to refine what was meant by 'one divine person subsisting in two
natures'. How Jesus could be fully human without being a human
person was answered by developing the concept of *enhypostasia*,
according to which the human nature of Christ acquired its hypo-
stasis, that is to say its identity and ability to function autonomously,
by being united to the divine person of the Son. Everything his
human nature did or was capable of doing was expressed in and
through the divine person of the Son, but without affecting his
divinity. The doctrine of *enhypostasia* codified what earlier theologians
had called 'the transfer of properties' (*communicatio idiomatum*) and
made it possible to say that on the cross the impassible and immortal
Son of God suffered and died in his human nature.

At the same time, it is because of the Son's divinity that his human
sacrifice has reconciled us to the Father. The benefits of that are
mediated to us by the Holy Spirit without either of those persons
being directly implicated in the sacrifice itself. Given that the sacrifice
is external to the being of God, this does not matter, because, thanks
to their mutual indwelling (Gk. *perichōrēsis*), all three persons act in
the light of its effects. To put it simply, the Father forgives me
because of his Son's sacrifice without having to experience that
sacrifice himself, and the Holy Spirit applies the sacrifice of the Son
to our lives and unites us to him, without feeling the pain of the
Son's sacrificial death.

Because the theologians of the immediate post-Chalcedonian
era did not think of feelings as anything more than a function of
the human body, they understood the feelings of Jesus for those
around him in the same way, and saw them as signs pointing to his
sacrifice on our behalf. It was inconceivable for them to think of
the Son as having feelings in his relationship to the Father and the
Holy Spirit, since he did not sacrifice himself for them in the way
he did for us. Their mutual relationships are eternal and therefore
perfect and immutable, so there is no room for interaction of the
kind that is normal among human beings. Admittedly, their relationships are grounded in love, which we think of as something
emotional, but this is not true of God because his love is perfectly
realized. Emotions are present in human love because our love is
imperfect and emotional involvement gives us a sense of security

and belonging that we would not otherwise have. But in God the three persons of the Trinity dwell in each other so completely that there is no 'spare room' (if we can put it that way) for them to express their mutual love within the Godhead. Whatever one of the persons does automatically embraces all three as co-actors with him, so it is only outside their shared divinity that they can express the love that they have for each other. Inside God, any expression of love by one person of the Trinity for the others would actually diminish that love because by drawing attention to it and defining it, it would make it less than all-embracing.

When it comes to personal relationships between God and man, things are more complicated. The Old Testament makes it clear that God did not have to become a man in order to relate to human beings, even if the incarnation of the Son changed the nature of that relationship. We express our feelings in our relationship with Jesus, and expect him to do the same in his relationship with us. We cannot isolate him from the other persons of the Godhead, because if we did, we would risk making the Father into a forbidding and inaccessible person. Since the Son came to show us the Father and establish us in a personal relationship with him, that would make no sense. We would also find it hard to explain how the feelings of the Son can be communicated to us by the Holy Spirit if the third person of the Trinity is incapable of sharing them. Thus we are back to the question we began with – are the feelings of Jesus human feelings that derive from his incarnation, or do they transcend the human and are therefore essentially divine? And can they be divine without compromising and diminishing the Godhead?

Modern questions

A generation ago the traditional doctrine of divine impassibility was almost universally rejected by theologians who had lived through the horrors of the Second World War and who, like Jürgen Moltmann, wondered where God was in Auschwitz. They tried to answer this question by reshaping their picture of God. Taking the crucifixion of Jesus as their model, they focused on his cry of dereliction, 'My God, my God, why hast thou forsaken me?'

(Matt. 27:46; Mark 15:34 AV).[2] and saw in this the ultimate identification of the divine with the human. The atoning purpose of
Christ's sacrifice was nudged out of the picture and replaced by
suffering as an end in itself. Only by seeing that there is a cross at
the heart of God could Moltmann and his colleagues come to terms
with what they themselves had lived through, but what they saw in
that cross was solidarity with human suffering more than redemption from human sin.

It is largely for this reason that their answer, while very understandable in the circumstances, was inadequate. We now know that
the horror of Nazi genocide was not an isolated aberration but the
harbinger of a new form of human behaviour made possible by
the invention of the means of mass destruction. Auschwitz, as it
turned out, was not unique, but the beginning of a trend. At the
same time, technological advances were not only or even mainly
applied to mass destruction. They could also be used for good, and
the great advances in the control of disease and the cure of scourges
like cancer, along with growing international cooperation in dealing
with crises caused by natural disasters and failed states, gave people
a new hope that physical suffering can be overcome. Horrible as
Auschwitz was, it is not and cannot be the last word on the subject
of suffering. In that context the impassibility of God can not only
be defended but can even be seen as a necessary precondition for
him to function effectively. If doctors and aid workers are suffering
from the conditions they are supposed to be curing, they are of little
practical use, and the same can be said of God. We want him to be
fit enough to get us out of the mess we are in, and considering how
great that mess is, his immunity to it can be regarded as a great relief
and source of hope.

In a brilliant monograph on the subject the Roman Catholic theologian Thomas Weinandy (1946–) has pointed out that a suffering
God would be of no help to us, not simply because he would cease
to be the transcendent Deity whose very non-involvement with
human suffering makes it possible for him to intervene effectively
to deal with it, but also – and most interestingly – because a suffering

---

2. The quotation is from Ps. 22:1.

God would have to suffer in his own divine way and not in ours.[3] In other words, his divine suffering would be no more like ours than his divine being is, and we would be just as unable to relate to it. Weinandy recognizes that Moltmann and his followers have the best intentions, but shows that their attempts to deepen our understanding of how God relates to the world have actually had the opposite effect!

Nowadays we have moved into a different kind of discussion. Our affluent societies are plagued not with physical suffering, though there is still plenty of that about, but with self-doubt, frustration and loneliness. We have gained the whole world, it seems, but in the process we have lost our souls. Our psychological unease is not new by any means, but it has become more pressing in an age when happiness and self-fulfilment have replaced survival as the priority for most people. We also live in a world where relationships are in crisis. The breakdown of the traditional family unit has reached epidemic proportions, and the full consequences have yet to be felt. New kinds of interconnectedness have appeared, ranging from gay marriage to communes that double as house churches. With greater freedom has come greater self-centredness, and how I feel about the situation I am in has become the primary criterion by which I judge it. In such a climate feelings are bound to take on an importance they never previously had. How does this affect our understanding of God?

Linked to this in some ways but independent of it in others is 'process theology', which pictures a dynamic God who is forever changing and growing in a constantly expanding universe. By adopting that principle, process theologians broke what had previously seemed to be the inescapable link between impassibility and immutability. Once it is assumed that change is an integral part of God's nature, the idea that he must be impassible because he is essentially immutable is neither inescapable nor even credible. He may still be impassible, but if so, it must be for some reason other than his immutability, at least as that has been traditionally

---

3. Thomas G. Weinandy, *Does God Suffer?* (Edinburgh: T. & T. Clark, 2000), pp. 1–39.

understood. A living, dynamic God is forever changing to meet the demands of his growing creation, which means that he is in constant interaction with his creatures. Orthodox Christians have been able to absorb some of this, but they insist that such interaction does not mean that God has to change in himself. They may even claim that process theologians who make movement natural to the being of God can be enlisted in support of their view. If internal development is a permanent reality in God, he would only change if he stopped growing. Since that is impossible, he can still be regarded as immutable, even though he is moving and growing all the time!

Dr Weinandy's criticisms of process theology follow lines very similar to his critique of Moltmann's theory of the suffering God, but process theology also suffers from being essentially impersonal and therefore insufficiently relational. To speak of atoms colliding and combining in new and different ways is to speak of a kind of relationship, but this is not what most of us understand by the term. For us, relationships are primarily personal and embrace feelings in a way that process theology finds it difficult to do. As a result, process theology remains the affair of philosophers, especially those interested in cosmology, although its emphasis on dynamism has penetrated more widely and is more compatible with the common modern understanding of relationships. It is hard to imagine any relationship being static or fixed, and Christians have always thought of our relationship with God in terms of growing in grace, holiness and sanctification. What we want to know is that if God makes a difference to our lives, do we not also make a difference to his? How can we say that he cares about us if we make no impression on him at all?

It is considerations like these that feed into the modern desire to find feelings in God. We cannot imagine having a relationship with an emotionally inert person. Images and memories of distant parents and formal relationships between children and adults, which we often associate with the Victorian era, disturb the modern mind and seem unnatural to us. If God is our Father, we do not want him to resemble the distant Victorian paterfamilias but to be more like an adult friend and mentor in whom we can confide. It is true, of course, that adults conceal things from children, and parents' emotional responses are almost bound to be more measured and guarded than their children's are, but for parents not to have any empathy with their offspring seems bizarre. Surely, therefore, there must be room for emotion in God?

This in brief is the case for saying that God has feelings. Relationships demand them, and if we are in a relationship with God our Father, there must be something in him that can connect with us at the emotional level if the analogy with human relationships is to have any meaning. The differences between God's nature and ours will put his feelings for us in their proper perspective but will not eliminate them altogether, because they are eternally present in the Trinity and were not created, but only temporally manifested to us in the incarnation of the Son.

A critique of the modern position

How valid is this modern demand for feelings in God? Do we have to revise or abandon the traditional understanding of his immutability in order to accommodate them, or should we instead aim our criticism at current perceptions of human desires on the ground that they are illegitimate and demean both God in himself and our relationship with him? Let me clarify the issue by starting with some self-evident truths.

First of all, if there are feelings in God that we can relate to, they must be present at the level of the divine persons, because that is how God relates to us. The divine nature is beyond our comprehension and experience, so any feelings it may have are unknowable and irrelevant to us. Secondly, the question of whether God has feelings must be distinguished from the question of his impassibility, because feelings are internal and can be self-generated, which was not true of suffering as that was traditionally understood. If human beings can have feelings without necessarily experiencing pain caused by an external influence, then surely the same must be true of God because we have been created in his image and likeness. Thirdly, do the feelings of Jesus, experienced by his divine person in his human nature, extend to the other persons of the Trinity or are they unique to him? If they involve the other members of the Godhead, did

Jesus have feelings as God as well as feelings as man, and if he did, were these two types of feeling distinct from each other?

No one doubts that in his human nature, the Son of God had the feelings of a man. He took that nature back into heaven with him at his ascension, so presumably his human feelings continue to exist along with his glorified human body and the wounds that it bore for our salvation. In our relationship with the glorified Son it should therefore still be possible for us to express our feelings and receive a sympathetic response from him. Of course, the feelings of the glorified humanity of Christ are purified and perfected in a way that ours cannot be, and they are freed from the limitations that he was subject to during his earthly life. To that extent, his heavenly feelings must be different from ours, but they are human feelings nonetheless. Our love for him is imperfect whilst his love for us is perfect, but our relationship is still one of mutual love and we connect with him on that basis.

That much is agreed by everyone, including those who want to maintain the classical doctrine of divine immutability. Even in heaven the divine person of the Son continues to experience feeling, just as he continues to experience suffering, at least in his glorified human nature. The question is whether, and how, the feelings experienced by the divine person of the Son in his human nature have a bearing on his relationship to the Father and the Holy Spirit within the Godhead. In other words, how does his personal relationship with us affect his personal relationship with them?

The Old Testament tells us that God loves his people and grieves when they turn away from him. His nature is not affected by our rebellion because although we change he does not. His grief over our sin is an expression of his love, because if he were indifferent or prepared to accept our behaviour, he would not feel that way. John 3:16 reminds us that it was because God loved the world that he gave his only begotten Son, allowing him to suffer and die so that we might be delivered from our sins and restored to eternal fellowship with him. It is important to interpret emotional language about God in the light of human sin and disobedience, because it might read very differently otherwise. In particular, the wrath of God would be a very different thing if it were divorced from the context of his love. God has not taken umbrage at our ingratitude and got angry because of it, as we might do in his situation. On the contrary, he has responded to us as a loving Father, and in his wrath he has determined to put right what has gone wrong in our relationship with him. Too often, modern critics of traditional Christian orthodoxy ignore or underplay this dimension; sin is not part of their vocabulary of suffering. And yet without sin, there would be no suffering at all. We do not suffer in direct proportion to our sins, as the story of Job reminds us, but we have all fallen in Adam and suffering is part of our common human inheritance.

However we look at it, our relationship with God is determined not only by our finitude, which conditions everything we say about him, but also by our sinfulness. God's relationship with us, on the other hand, is determined by his infinitude, which makes him free of all our basic creaturely limitations, and also by his sinlessness, which means that it does not fluctuate according to his mood-swings but remains fixed and perfect in spite of everything. Because of this we can trust him in a way that we cannot trust each other or even ourselves, and it is that trust which is the basis of our relationship with him.

Within the Trinity we know that the Father relates to the incarnate Son in his human finitude, which the Son shares with us, but not in his sinfulness, because even as a human being he was not sinful. Only when the Son voluntarily became sin for us did the Father's wrath fall on him, but this was not because the relationship between them was broken. On the contrary, the wrath of God could fall on the Son in the way it did precisely because the relationship of love between the Father and the Son was strong enough to bear it. The Father did not punish the Son because he turned against him in anger, but because the Son voluntarily took our place on the cross and accepted our punishment. His suffering was an act of obedience, and that obedience was a mark of his love for the Father.

That love is eternal inside the Trinity, which is why the Father and the Holy Spirit were not cut off from the Son's human suffering on our behalf, nor were they unaffected by it. Their love for the Son and his love for them meant that they were deeply involved in his agony, even if they did not feel it themselves. That involvement did not change or diminish them, but revealed the depth and power of the love that binds them together. At the same time, that love is, and must be, both impassible and immutable. It is impassible, because if it were to suffer it would be diminished and made less effective; it is immutable, because if it changed it would cease to be what it is and our salvation would be compromised, if not lost altogether.

As I have already stated, God's love cannot grow or develop internally because it is perfect, but it can and does express itself externally – in the creation of the world and in the redemption of humanity. God did not bring us into being because he needed something to love, but because he chose to express his love outside his own being. What we experience as a feeling is to him a plan and purpose that does not change and cannot be deflected by our rebellion against him. God is faithful even though every man were a liar, and he is faithful because he does not change (Rom. 3:4). By sending his Son to die for us he showed us what the limits of that faithfulness are – there are none! Everything about him is infinite, and so his love for us is infinite too.

Emotions as we know them are finite and fickle. They can swing from one extreme to another, and may be good, bad or some mixture of the two. God is not, and cannot be, like that. His love for us is not a passing feeling but an eternal purpose. If it appears to change because of our sin, the fault is ours, not his and the change is in us, not in him. Attempts to project human emotions onto God may be well meaning, but in the end they destroy what they have set out to achieve. Instead of gaining a deeper insight into God and his ways, we find that we have brought him down to our level and thus lost him altogether. God did not send his Son into the world merely to share our sufferings but to deliver us from them. In the kingdom of heaven every tear will be wiped away and sorrow and sighing will be no more (Rev. 21:4). The ups and downs of emotion will give way to the perfect joy of union with God in which we shall be perfect even as he is perfect, and share in the fullness of a love that has neither beginning nor end.

5. WHOSE TEARS? THE EMOTIONAL LIFE OF JESUS

Richard J. Gibson

The Gospels constitute rich sources for study of the emotions. The Evangelists often attribute emotional responses to disciples, opponents, supplicants and to Jesus. Taken together, the four portraits of Jesus attribute an impressive range of emotions to him. As James Stalker observed in the late nineteenth century, 'the notices of how He felt in different situations in which He was placed are far more numerous than anyone whose attention has not been specifically directed to them would believe'.[1]

When the Gospel accounts are compared and contrasted, intriguing issues emerge. As might be expected, John provides a distinctive perspective. Comparison of Mark and Luke generates a perplexing puzzle. On the assumption of Mark's priority, Luke's systematically deletes all of Mark's references to Jesus' emotions. As Fitzmyer puts it, 'the description of Jesus moved by human emotions in the Marcan Gospel is normally eliminated in the Lucan story, even if they are

---

1. James Stalker, *Imago Christi: The Example of Jesus Christ*, 3rd ed. (London: Hodder & Stoughton, 1890), pp. 312–313.

expressions of love, compassion, or tenderness'.[2] The phenomenon
is significant for early Christian evaluations of emotion. Does Luke
object to Mark's portrayal of Jesus as angry, compassionate and
stricken with grief? Does this reflect a divergent, competing assessment of the value and validity of emotion?

Gospel portraits of Jesus

It hardly needs to be argued that Jesus ought to be significant for
any Christian account of the emotions. The way in which Jesus is
portrayed is crucial to any Christian evaluation of the significance
of emotions more generally. Whether our interest is in Jesus as the
'one who in every respect has been tempted as we are, yet without
sin' (Heb. 4:15 ESV) or as the 'exact imprint of [God's] nature' (Heb.
1:3 ESV), we cannot afford to neglect the way early Christian writers
presented Jesus' emotional experience and expression.

Yet despite this, and the ample material pointed to by Stalker,
the topic has been decidedly neglected. Sustained, scholarly studies
of Jesus' emotions are rare. Two exceptions spring to mind. In the
early twentieth century B. B. Warfield published a 52-page study
entitled, 'On the Emotional Life of our Lord'.[3] Much more recently
Stephen Voorwinde published the fruit of his doctoral research,
Jesus' Emotions in the Fourth Gospel.[4] There have been numerous
articles focusing on particular episodes, canvassing specific issues.
Of course, commentaries discuss particular emotions as they
arise. Yet the last century has witnessed little sustained attention to
the topic.

---

2. Joseph A. Fitzmyer, *The Gospel According to Luke I–IX* (Garden City,
    N. Y.: Doubleday, 1981), p. 95; cf. Joseph A. Fitzmyer, *The Gospel
    According to Luke X–XXIV* (Garden City, N. Y.: Doubleday, 1985),
    p. 816).

3. Benjamin Breckinridge Warfield, *The Person and Work of Christ*
    (Philadelphia: Presbyterian & Reformed, 1950), pp. 93–145.

4. Stephen Voorwinde, *Jesus' Emotions in the Fourth Gospel: Human or
    Divine?* (London: T. & T. Clark, 2005).

A number of reasons are suggested for this relative neglect. Some would regard it as consistent with a pervasive western bias against emotion.[5] Matthew Elliott traces the neglect by New Testament scholars to a preference for a non-cognitive account of emotion, which 'simplifies the academic process and may promote a feeling of irrational infallibility'.[6] In pleading for a cognitive approach, Elliott points to a growing acceptance of such theories among psychologists, philosophers and anthropologists. He argues that the New Testament evidence points in the same direction.[7]

The lack of interest could also reflect assessments of the Gospel accounts. For much of the twentieth century the historical and bio-graphical value of the Gospels were dismissed by New Testament scholars. This was in part in reaction to the excesses of popular attempts to reconstruct the life and psychology of Jesus in the preceding century. It is not my intention here to revive psychological profiling of Jesus. What the Gospels do attribute to Jesus is of interest for what we learn about early Christian evaluation of emotion, and certain emotions in particular. How is Jesus presented? Is he depicted as an ideal Hellenistic sage, emotionally unaffected by his circumstances? Is Jesus subject only to 'positive' emotions or mild, restrained versions of typical human experiences? Does he enter into the full range of human emotion? Are we entitled to construe anything about the nature of God?

Mark's portrait of Jesus

Despite its relative brevity, Mark's Gospel attributes an impressive range of emotions to Jesus. On thirteen occasions, in nine separate episodes, Mark indicates an emotional response. On two of these occasions Jesus expresses the emotion himself (indicated below by italics).

---

5. *James E. Gilman*, 'Reenfranchising the Heart: Narrative Emotions and Contemporary Theology', *JR* 74 (1994), p. 219.
6. Matthew Elliott, *Faithful Feelings: Emotion in the New Testament* (Leicester: Inter-Varsity Press, 2005), p. 53.
7. Ibid., pp. 53–55.

Table 5.1 Jesus' emotions in Mark's Gospel

Context	Emotion (TNIV)	Greek
1:40–45 Healing leprosy	41 Jesus was indignant (moved with pity, NRSV) 43 with a strong warning	*orgizō* (*splanchnizomai*) *embrimaomai*
3:1–6 Healing a hand	5 in anger 5 deeply distressed	*orgē* *syllypeō*
6:1–6a In Nazareth	6 he was amazed	*thaumazō*
6:30–44 Feeding 5,000	34 he had compassion	*splanchnizomai*
8:1–10 Feeding 4,000	2 *I have compassion*	*splanchnizomai*
8:11–13 Demand for a sign	12 he sighed deeply	*anastenazō*
10:13–16 Blessing children	14 he was indignant	*aganakteō*
10:17–31 Rich man	21 [he] loved	*agapaō*
14:32–42 In the Garden	33 began to be deeply distressed 33 began to be troubled 34 *My soul is overwhelmed with sorrow to the point of death*	*ekthambeō* *adēmoneō* *perilypos*

The briefest of the four Gospels paints this portrait with great economy. While mentions of emotion are spread through the major sections of the Gospel, chapters pass without any. In most contexts a single word conveys Jesus' reaction. Only the scene in Gethsemane could be considered an extended account of Jesus' emotional state, reinforced by Jesus' own expression of the depth of his distress. Literary critics point out that sparseness of description may yield 'a more dynamic and personal view of character' than if more information is given. As Merenlahti points out, 'the mystery of the biblical characters is the mystery of the mustard seed: how does so much come out of so little'.[8]

This potential dynamism is reinforced by the sheer breadth and variety of Mark's presentation. There is no hint of stereotypical emotional responses. Only one term, 'compassion', is repeated (6:34; 8:2). The thirteen instances range across four shades of anger (1:41, 43; 3:5; 10:14), grief (3:5; 14:33–34), amazement (6:6), compassion (6:34; 8:2), frustration (8:12), warm affection (10:21) and distress (14:33). Analysed according to the taxonomy provided by Louw and Nida's *Greek–English Lexicon*, Mark's thirteen references employ five semantic subdomains: Love/Compassion, Groan/Cry, Amazement, Distress, Sorrow and Anger.[9]

Jesus emerges as a 'round' character, with complex temperament and motivation. Most references lend support to a cognitive approach. Jesus' emotional reactions make sense: they are not presented as irrational or inexplicable. Mark supplies reasons for Jesus' construal of, and response to, these circumstances. He feels anger and grief 'at' (Gk. *epi* + dative) the hard-heartedness of Israel's leadership (3:5). His amazement is caused (Gk. *dia* + accusative) by the unbelief of his home town (6:6). On surveying the ragged crowd in 6:34 'he had compassion on them, because [Gk. *hoti*] they were like sheep without a shepherd' (ESV). In 8:2–3 compassion springs from the perception of the crowd's hunger and vulnerability. Even when grounds are not made explicit, it is not difficult to understand Jesus' frustrated sigh as a reaction to the perversity of his opponents (8:11–12) or his indignation at his disciples as dismay at their practice of the politics of exclusion favoured by the Pharisees (10:14; cf. 7:1–5). Jesus' emotions in Mark, to borrow the words of Martha Nussbaum, 'are not blind animal forces, but intelligent discriminating parts of the personality, closely related to beliefs of a certain sort'.[10]

---

8. Petri Merenlahti, *Poetics for the Gospels? Rethinking Narrative Criticism* (London: T. & T. Clark, 2002), pp. 78–80.

9. J. P. Louw and E. A. Nida (eds.), *Greek–English Lexicon of the New Testament: Based on Semantic Domains*, 2nd ed., 2 vols. (New York: United Bible Societies, 1988–9).

10. Elliott, *Faithful Feelings*, p. 65.

Yet part of the roundness of Jesus as a character is the surprising nature of some of his responses. Some find Jesus 'amazement' (6:6) difficult to square with his omniscience.[11] Leon Morris follows Calvin in ascribing this wonder to Jesus' humanity.[12] Joel Marcus puts it down to a 'mood swing'.[13] Curiously, the only emotion expressed towards his disciples is one of angry indignation (10:14). Compounding this strangeness is Jesus' most affectionate response in Mark, just verses later (10:21), rendered by van Iersel as 'his heart warmed to him'.[14] It is prompted by a wealthy materialist who will walk away from the offer of eternal life.

The most perplexing occurs in Mark 1:40–45. Most English versions follow a textual tradition that has Jesus 'moved with compassion' when confronted by the man with leprosy. The TNIV follows the Western reading, 'indignant' (1:41, Gk. *orgizō*). While the evidence is finely balanced, commentators increasingly find in favour of the Western reading.[15] It is much harder to imagine a scribe changing 'anger' to 'compassion'. Anger is also consistent with another verb in verse 43 (Gk. *embrimaomai*) that often expresses 'anger and displeasure'.[16]

Jesus' reason for responding so severely to a supplicant has mystified commentators. It is not immediately apparent why he should be angry, hence the amendment by some scribe to the more acceptable 'compassion'. Did the man endanger a whole community

---

11. A. Plummer, *A Critical and Exegetical Commentary on the Gospel According to S. Luke*, 5th ed. (Edinburgh: T. & T. Clark, 1922), pp. 196–197; J. Nolland, *Luke*, 3 vols. (Dallas: Word, 1989), vol. 1, p. 318.

12. Leon Morris, *The Gospel According to Matthew* (Grand Rapids: Eerdmans, 1992), p. 194.

13. Joel Marcus, *Mark 1–8: A New Translation with Introduction and Commentary* (New York: Doubleday, 1999), p. 377.

14. Bas van Iersel, *Reading Mark* (Edinburgh: T. & T. Clark, 1989), p. 237.

15. Carl R. Kazmierski, 'Evangelist and Leper: A Socio-Cultural Study of Mark 1.40–45', *NTS* 38 (1992), p. 40; Marcus, *Mark 1–8*, p. 209; R. T. France, *The Gospel of Mark: A Commentary on the Greek Text* (Grand Rapids: Eerdmans, 1998), p. 115.

16. BDAG, CD-ROM, 4th ed. (Florida: Oak Tree, 2000).

with contamination and ritual impurity? Was Jesus anticipating the
man's disobedience in spreading the news everywhere? Was there
simply something about the man that antagonized Jesus?

In seeking an explanation, it is worth noting the placement in
Mark's narrative of these indications of Jesus' emotion. A number
appear to function significantly in Mark's literary strategy, offering
implicit commentary on surrounding material. According to Barnett,
the healing of the man with leprosy brings to completion 'the first
phase of Jesus' Galilean ministry' (1:14–45).[17] One possible explanation of Jesus' anger is that this final episode provides commentary
on events narrated in the preceding unit. Rather than being directed
at the man, Jesus' anger is aroused by the state of first-century
Judaism, where the scribes lack authority (1:22), evil spirits inhabit
synagogues (1:23) and demons and disease oppress the people
(1:32–33). The man with leprosy confronts Jesus again with the
desperate plight of those severed from the worshipping community.
So Jesus' angry response reflects the tragic and widespread plight
the man embodies and culpable failure of Israel's teachers.

This impression is strengthened by the anger and grief expressed
at the stubbornness of the Pharisees (3:5). Again, this episode brings
a unit to a close, a cycle of five conflict stories extending from 2:1 to
3:6. The climactic nature of the healing of the withered hand is
underlined by the instigation of the plot to destroy Jesus in 3:6. Anger
and grief offer appropriate commentary on the mounting conflict
of the section. Mark provides Jesus' perspective on this mounting
opposition. It is stiff-necked rebellion that motivates scribes and
Pharisees. The Son of Man is angered and saddened by the spectacle.

According to Hurtado, Mark 6:1–6a 'can be seen as concluding
a section that may include everything from 3:7–6:6'.[18] The 'section
seems designed to give further samples of Jesus' ministry and more
indication of the polarizing effects it had on the people who
witnessed it'.[19] The focus of the section is how people respond to

---

17. Paul Barnett, *The Servant King: Reading Paul Today* (Sydney: Anglican
    Information Office, 1991), p. 41.

18. Larry W. Hurtado, *Mark* (Peabody, Mass.: Hendrickson, 1989), p. 88.

19. Ibid., p. 56.

Jesus, whether they do God's will (3:35), are like the good, receptive soil (4:20), trust Jesus in the midst of disaster (4:40) or have faith that he can heal (5:34, 36). Having demonstrated his authority and power, Jesus registers his astonishment (6:6) at the unbelief in his home town. The closing episode of the section offers insight into Jesus' incredulity at human perversity.

It is plausible that Mark intended 6:6b – 8:21 as another unit of the narrative, unified by the theme of 'bread' (Gk. *artos*: 6:8, 37, 38, 41, 44, 52; 7:2, 5, 27; 8:4, 5, 6, 14, 16, 17, 19). The enigmatic interrogation about their possession of bread and the disciples' incomprehension in the ultimate episode (8:14–21) highlights this as a theme of great importance to Mark. While there is no mention of Jesus' emotion in this final episode, the repetition of Jesus' compassion in 6:34 and 8:2 proves significant, embedded as they are in the two feeding miracles. The similarity of the two led earlier form-critical scholars to treat the latter as a doublet, clumsily duplicated by a confused Mark.[20] However, Mark's literary craft suggests another more probable explanation. The first feeding takes place in Jewish territory. The second evidently occurs on the other side of the lake, among a great crowd that 'have come from a great distance' (8:3 NRSV; cf. Josh. 9:6 LXX; Isa. 60:4 LXX; Acts 2:39; Eph. 2:13). The phrase and location point to the presence of Gentiles in the crowd. The only instance of repetition of a particular emotion term (Gk. *splanchnizomai*: 6:34; 8:2) serves to anticipate the Gentile mission.[21] The same compassion shown to the scattered sheep Israel is extended to Gentiles. They share in the children's bread, just as the Syro-Phoenician woman pleaded (7:27–29).

The broad range and literary significance of Jesus' emotions strongly suggest that Mark regarded them as an integral and important aspect of Jesus' presence during his ministry. Mark gives no details of Jesus' physical appearance. We cannot be sure which languages Jesus spoke in any situations. Yet Mark ensures that his

---

20. Robert A. Guelich, *Mark 1–8:26* (Dallas: Word, 1989), p. 401.

21. Eric K. Wefald, 'The Separate Gentile Mission in Mark: A Narrative Explanation of Markan Geography, the Two Feeding Accounts and Exorcisms', *JSNT* 60 (1995), pp. 3–26; Marcus, *Mark 1–8*, p. 487.

readers are aware of a wide range of emotional responses at crucial moments. Mark's Jesus is robustly emotional, responding with feeling to supplicants, opponents, crowds and disciples alike. There is no hint of these reactions as signs of weakness or cowardice, even with the intensity of Jesus' distress and sorrow in Gethsemane.

If, as Papias claimed early in the second century, and Bauckham has recently argued, Mark had access to Peter's eyewitness testimony, then we may assume that Jesus' emotional responses had made a deep impression on the apostle.[22] No one was better placed to observe Jesus closely, even question him about how and why he reacted in various situations. Strikingly, all of Mark's references to Jesus' emotion occur in situations where Peter was recorded as being present or can be assumed to have been. At no point does Mark provide access to Jesus' inner emotional life when the Saviour is unaccompanied.

Mark's Jesus and Hellenistic ideals

The intensity and range of Jesus' emotions invite comparison with the Hellenistic schools of the first century. As Elliott observes, 'Emotions were considered a major topic of philosophical inquiry at the time of the New Testament. The emotions also had an important place in literature and society.'[23] The writings of a contemporary of Jesus, Lucius Annaeus Seneca, serve to illuminate this cultural context. As a Roman Stoic, Seneca displays a keen interest in theories of the passions and their place in the life of the true sage.[24]

From his writings emerge three major schools of thought. Those who stood in the tradition of Plato regarded emotions as irrational impulses that must be reined in by reason. Plato was a realist and

---

22. Eusebius, *The History of the Church*, tr. G. A. Williamson (London: Penguin, 1989), 3.39.14–16; Richard Bauckham, *Jesus and the Eyewitnesses: The Gospels as Eyewitness Testimony* (Grand Rapids: Eerdmans, 2006), pp. 202–239.

23. Elliott, *Faithful Feelings*, p. 78.

24. Richard J. Gibson, 'As Dearly Loved Children: Divine and Human Emotion in Early Christian Thought and Its Hellenistic Context' (PhD diss., Macquarie University, 2005), pp. 13–58.

did not envisage the elimination of emotion. The truly wise man
would 'master' the passions and 'minimize' their impact. Aristotle
and the Peripatetic school advocated 'moderation' or 'the mean'.[25]
Aristotle offered the earliest cognitive account of emotions, arguing
that emotions were distinguished by the belief that generated them.[26]
As a result, emotions were not dismissed as irrational but valued as
integral to the flourishing life. The challenge for the virtuous was to
display the right response, to the appropriate degree, in valid
circumstances.[27]

Hardline Stoicism, as espoused by Chrysippus, regarded both
Plato's and Aristotle's approaches as cowardly half measures.[28] The
four great passions – 'fear', 'desire', 'pleasure' and 'grief' – along
with their subspecies were to be eliminated from the life of the
sage.[29] There were acceptable 'rational' versions of the first three,
namely 'caution', 'wishing' and 'joy', but no form of grief was
ever acceptable.[30] Seneca himself followed a qualified, softened
Stoicism, under the influence of Posidonius. While Seneca regarded
emotions as 'diseases of the mind',[31] he did allow for some expressions grief.[32]

It is impossible to reconcile Mark's presentation of Jesus with
the Stoic ideal elimination of the passions, even the qualified
approach adopted by Posidonius and Seneca. As a subspecies of
desire, Jesus' anger would rule him out of eligibility as a sage. Even
his compassion would be seen as 'a weakness of mind that is
over-much perturbed by suffering'.[33] It is, however, his grief

---

25. Seneca, *Ep.* 85.3–4, in *Seneca*, tr. J. W. Basore et al., 10 vols. (Cambridge,
    Mass.: Harvard University Press, 1917–72).
26. Elliott, *Faithful Feelings*, pp. 66–70.
27. Aristotle, *Eth. nich.* 2.1106b17–25.
28. Seneca, *Ep.* 85.3–4.
29. Ibid. 116.8.
30. Diogenes Laertius, *Lives of Eminent Philosophers*, tr. R. D. Hicks, vol. 7
    (Cambridge, Mass.: Harvard University Press, 1991), pp. 116–118.
31. Seneca, *Ep.* 75.12.
32. Seneca, *Marc.* 4.1; *Polyb.* 18.5.
33. Seneca, *Clem.* 2.6.4.

manifested in Gethsemane that simply disqualifies Jesus from any claim to be a Hellenistic wise man. Mark's portrayal also places Jesus out of step with the Platonic goal of minimization. There is no hint of irrationality in Jesus' responses. He acts and reacts as the Holy One and Son of God. There is no attempt to restrain his expression of sadness and despair in the garden. Aristotle's cognitive approach and ideal of moderation is more consistent with Jesus' emotions, yet even then it hardly seems that Mark's intention is to portray Jesus as a model of moderation.

Mark's Jesus and the God of Israel

It is more difficult to determine whether these emotions point to the reality of Jesus' incarnation or to his revelation of the divine nature. Commentators are often quick to attribute any emotional response to Jesus' humanity. Mark does not invent a new vocabulary to describe Jesus. He experiences recognizably human emotions. In some instances, it is difficult to see them as other than human. Jesus' amazement provides one example. Traces of fear and distress in the face of death also point in a distinctively human direction (14:33–34).

However, a number of incidents are reported in ways that echo Yahweh in the Hebrew Scriptures. With respect to Jesus' anger in 1:40–45, Stählin avoids making the choice between human and divine: Jesus' anger 'is in the first instance a sign that He was a man of flesh and blood. Nevertheless, this is not just human anger. It always has about it something of the nature of God's wrath'.[34] Edwards cites as parallel the NRSV of Judges 10:16, where Yahweh 'became indignant over the misery of Israel'.[35]

Jesus' mixture of anger and perhaps sympathetic sadness towards the Pharisees (3:5) can also be construed as divine. According to Marcus, their hardness of heart towards the Bridegroom recalls Pharaoh's towards Yahweh (Exod. 7:3, 13, 22; 8:15).[36] For Lane,

---

34. Gustav Stählin, '*orgē*', in *TDNT* 5, p. 427.
35. James R. Edwards, *The Gospel According to Mark* (Grand Rapids: Eerdmans, 2002), p. 70.
36. Marcus, *Mark 1–8*, p. 253.

Jesus' grief 'expressed the anger of God',[37] recalling Yahweh's wrath at the corruption of Israel's leadership and the plight of his people (cf. Isa. 3:13–15; Jer. 8:10–12, 18–22; 32:31–32; Lam. 2:6; Hos. 4:4–6). Similarly, Jesus' grief recalls God's heartache in Genesis 6:6 and Ezekiel 16:43 (LXX; cf. 1 Esdras 1.22 Gk.).

Old Testament background also illuminates Jesus' 'deep sighing in his spirit' (8:12, my tr.). The Pharisees' demand for a sign in order to test (Gk. *peirazontes auton*) Jesus follows directly after a feeding miracle. At Massah and Meribah (Exod. 17:1–7) the Israelites 'tested' Yahweh (Gk. *peirazete kyrion*). Psalm 95:9 recalls the rebellion of 'that generation' (Gk. *tē genea ekeinē*). Jesus' exasperated sighing is followed by the question 'Why does this generation [Gk. *tē genea tautē*] seek a sign?' (8:12). Readers of Mark know that the Pharisees have succumbed to the hardness of heart warned against in the preceding verse of the psalm (Mark 3:5). Edwards describes Jesus' sigh as a 'nadir of dismay'.[38] For Marcus, 'Jesus himself is tested and thus assumes the role of God in the Exodus narrative'.[39]

Understandably, commentators are also inclined to detect divinity in Jesus' compassion (6:34; 8:2). For Köster, this compassion 'is always used to describe the attitude of Jesus and it characterizes the divine nature of his acts'.[40] Likewise, in commenting on parallels in Matthew, Morris finds 'not purely human pity, but divine compassion for troubled people'.[41]

For those with ears to hear, Jesus' emotional responses in Mark identify him with Yahweh at a number of crucial points, chiefly displays of anger at the failure of Israel's leadership, grief and dismay at their hardness of heart, and compassion at the tragic plight God's people. Yet the genius of Mark's presentation is that these hints do not undermine the humanity of Jesus' responses. In most cases we are not forced to choose either–or.

---

37. William L. Lane, *The Gospel According to Mark* (Grand Rapids: Eerdmans, 1974), p. 123.

38. Edwards, *Gospel According to Mark*, p. 236.

39. Marcus, *Mark 1–8*, p. 504.

40. H. Köster, '*splanchnon*, etc.', in *TDNT* 7, pp. 553–554.

41. Morris, *Gospel According to Matthew*, p. 239.

Parallel passages in Luke's Gospel

In the light of the breadth, richness and significance of Jesus' emotions in Mark, Luke's treatment of these same episodes is striking. The table overleaf reiterates Mark's context, identifies the parallel passage in Luke according to the fourth edition of the United Bible Society *Greek New Testament* and Aland's *Synopsis*.[42] Comparison of the passages in the English confirms the claim that these represent parallel accounts. Assuming Mark's priority and Luke's access to Mark, Luke wilfully deletes every reference to emotion.

The table reveals Luke's systematic excision. Of course, some modification of Mark's material is expected. Luke followed his own plan of composition and drew on other sources. In some contexts he may have felt mention of Jesus' emotion contributed little. Yet, when these factors are taken into account it remains undeniable that Luke consistently deletes the emotions of Mark's Jesus. There is something programmatic about this redaction, which targets the emotions of Jesus.

Perhaps the most remarkable feature of Luke's parallels is the apparent transference of emotions attributed to Jesus in Mark to other characters. When Jesus heals the man with the withered hand (Luke 6:6–11), Luke makes no mention of Jesus' anger and grief. Instead, Pharisees and scribes are furious. Rather than closing with Jesus' astonishment (Mark 6:6), Luke's Nazareth narrative concludes with the fury of the crowd (Luke 4:28). Most glaringly, the grief of Mark's Jesus is displaced to the disciples, who are exhausted from sorrow (Luke 22:45).

Intriguingly, Luke appears to treat these emotions as a class of phenomena. Not only difficult or unexpected emotions, such as anger and amazement, are excised. The process does not distinguish 'bad' and 'good' emotions, or 'violent' and 'mild' emotions. All of the terms labelled 'passions' by Stoic theorists and 'emotion' by modern scientific taxonomies are eliminated. What accounts for Luke's consistency? What motivation could there be? Does Luke correct Mark's misguided Christology? Is he informed by a radically different assessment of emotion?

---

42. Kurt Aland, *Synopsis of the Four Gospels* (New York: United Bible Societies, 1985).

Table 5.2 Luke's parallels to Mark

Context (Mark)	Jesus' emotion	Luke	Jesus' emotion (TNIV)	Others (TNIV)
1:40–45 Healing leprosy	Anger Severity	5:12–16		
3:1–6 Healing a hand	Anger Grief	6:6–11		11 Pharisees and the teachers of the law were furious (Gk. *anoia*)
6:1–6a In Nazareth	Wonder	4:16–30		22 all . . . were amazed (cf. Mark 6:2) 28 all the people . . . were furious (Gk. *thymos*)
6:30–44 Feeding 5,000	Compassion	9:10–17		
8:1–10 Feeding 4,000	Compassion	None		
8:11–13 Demand for a sign	Dismay	None		
10:13–16 Blessing children	Indignation	18:15–17		
10:17–31 Rich man	Love	18:18–30		
14:32–42 In the garden	Distress Anxiety Grief	22:39–46 [22:43–44]	[44 being in anguish, Gk. *agōnia*]	45 the disciples . . . exhausted from sorrow (Gk. *lypē*)

On the assumption of Mark's priority and the belief that Luke had access to Mark's Gospel, commentators have construed this as Luke's conscious 'avoidance', 'elimination' or 'removal' of the emotions of Mark's Jesus. Most commentaries, especially those written out of a redaction-critical approach, observe the tendency. Fitzmyer explains that

> the description of Jesus moved by human emotions in the Marcan Gospel is normally eliminated in the Lucan story, even if they are expressions of love, compassion, or tenderness. The Marcan episodes depict Jesus in a more human way, perhaps too human for the nobility of character that Luke sought to depict.[43]

In the same vein Bock notes, 'It is also unlike Luke to note Jesus' emotions, since he lacks such remarks, unlike the Marcan parallels.'[44] Some go beyond comparison to speak in an unqualified way. According to Tannehill, 'the narrator seldom indicates the emotions of Jesus'.[45] Marshall goes still further, claiming that Luke 'avoids expressions of Jesus' emotions', a feature observed repeatedly.[46] Others detect an aversion to the violent. For Sanders and Davies, Luke's criterion is the removal of 'emotional violence attributed to him'.[47] Fitzmyer's Luke is guided by 'a delicate sensitivity which tends to make Luke eliminate anything that smacks of the violent, the passionate, or the emotional'.[48] Elsewhere, Fitzmyer opines that it

---

43. Fitzmeyer, *Gospel According to Luke I–IX*, p. 816.

44. Darrell L. Bock, *Luke 9:51–24:53* (Grand Rapids: Baker, 1996), p. 1193, n. 10.

45. Robert C. Tannehill, *The Narrative Unity of Luke-Acts: A Literary Interpretation*, vol. 1: *The Gospel According to Luke* (Minneapolis: Fortress, 1986), p. 92.

46. I. Howard Marshall, *The Gospel of Luke: A Commentary on the Greek Text* (Exeter: Paternoster, 1978), p. 209; cf. pp. 236, 359–360, 682, 685, 828.

47. E. P. Sanders and M. Davies, *Studying the Synoptic Gospels* (London: SCM, 1992), p. 287.

48. Fitzmeyer, *Gospel According to Luke I–IX*, p. 95.

may be related to the lapse of time between the two Gospels, during which a higher Christology emerged.[49]

In search of an explanation: Luke's Jesus as Stoic sage
The fullest and most coherent attempt at explaining Luke's motivation is provided by Jerome Neyrey.[50] Given the currency of the Hellenistic passion theories in the first century it must be granted some plausibility. Neyrey makes much of the textual variant preserved as Luke 22:43–44, verses regarded by many as a later interpolation:

> Then an angel from heaven appeared to him and gave him strength.
> In his anguish [Gk. *en agōnia*] he prayed more earnestly, and his sweat became like great drops of blood falling down on the ground. (Luke 22:43–44 NRSV)

These verses come in the midst of Luke's account of Jesus in the garden, which otherwise omits any reference to Jesus' overwhelming distress, anxiety and grief. In keeping with the consensus noted above, Raymond Brown remarks, 'Not surprisingly, Luke (who would never attribute psychological disarray to Jesus) omits the whole Marcan description.'[51]

Neyrey goes still further. He argues that Luke implements a very deliberate programme to harmonize Jesus with the highest Hellenistic ethical standards, regarding the emotions. Luke 22:43–44 is original and significant for Luke's presentation of Jesus in terms compatible with Stoic ideals, informed by negative perceptions of the passions, especially grief, in the Hellenistic schools and Judaism.[52] As judgment

---

49. Ibid., p. 572.

50. Jerome H. Neyrey, 'The Absence of Jesus' Emotions: The Lucan Redaction of Lk 22, 39–46', *Bib* 61 (1980), pp. 153–171.

51. Raymond E. Brown, *The Death of the Messiah: From Gethsemane to the Grave: A Commentary on the Passion Narratives in the Four Gospels*, 2 vols. (Garden City, N. Y.: Doubleday, 1994), p. 153.

52. Gen. 4:6 LXX; Isa. 1:5 LXX; Sirach 30.21, 23; 38.18; Philo, *Her.* 270; *Mos.* 1.139; *Prob.* 159; *Virt.* 88; *Ios.* 214 (in *The Works of Philo: Complete and Unabridged*, tr. C. D. Yonge [Peabody, Mass.: Hendrickson, 1993]).

for sin, indication of guilt, and one of the tetrachord of Stoic passions, 'grief' (Gk. *lypē*) was simply unacceptable in the life of a virtuous sage. So Luke expunges the passion, to commend Jesus to the philosophically aware reader.

Consequently, Luke depicts Jesus as the model of the cardinal virtue, 'courage'. Jesus' sorrow is transferred to the disciples, who sleep 'because of grief'. The introduction of 'if it be your will' and 'I wish' indicates that Jesus experiences 'correct rational longing', but is determined to do his duty. Luke also uses *agōnia*, for which Neyrey prefers 'contest, struggle, gymnastic exercise' to 'debilitating fear'. Like the ideal Hellenistic and Philonic sage, Luke's Jesus is the courageous victor in this struggle with temptation.[53] Jesus' sweat recalls the effort of an athlete, and the Maccabean heroes (2 Maccabees 2.26), including Eleazar, who died defending the Jewish way of life, 'with their own blood and noble sweat' (4 Maccabees 7.8 NRSV).[54] Neyrey concludes, 'Jesus, therefore, is not a victim, out of control, subject to irrational passion; on the contrary, he is portrayed as practicing virtue, singleheartedly searching for God's will and being manfully obedient to God.'[55]

Neyrey's influence is apparent in Luke Timothy Johnson's commentary. Johnson notes two changes from Mark's account. First, the focus is shifted from the disciples to Jesus. Secondly, Luke shapes the image of Jesus so that he lacks the need for companionship and the distress so prominent in Mark. Luke and his Hellenistic readers regarded these as vices rather than virtues. Luke's goal is to present Jesus as 'not only prophet but true philosopher (*sophos*)'. Johnson adds:

> We notice, therefore, that the emotion of 'sorrow' (*lypē*) which is associated in Hellenistic moral literature with fear and cowardice as well as envy, is shifted from Jesus to the disciples. They fail to pray as he told them, because their 'sorrow' (read: fear/anxiety/cowardice) has weighed them down with sleep. In contrast, Luke presents Jesus

---

53. Neyrey, 'Absence of Jesus' Emotions', pp. 159–161.

54. Ibid., p. 167.

55. Ibid., p. 171.

as the spiritual athlete. He enters the *agōn* of prayer before God, bringing his mind and will into line with the Father, releasing his deep desire to live and avoid suffering, and accepting what has been determined for him.[56]

If Neyrey and Johnson accurately discern Luke's intention, this has important implications for what the Gospels teach us about early Christian attitudes to emotions. The two Gospels would represent very divergent approaches. Mark validates a wide range of emotions, sometimes experienced with great intensity, by attributing them to Jesus. This leads to a very positive evaluation of emotion in Jesus, and even God, implying a valid and vital place in Christian experience. In contrast, Luke at least offers a widely divergent assessment, stripping Jesus of emotions attested to in Mark, and where possible, displacing them to human characters. Emotions emerge as a sign of weakness and cowardice, not fitting for Jesus, with an implied endorsement of Stoic efforts to eliminate them from the virtuous life.

However, there are a number of problems with the evidence on which Neyrey and Johnson base their conclusions, chiefly their reliance on a dubious textual variant, dependence on a particular construal of *agōnia*, and neglect of the emotions Luke does attribute to Jesus. Despite the arguments of some for inclusion,[57] most agree that the textual evidence does not favour the originality of 22:43–44 in Luke's Gospel. Significant ancient and diverse witnesses omit them altogether. Others suggest their spuriousness. Some lectionaries relocate them after Matthew 26:39. Metzger has little doubt they constitute a later addition to the text.[58]

---

56. Luke T. Johnson, *The Gospel of Luke* (Collegeville, Minn.: Liturgical Press, 1991), p. 554.

57. Bock, *Luke 9:51–24:53*, pp. 1763–1764; Christopher M. Tuckett, 'Luke 22,43–44: The "Agony" in the Garden and Luke's Gospel', in Adelbert Denaux (ed.), *New Testament Textual Criticism and Exegesis: Festschrift J. Delobel* (Leuven: Leuven University Press, 2002), p. 144.

58. Bruce M. Metzger, *A Textual Commentary on the Greek New Testament*, 2nd ed. (Stuttgart: United Bible Societies, 1994), p. 151.

Instructively, Metzger rejects the suggestion that these verses were deleted 'by those who felt that the account of Jesus being overwhelmed with human weakness was incompatible with his sharing the divine omnipotence of the Father'.[59] For most inclusion of these verses introduces a strong emotional reaction. Neyrey and Johnson insist that *agōnia* describes Jesus' courageous, athletic struggle with the passions. Certainly, the related forms *agōn* and *agōnizomai* in the New Testament carry the ideas of 'contest' (Phil. 1:30; Col. 2:1; 1 Thess. 2:2; 1 Tim. 6:12; etc.) and 'struggle' (Luke 13:24; John 18:36; 1 Cor. 9:25; Col. 1:29; etc.). But this does not determine the meaning of the rarer noun *agōnia*, only used here in the New Testament. BDAG offers only 'apprehensiveness of mind, esp. when faced with impending ills, *distress, anguish*' as a gloss.[60] Neyrey and Johnson also invoke parallels with the Maccabean martyrs. In 2 Maccabees *agōnia* is reserved for personal distress and anguish: 'To see the appearance of the high priest was to be wounded at heart, for his face and the change in his color disclosed the anguish [Gk. *agōnia*] of his soul' (2 Maccabees 3.16 NRSV; cf. 3:14). 2 Maccabees 15.19 links this directly to anxiety: 'And those who had to remain in the city were in no little distress, being anxious over the encounter in the open country' (NRSV). Rather than 'entry into the contest' the noun implies deep personal distress.

By far the most compelling argument against the interpretation of Neyrey and Johnson is Luke's failure to complete his alleged programme. Undeniably, Luke excises Mark's indications of Jesus' emotion. This does not mean, however, that Luke fails to attribute emotions to Jesus. In a range of texts often overlooked in these discussions, Luke does portray Jesus as reacting emotionally, at times with great intensity, and often in ways inconsistent with the self-sufficient sage.

Luke's portrait of Jesus

On eight occasions in seven contexts (see table 5.3 below), Luke attributes emotion to Jesus. When this material is taken into account,

---

59. Ibid., p. 151; cf. Fitzmyer, *Gospel According to Luke X–XXIV*, p. 1444.
60. BDAG, p. 17.

a distinctive portrait of Jesus emerges, painted with different colours, but with significant overlap with Mark (again, italics indicate where Jesus expresses the emotion himself).

Table 5.3 The seven contexts where Luke attributes emotion to Jesus

Context	Emotion (NRSV)	Greek	Emotion
7:1–10 Centurion's slave	9 he was amazed	*thaumazō*	Wonder
7:11–17 Widow's son	13 he had compassion	*splanchnizomai*	Compassion
10:21–24 The Son reveals	21 rejoiced	*agalliaō*	Joy
12:49–53 Come to divide	49 *how I wish* 50 *what stress I am under*	*thelō* *synechō*	Desire Anxiety
13:31–35 To Jerusalem	34 *have I desired*	*thelō*	Desire
19:41–44 Over Jerusalem	41 he wept	*klaiō*	Grief
22:14–23 Last Supper	15 *I have eagerly desired*	*epithymia epithymeō*	Desire

Easily overlooked is the fact that Luke draws attention to the emotions of his characters more often than the other Gospels. Relative to mentions of Jesus' emotions, Voorwinde estimates the ratio of attribution to other characters at 17:1. This compares with Matthew's 5:1, Mark's 3:1 and John's 4:1.[61] For this reason, Dibelius called Luke 'the evangelist who depicts feelings'.[62]

Yet it remains true that Luke indicates Jesus' emotions significantly less frequently than Mark. Mark's thirteen emotion terms are

---

61. Voorwinde, *Jesus' Emotions*, p. 56.
62. Martin Dibelius, *From Tradition to Gospel*, tr. B. L. Woolf (London: Nicholson & Watson, 1934), p. 75.

scattered through just sixteen chapters; Luke's eight, through twenty-four. The range also varies. There is some overlap. Jesus responds with amazement at the faith of the centurion's slave (7:9) and has compassion on a bereft widow (7:13). His tears express a grief response (19:41) and Jesus communicates his anguish over completion of his mission (12:50). Absent are the anger, indignation, frustration and profound sadness in Gethsemane of Mark's Jesus.

If there is a characteristic tenor to Luke's Jesus it is 'desire'. Twice the verb *thelō* (12:49; 13:34) is employed, and once, the striking cognate dative *epithymia epithymeō*. The net effect is to underline the extent to which Jesus is gripped by his mission. In 12:49–50 he announces, 'I came to cast fire on the earth, and would [Gk. *thelō*] that it were already kindled! I have a baptism to be baptized with, and how great is my distress [Gk. *synechō*] until it is accomplished!' (12:49–50 ESV). This is potentially one of the most emotional expressions in the Gospels, but notoriously ambiguous. The language of 'wishing' for something can imply little more than volition or intent (Luke 5:13). The verb translated 'distress' can signal preoccupation with a task (Acts 18:5). The tortuous grammar of the saying suggests strong affective content. The interrogative pronoun intensifies the sense of desire, while Louw and Nida provide as a gloss for *synechō*, 'to experience great psychological pressure and anxiety'.[63] In other words, it is likely that Jesus signals an intense longing for relief from emotional strain.

The intensity of Jesus' desire is also on view in the Last Supper. The cognate dative construction of Luke 22:15 intensifies Jesus' longing (Gk. *epithymia epethymēsa*). The verb is used elsewhere in Luke for the prodigal son's desperate longing for pig's food, Lazarus's craving for scraps from the rich man's table, and the disciples' yearning for the coming of the Son of Man. The noun is used pejoratively in Mark 4:19 and John 8:44. The combination recalls Numbers 11:4 and Psalm 106:14. In Numbers the faithless rabble had 'a strong craving' (Gk. *epethymēsa epithymian*) for meat. Psalm 106 (LXX Ps. 105) recalls that time when that generation had a 'wanton craving' and put God to the test. As counterpoint to their

---

63. Louw and Nida, *Greek–English Lexicon*, 1.315.

faithlessness, Jesus 'intensely desires' a very different meal that cele-
brates his death as a pledge of a future, fully satisfying, meal together.

Also distinctive to Luke, and related to the fulfilment of his mission,
is Jesus' joy in 10:21. Jesus 'delighted' or 'exulted in the Holy Spirit' as
he thanks the Father for revealing hidden things to infants. The source
of the emotion lies in his relationship to his Father and the authority
granted to Jesus to draw believers into that relationship.

Luke's Jesus is also moved to compassion, towards the widow
of Nain as she accompanies the lifeless body of her only son.
Remarkably, commentators tend to see little significance for Luke's
portrait of Jesus. Marshall follows Dibelius in concluding:

> This evidence suggests that Luke is here making use of a source, and that
> the verse should not be ascribed to Luke's own desire to express emotion
> and draw attention to Jesus' care for women; on the contrary, this desire
> is characteristic of his source.[64]

It seems that Marshall has it both ways. Luke's avoidance of emotion,
especially when drawing from Mark, is a notable feature of his
composition. But here, inclusion is dismissed as nothing more than
Luke's repeating his source.

Evidence suggests the emotion has great significance for Luke.
Menken points out the significance of the verb 'I have compassion'
(Gk. *splanchnizomai*) and the cognate noun 'tender-hearted' (Gk.
splanchna) in Luke's Gospel. In each instance (1:78; 10:33; 15:20) these
are at the centre of a unit. In 7:11–17 the verb marks the turning
point in the story, turning from death to life. Menken counts 106
syllables before the phrase and 105 after it, and offers further support
from word counts. For Menken, 'Luke wants to present Jesus as the
compassionate benefactor of the mother rather than as a performer
of mighty acts.'[65]

This literary significance is underpinned by theological associations not evident in Mark's Gospel. The noun is used in Luke 1:78

64. Marshall, *Gospel of Luke*, p. 286.

65. M. J. J. Menken, 'The Position of SPLANCHNIZESTHAI and
    SPLANCHNA in the Gospel of Luke', *NovT* 30 (1988), pp. 111.

for the 'tender mercy of our God' (ESV). The compassion of the prodigal son's father evokes God's tenderness towards sinners (15:20). Brodie concludes that Jesus' sympathy is the very compassion of Yahweh. Again, Old Testament background is key. Luke 4:25–27 juxtaposes references to Naaman and the widow of Zarephath. These are again echoed in Luke's account of the Roman centurion and the widow of Nain.[66] As the first context in Luke where Jesus is identified as 'Lord', it is probable that Luke regards compassion as a distinctively divine characteristic, peculiarly expressed in Jesus.[67] As Bovon puts it, 'Just as God is compassionate (6:36) so is the healing Messiah who here shows great sympathy.'[68]

The most poignant expression is found in Jesus' laments and weeping over the unresponsiveness of Jerusalem. The affective content of Jesus' 'wish' in 13:34 is suggested by the pathos of the context. Jesus knows he will die in Jerusalem, giving rise to a lament over the city's perverse rejection of the prophets and her future judgment. It is a context riddled with desire. Herod wants to kill Jesus (13:31). Jesus reflects, 'How often would I have gathered your children together as a hen gathers her brood under her wings' (ESV). This is met only by their perverse 'unwillingness'. The poignancy reaches its zenith with the image of the mother bird's striving to gather her brood. Psalm 90:4 LXX promises refuge under Yahweh's wings. It is a psalm already used by Satan in Luke 4:10–11 to tempt Jesus. Similar language is used in Deuteronomy 32:11. There the eagle's 'yearning' to protect parallels Jesus' longing in Luke 13. For Bock, the image 'reveals God's heart. God's constant desire is to intimately care for, nurture, and protect his people.'[69]

---

66. Thomas L. Brodie, 'Towards Unravelling Luke's Use of the Old Testament: Luke 7.11–17 as an *Imitatio* of 1 Kings 17.17–24', *NTS* 32 (1986), p. 254.

67. Johnson, *Gospel of Luke*, p. 118.

68. François Bovon, *Luke 1: A Commentary on the Gospel of Luke 1:1–9:50*, tr. C. M. Thomas (Minneapolis: Fortress, 2002), p. 272.

69. Darrell L. Bock, *Luke 1:1–9:50*, BECNT (Grand Rapids: Baker, 1994), p. 1249.

Jesus' tears over Jerusalem (19:41) recall the pathos of 13:34 and build on it. Luke makes no effort to obscure Jesus' bitter sadness at Jerusalem's unresponsiveness. Many discern the tears of a prophet, leading to prophetic lament. Tiede regards it as 'the sympathy of the suffering prophet, of Deuteronomy's Moses, of Jeremiah, Isaiah, and Hosea, caught up in the rage, anguish, frustration, and sorrow of God for Israel'.[70] In the weeping of Jesus (Matt. 23:37–39) Keener discerns the tears of God: 'as often in the case of God in the Old Testament, Jesus' love for Jerusalem gives way to the brokenhearted pain of rejection. God also weeps over his judgment of Israel (e.g., Jer 8:21–22; 9:1, 10).'[71]

Luke's Jesus and Hellenistic ideals

When his whole Gospel is considered, it is apparent that Luke's Jesus ultimately falls short of Hellenistic ideals. Comparison of Luke's parallels to Mark creates an illusion that Luke is uncomfortable with Jesus' emotion. Like Mark, Luke ranges over five of Louw and Nida's semantic subdomains, four of which overlap with Mark: Desire, Love/Compassion, Groan/Cry, Amazement, Distress and Sorrow. Luke's portrait may lack the anger of Mark's Jesus, but his emphasis on desire was just as scandalous to the Hellenistic mindset, since anger was a species of the master passion, desire. If Luke did set out to present Jesus as the self-sufficient sage, then he failed miserably in the implementation. Luke's Jesus feels anguish, weeps tears of grief, is astonished by responses to his preaching, and yearns to fulfil his mission.

In search of an explanation

If, as the evidence of the Gospel suggests, Luke is prepared to present Jesus as one subject to intense emotion, how is his systematic deletion of Mark's references to be explained? Two possible

---

70. David L. Tiede, *Prophecy and History in Luke-Acts* (Philadelphia: Fortress, 1980), p. 78.
71. Craig S. Keener, *A Commentary on the Gospel of Matthew* (Grand Rapids: Eerdmans, 1999), p. 558.

explanations remain: Luke's awareness of Mark's literary strategy and his attitude to his sources.

Mark's indications of Jesus' emotions, as discussed above, seem to have a significant function in Mark's narrative, often serving as implicit commentary preceding sections or offering insights into the meaning of an incident. On the assumption that Luke was aware of Mark's literary strategy and determined to pursue his own, it is reasonable to expect that some references did not serve Luke's purpose. Jesus' emotions in Mark serve to highlight the desperate plight of the Jewish people under corrupt political and religious leadership. Jesus is presented as the righteously indignant and tender-hearted shepherd Israel has longed for, a Suffering Servant subject to anger, wonder and sorrow at the horrors of sin and death. Complementing this account is Luke's portrayal of the prophet and Son of God, gripped by his mission to 'seek and save the lost', earnestly desiring to reach Jerusalem where he knows tragedy and rejection await. This difference in perspective would explain a number of Luke's exclusions, but hardly accounts fully for systematic removal.

Perhaps an attitude towards his sources could account for this. In his recent volume subtitled *The Gospels as Eyewitness Testimony* Richard Bauckham cites and builds on the contribution of Samuel Byrskog. Byrskog likened ancient historiographical practice to the modern discipline of 'oral history'. Ancient historians 'were convinced that true history could be written only while events were still within living memory, and they valued as their sources the oral reports of direct experience of the events by involved participants in them'.[72] Bauckham builds a case for the Gospel authors adopting this principle, concluding that the Gospels are much more dependent on eyewitness testimony than modern scholarship has assumed, largely under the influence of form criticism.

Luke acknowledges his use of sources (1:1–4) and, in the case of Mark at least, probably encountered it as a written source. The implication of Bauckham's study is that Luke would prefer to draw on surviving eyewitnesses where possible, while incorporating

72. Bauckham, *Jesus and the Eyewitnesses*, pp. 8–9.

written sources where necessary to offer 'an orderly account' (Luke 1:3 ESV). We noted above that the completeness of Luke's exclusion of emotion from Mark's account pointed to recognition of them as a class of phenomena. If Luke regarded Jesus' emotion as a significant but peculiarly personal detail, it is feasible that he would include such details only if confirmed by a surviving eyewitness. Since Peter was no longer alive this was not possible. So Luke is prepared to follow Mark for much of the framework and content of his narrative, but refrains from inclusion of the attribution of emotion, on the principle that he did not have eyewitness testimony for such intimate personalia. This must remain a tentative and speculative solution but is more promising than theories of a programme to conform Jesus to Stoic tranquility.

Evaluating emotions in the light of the Gospels

The goal of this discussion has not been reconstruction of a psychological profile of Jesus. Rather, the presentation of Jesus in these two Gospels offers precious insight into the way emotions were evaluated in early Christianity.

At a minimum these portraits dignify our experience of human emotion. No shame is attached to Jesus' experience of bitter sadness, exuberant joy, gut-wrenching compassion, deep distress and anxiety, even fierce anger. These are not necessarily signs of failure or sin. There is no encouragement to repress these strong emotions in the name of courage, manliness or virtue. These things resided in the perfect human being with a wide range and real intensity. Emotions are integral to being human. The Evangelists insist on informing us about Jesus' experience of these emotions. Their presentations of Jesus encourage us to acknowledge, reflect on, discuss, even covet, experience of a rich array of emotions.

These portraits also expose some widely held but spurious distinctions, such as 'good' and 'bad', or 'positive' and 'negative', emotions. By positive emotions people often have in mind joy, compassion and love. Negative emotions usually include sadness, grief, anger and excessive desire. Jesus exposes the inadequacy of these dichotomies. According to Mark and Luke, all these emotions

THE EMOTIONAL LIFE OF JESUS

had their place in the life of Jesus. Much more important for the evaluation of any emotion is its object orientation. It was right for Jesus to desire the fulfilment of his mission or the meal with his disciples intensely. It was right for him to be angry at hypocrisy, religious cant and the exploitation of the vulnerable. It was right for him to be grieved by hardness of heart and the prospect of his own death. The challenge for those who would follow Jesus is to learn to rejoice at what Jesus rejoiced at, to have compassion on, to love, to be angry at, grieved by and yearn for the things that Jesus did. Conversely, this means keeping ourselves from the idols to which we are attached, with the petty and unworthy desires, fears, loves, resentments and anxieties through which they subjugate and rule over us.

These Gospel portraits also explode certain myths. Among them are deeply entrenched convictions that rationality and emotion are inexorably at odds, that emotional involvement clouds good judgment, or that experience of intense emotion distracts us from virtue and duty. Despite the intensity of Jesus' grief, compassion and anger, he always did the Father's will, always pleased him, and fulfilled the very mission that filled him with anxiety, distress and sorrow. These responses often galvanize Jesus to act, to heal, to raise the dead, to rebuke, to communicate affection, to beg others to pray.

Finally, there is much in these Gospel portraits to justify the confidence that Jesus exegetes the Father, even as he responds emotionally. His anger, compassion, and even his tears, cannot simply be corralled within his human nature. At the end of his excellent study of Jesus' emotions in John's Gospel, Stephen Voorwinde concludes:

> All the emotions of the Johannine Jesus therefore have both human and divine dimensions, albeit in differing ways. His zeal is that of both the righteous sufferer and the jealous Lord of the covenant. His joy, his troubled soul/spirit, and his rage are human emotions that depend for their motivation on his divine foreknowledge.[73]

---

73. Voorwinde, *Jesus' Emotions*, pp. 268–269.

Voorwinde's findings resonate with Mark and Luke. Without undermining the genuine humanity of Jesus, his emotional responses often recall Old Testament events and align Jesus with Yahweh. Only one Old Testament figure, Yahweh, comes to mind at the cumulative sight of Jesus' anger at religious cant and corruption, his jealousy for the temple, his grief and groaning at the hard-heartedness of Israel's leadership, his compassion for helpless and harassed people, and his longing to gather the inhabitants of Jerusalem, through tears. Jesus exegetes the Father as he experiences these intense emotions.

6. THE SPIRIT'S PERFECTING WORK ON THE EMOTIONS

David A. Höhne

The Spirit of the times

Throughout the last century and across the whole world Christians from different walks of life, diverse cultural and ethnic backgrounds, have expressed 'a hunger for a concrete, lived experience of [God's] life-giving Spirit'.[1] As the gospel of the Lord Christ Jesus spreads further and further throughout the globe, hundreds of millions of Christians want (at least according to Jürgen Moltmann) 'an awareness of God in, with and beneath the experience of life, which gives us assurance of God's fellowship, friendship and love'.[2] That is, ordinary Christians want some real evidence that God's Spirit is with them and that God's Spirit is for them – they want to *feel* that God's Spirit is genuinely active in the world. Alternatively, they want

---

1. Veli-Matti Kärkkäinen, *Pneumatology* (Grand Rapids: Basker, 2002), p. 14.
2. Jürgen Moltmann, *The Spirit of Life: A Universal Affirmation* (London: SCM, 1992), p. 17.

to understand their experiences as, in some way or other, the actions of God's Holy Spirit in the world.

The Pentecostal theologian Michael Welker summarizes these experiences in terms of 'experiences of a life that is threatened and endangered, but also a life that has been delivered and liberated'.[3] Along a continuum of life events marked by these two poles Welker includes the following:

> A people are threatened with annihilation. A political system collapses or is abruptly reshaped. The moral network of a community is rent asunder. The sun sets on a historical world. People receive a new identity. A dispersed people are led together again. People who are strange or even hostile to each other open God's reality for each other. A disintegrated world grows together.[4]

The last hundred years have seen remarkable events of both great horror and great wonder – two world wars, the rise of the American state as the driver of a more general western capitalism and the consequent fall of Communism (although not entirely as in the case of China), the end of European colonialism and the civil rights movements of the 1960s. Throughout all of these events with all their social and political consequences Christians have, rightly or wrongly, sought evidence and assurance that the promised Holy Spirit '*has been* poured out, on what *they* both see and hear' (Acts 2:33, my emphases).[5]

It seems fair to say that no one has been asking this question louder than the Pentecostals or those identified and identifying as Pentecostal Christians. Having grown in numbers from zero to around 500 million adherents in less than a century,[6] this worldwide movement has a number of characteristics, but the most obvious and central

---

3. Michael Welker, *God the Spirit* (Minneapolis: Fortress, 1994), p. x.
4. Ibid.
5. Unless stated otherwise, Scripture translations in this chapter are my own.
6. Walter J. Hollenweger, *Pentecostalism* (Peabody, Mass.: Hendrickson, 1997), p. 1.

among them is a particular concentration on the person and work of the Holy Spirit, especially in relation to human experience. Whether it is the general Pentecostal habit of focusing on 'the eschatological in-breaking of the Spirit in ways that are extraordinary, unpredictable and radically new',[7] or the more recent charismatic[8] habit of focusing on the powerful presence of Christ by the Spirit that continually transforms and improves the individual, more than 10% of the world's population seek and, in fact, require concrete explanations of their ordinary experiences in terms of the activities of God's Spirit.

In order to make some contribution to a seemingly vast need, in this chapter, in conversation with some of the elders of the Reformed tradition, I shall outline a way of describing the work of God's Spirit in human creaturely experiences in general, in order to make space for a description of the Spirit's agency in human emotions, affections or passions in particular. Previous chapters in this book have covered much concerning the affections of God, and subsequent chapters will provide opportunities to discuss human emotions. For now, I shall take a broad approach to the question of interaction between Creator and creation, between God's Spirit and human emotions for the simple reason that human feelings are a specific subset of the broader category of human experience or the way human creatures act and react in order to give expression to the many and various relationships in which they find themselves. From this perspective I shall take it as a given that whatever is true about the interaction between God's Spirit and human experience

---

7. Frank D. Macchia, 'God Present in a Confused Situation: The Mixed Influence of the Charismatic Movement on Classical Pentecostalism in the United States', *Pneuma* 18.1 (1996), p. 39.

8. According to Walter Hollenweger, a Swiss Pentecostal, the charismatic movement is a predominantly western, or westernized, and middle-class subset of Pentecostalism. While not exclusively Protestant, it is predominantly so and likewise found most commonly in North America, although there are increasingly significant pockets of it in Europe, East Asia and Latin America (Hollenweger, *Pentecostalism*, pp. 194–199).

is also true of the interaction between God's Spirit and human emotion. The affections were a matter of great importance to the Puritan divines, so we shall turn to one of their greatest, John Owen, to begin this study.[9]

The Spirit and creation

God's perfecting cause

In the tenth chapter of John Owen's *Greater Catechism* the fifth question asks, 'How prove you that he [Jesus] was a perfect man?' The third part of the answer is 'By the Scriptures assigning to him those things which are required to a perfect man.'[10] These are a body and then a soul consisting of a will, affections and cognitive endowments. When it comes to evidence for the perfection of Jesus' affections, Owen cites Luke 10:21: 'In that same hour he [Jesus] rejoiced in the Holy Spirit'). From what we can read elsewhere in Owen's work the implication is that Owen thought it was a particular work of the Holy Spirit to perfect the affections of Christ Jesus in order to enable him to be the perfect mediator between God and humanity. In fact, Owen held that it was the particular work of the Holy Spirit to perfect all of creation in the Bible story.

To appropriate to the Spirit the work of perfecting creation was first proposed by Basil of Caesarea who wrote, 'and remember that in creation . . . the Spirit is the perfecting cause'.[11] The idea was subsequently adopted and adapted into the Reformed tradition by John Calvin. In the *Institutes* we read:

> To the Father is attributed the beginning of activity and the fountain and wellspring of things; to the Son, wisdom, counsel, and the ordered

---

9. See also chapter 3 in this volume.
10. John Owen, 'The Greater Catechism', in *John Owen Collection* (Rio, Wis.: AGES Software, 2004), p. 29.
11. Basil, *Sur Le Saint-Esprit*, tr. Benoît Pruche, 2nd ed. (Paris: Cerf, 1968), 16.38.15.

disposition of all things; but to the Spirit is assigned the power and efficacy of the activity.[12]

The only distinction between Basil and Calvin was that Basil's description of the Sprit's empowering and effecting activity has an obvious eschatological direction – God acts in the Spirit to move creation in a certain direction. In Basil's writing, perfection is not a static notion of changeless, faultlessness but rather the more obvious biblical notion that things or promises have reached fulfilment in the purposes of God. In the *Institutes* Calvin seems more reserved, describing the Spirit's agency in a way that sounds more like a simple sustaining work in creation. That is hardly surprising considering Calvin's disciplined approach to reading the Bible, particularly when we consider the words of the psalmist:

> When you send your Spirit,
> they are created,
> and you renew the face of the ground.
> (Ps. 104:30 TNIV)

Here the Spirit gives life to the creation, and where the Spirit's actions are absent then so is life. Calvin recognized this sustaining work while commenting on the presence of the Spirit in Genesis 1:2, where he was 'hovering over the waters'. For Calvin, Genesis is teaching us that the power of the Spirit was necessary to sustain the world, to keep the confused mass stable.[13] On the whole Calvin tended to associate the perfecting work of the Spirit with God's providential works in creation, but we can find evidence of a more nuanced description. For example, while reading Romans 8:14 ('For those who are led by the Spirit of God are the children of God', TNIV) Calvin delineated the Spirit's work along three lines:

---

12. John Calvin, *Institutes of the Christian Religion*, ed. J. T. McNeil, tr. F. L. Battles, LCC 20, 21 (Philadelphia: Westminster, 1969), 1.13.14.
13. John Calvin, 'Genesis', in *Biblical Commentaries* (Albany, Ore.: AGES Software, 1997), p. 32.

But it is right to observe, that the working of the Spirit is various: for there is that which is universal, by which all creatures are sustained and preserved; there is that also which is peculiar to men, and varying in its character: but what Paul means here is sanctification, with which the Lord favours none but his own elect, and by which he separates them for sons to himself.[14]

In general the Spirit's power sustains all creaturely life. There is a particular aspect of that work that affects the human creature and this is most clearly seen in the elect. To understand the nature of the work that God does for the human creature we need to recall what Calvin wrote in the *Institutes*: that the Spirit is the one who effects, in Calvin's words noted above, 'the ordered disposition of all things' – their wisdom and council. The culture that human beings share together is a gift from God by His Spirit.

The Spirit of God and human culture
Since there is a strong Old Testament tradition of wisdom coming from God to human beings, often in the context of the Spirit's actions,[15] Calvin felt free to say that any and all of the wisdom we need to live in the world comes to us by God's Spirit:

Just as the experience of all ages teaches us how widely the rays of divine lights have shone on unbelieving nations, for the benefit of the present life; and we see at the present time, that the excellent gifts of the Spirit are diffused through the whole human race.[16]

God's Spirit gives human beings the gifts of knowledge and skill. He mediates to them 'the wisdom and council' that comes through

---

14. John Calvin, 'Romans', in *Biblical Commentaries* (Albany, Ore.: AGES Software, 1998), pp. 227–228.
15. God grants Solomon wisdom to be His great chosen King in 1 Kgs 3, and in the narrative he becomes an embodiment of the wisdom of Proverbs and Ecclesiastes. Elsewhere Isaiah consistently identifies the abilities of the Messiah/Servant in terms of the Spirit's gifts of wisdom (Isa. 11; 42; 61).
16. Calvin, 'Genesis', p. 139. See also Calvin, *Institutes* 2.2.15.

God's Son that they need to continue living in the world. The Spirit preserves humanity in a particular way in relation to the rest of creation. Of course, Calvin maintained a very clear distinction between the work of the Spirit and the fashions and trends of human culture. The Spirit sustains human creatures by giving them the gifts they need to build a culture.[17] However, God judges human beings according to the *kind* of culture they have established with the wisdom and council he gives them through his Son.

So the Spirit enables human beings to be themselves as creatures living together in God's good creation. They undertake the various activities that make for society and culture, sometimes showing remarkable insight into the workings of the world and each other. There are great discoveries of the truth about nature; great advances in good care for the sick or the ordering of society, great master-pieces of the representation of beauty. The greatness of any and all of them is due to the gracious acts of God by his Spirit.

The conversation with Calvin has given us some insight into what it might mean to appropriate to the Spirit God's work of perfecting creation. We've seen that there is a definite sense in which the Spirit sustains and preserves creaturely life, especially human life in all its ways. However, there is still some distance to go before we reach the sense of perfection or fulfilment that Basil suggested and Owen incorporated in his description of the emotions of Jesus. Before we get there though we can make a couple of observations regarding human experience and the interaction of divine and creaturely life.

The Spirit's agency, not his emanation

The first observation to make is that when we speak of God's giving or even breathing life into creation by his Spirit, and here we could refer to Psalm 33:6, which says, 'The heavens were made by the word of the LORD, / and all the stars, by the breath of His mouth' (HCSB),

---

17. In effect the Spirit consistently negates the negative actions of sin, death and evil inherent in human culture in order to sustain life. See John Bolt, 'Spiritus Creator: The Use and Abuse of Calvin's Cosmic Pneumatology', in P. De Klerk (ed.), *Calvin and the Holy Spirit* (Grand Rapids: Calvin Studies Society, 1989), pp. 23–24.

orthodox Christianity has always required a definite separation between the life of God who is the Spirit and the life of creation that is mediated to it by the Spirit. The life of creation is not some kind of emanation of God's being into a material creaturely form. Emanationism is an ancient pagan notion that the Church Fathers were determined to eradicate from Christianity through the doctrine of creation *ex nihilo*.[18] Some Pentecostal Christians have not been entirely vigilant in adhering to the patristic precedent.[19] For example, Pinnock writes, 'We encounter Spirit in the life of creation itself, in the vitality, the joy, the radiance, the music, the honey, the flowers, the embrace.'[20] Despite the power of the images involved here, this kind of description has crossed a line, or actually a division has been removed between God's life and the life of creation. The Spirit mediates God's power to creation to make it animate, but the prophet Elijah discovered the following:

> A great and mighty wind was tearing at the mountains and was shattering cliffs before the LORD, but the LORD was not in the wind. After the wind there was an earthquake, but the LORD was not in the earthquake. After the earthquake there was a fire, but the LORD was not in the fire. (1 Kgs 19:11–12 HCSB)

The second observation to make about the Spirit and creation, which flows on from the first, relates to the interaction between the

---

18. 'Athanasius . . . would have nothing to do with any attempt to reach an understanding of the Spirit beginning from manifestations of the Spirit in creaturely existence, in man or in the world' (T. F. Torrance, *The Trinitarian Faith* [Edinburgh: T. & T. Clark, 1995], p. 201).

19. See Kärkkäinen, *Pneumatology*, pp. 156–158.

20. Clark H. Pinnock, *Flame of Love: A Theology of the Holy Spirit* (Downers Grove: InterVarsity Press, 1996), p. 50. While Pinnock does not necessarily own the label of Pentecostal, his work has certainly found favour in the eyes of many charismatics. Likewise, Moltmann's pneumatology (cf. Moltmann, *Spirit of Life*), while exhibiting similar theological difficulties, has gained similar support from Pentecostals (Hollenweger, *Pentecostalism*, p. 4).

Spirit and human culture. Charismatics have a strong emphasis on the freedom of individual imagination to pursue the possibilities for life with God in the world and, in fact, a heightened sensitivity to the immanent presence of God in the world in general. Charismatics tend to favour affectionate confirmation of God's presence and action, they tend to give priority to personal intuition when it comes to interpreting God's actions even as they are described in the Bible.[21] At the beginning of this chapter I quoted Michael Welker's description of the Spirit's activities in various social, political and economic events throughout the twentieth century. Calvin helped us to see how we could interpret the various skills, abilities or knowledge that humans use to create their culture as a gift of the Spirit. However, Calvin also reminded us that there is a critical difference between receiving a gift from the Spirit and exercising that gift for the glory of God. In terms of how the Spirit acts to bring or preserve the good in a culture distorted by sin, death and evil Calvin wrote:

> Although he does not govern them (wicked and devils) by his Spirit, yet he checks them by his power as if with a bridle, so that they are unable to move unless he permits them to do so. Further he even makes them ministers of his will.[22]

The Spirit sustains life and preserves God's creation as good over and against rebellious creaturely efforts to despoil it. This means that Christians should be quite circumspect about interpreting the results of human culture as a perfecting work of God's Spirit – the Spirit has no specific political affiliation and no socio-economic preference. We ought to uphold that God's Spirit works in the world to preserve truth, beauty and goodness. In fact, we could go so far as to say, 'the divine economy embraces the being of the world in its relations to God and the actions of God in relation to the world'.[23] Nevertheless, while the

21. Hollenweger, *Pentecostalism*, pp. 194–195. See also Macchia, 'God Present', p. 36.

22. *Catechism of the Church of Geneva* (cited in Bolt, 'Spiritus Creator', pp. 26–27).

23. Colin E. Gunton, *The One the Three and the Many* (Cambridge: Cambridge University Press, 1993), p. 160.

Spirit is the mediator of God's perfecting work in creation, the nature of that perfection is determined by the fulfilment of God's intentions in the Lord Jesus. It is exclusively in the incarnate Son that the being of God and the being of creation come together. Both Calvin and Basil described God as effecting His intentions by the Spirit and through the wisdom, council or creative cause of his Son. Thus far I have mentioned this only in fairly abstract terms, but the gospel of the Lord Christ Jesus makes concrete what it means for God to relate to the world through his Son. More importantly, as Owen suggested, it is in the gospel events that we get a tangible sense of what it means for human experiences to be perfected as a result of the relations between the Spirit and the incarnate Son, Christ Jesus.

The Spirit perfects the Son

So far, with Calvin's help, we have the beginnings of a description of the Holy Spirit as God's perfecting cause in creation. Admittedly, in the snippets of Calvin's writings considered, the Reformer was focused mostly on describing the Spirit as the agent by whom God providentially cares for creation. The Spirit's work still needs a specifically eschatological direction in order to fit in with Basil's notion of perfecting creation and this direction must take shape in the context of relations between Jesus and the Spirit to fit with Owen's suggestion that the Spirit perfects the humanity of Jesus.

The task of defining the eschatological direction of God's actions in the economy of salvation is made straightforward for us by the apostle Paul, who wrote in his letter to the Ephesians that it was God's intention since before the creation of the world to sum up all things in the Lord Jesus Christ (Eph. 1:9–10). If the Spirit is the perfecting cause in creation, then the universal and everlasting lordship of Jesus over creation is the direction to which the Spirit is moving all creation.[24] At the same time, Paul's words to the Colossians, which were echoed by Basil and Calvin, state that all things in creation were made through the Lord Jesus, all things are for him, and in him all things hold together (Col. 1:16–17). If the

---

24. Colin E. Gunton, *The Triune Creator*, ESCT (Grand Rapids: Eerdmans, 1998), p. 223.

power of God is mediated to creaturely life by the Spirit so that it can 'live and move and have its being', then the shape that life takes in creation is found in the incarnate Son, for as Paul says, 'In him all things hold together.' What God perfects in the Lord Jesus by the Spirit, he perfects for all creation, for in the incarnate Son the being of God and the being of creation come together like never before. Colin Gunton observed, 'God the Father through His Spirit shapes this representative sample of the natural world for the sake of the remainder of it.'[25] With this in mind we turn to the Gospel accounts to consider the Father's Spirit working in and for the Son.

The Spirit and the experiences of Jesus

Let us return to the original suggestion from John Owen that the Spirit is the one by whom the humanity of Jesus is perfected.[26] Owen suggested that Jesus was joyful at the news of the seventy-two missionaries because the Spirit inspired him to be so, to react this way. How might that work? A key thing to note in this episode is the fact that Jesus is speaking or relating to the Father:

> At that time Jesus, full of joy through the Holy Spirit, said, I praise you, Father, Lord of heaven and earth, because you have hidden these things from the wise and learned, and revealed them to little children. (Luke 10:21)

God's triunity is on display here again as the Son relates to the Father in the Spirit and the emotional responses of Jesus and any

---

25. Colin E. Gunton, 'Creation (2): The Spirit Moved over the Face of the Waters. The Holy Spirit and the Created Order', in *Father, Son and Holy Spirit: Toward a Fully Trinitarian Theology* (London: T. & T. Clark, 2003), p. 199.

26. Owen, 'Greater Catechism'. Significantly for later discussion, Owen also notes Mark 3:5 where Messiah Jesus grieves the hard-heartedness of the synagogue rulers at the plight of a disabled man. It would appear that Owen considered the full gamut of Jesus' emotional states as a sign of the Saviour's perfection. Therefore, by way of inference it would appear possible to attribute lament over sin to work of the Spirit.

part the Spirit might play in those needs to be understood within the context of divine interpersonal relations on the one hand and the purpose of God for salvation on the other.

The seventy-two return with joyful tales of the in-breaking of the kingdom of God, and, moved by the Spirit, Jesus interprets this as both a sign of God's favour towards the poor and vindication of his own authority as the Son of God – the Messiah (Luke 10:21–22). It is the Spirit's gift both to enable Jesus to make this interpretation and consequently to experience this joy as he offers thanks to his heavenly Father. By this stage in the gospel story – especially in Luke's Gospel – we should expect the Spirit to equip, empower or enable Jesus to respond to God in this manner since much of what has occurred in the gospel story thus far prepares us to understand Jesus as the Spirit-empowered Son and Servant.[27] From the perspective of the gospel story at least, the Spirit is the one who acts in and for Jesus to empower him to be God's specially chosen one – he is the Spirit of Sonship. We see this first in the events comprising Jesus' baptism, testing and maiden sermon in Nazareth.

At the Jordan, Jesus is distinguished amongst all the other supplicants gathered before the baptizer when God speaks to him by the Spirit and designates him as the beloved Son (Luke 3:22; Matt. 3:17; Mark 1:11). The incident brings together a variety of Old Testament contributions to the identity of Jesus in so far as the psalms, the Samuel narratives and the Isaiah prophecies anticipate a particular relationship between the son of David as King of Israel, empowered by God's Spirit, and YHWH.[28] This Messiah will bring salvation and defeat the enemies of God's people. This Son of God will be empowered by the Spirit to judge but also to suffer on the way to fulfilling the promises of God for his people. That is, the Spirit is the agent by whom God will empower his Son to perfect the long-promised salvation.

---

27. See David A. Höhne, *Spirit and Sonship: Colin Gunton's Theology of Particularity and the Holy Spirit* (Farnham, UK: Ashgate, 2010), ch. 3.

28. See Pss 2:7; 89:26–27; Isa. 11:2; 42:1; 1 Sam. 6:13; 2 Sam. 7:12. Myk Habets, *The Anointed Son* (Eugene, Ore.: Pickwick, 2010), pp. 131–132.

Having been specially chosen by God at the Jordan River, the faithfulness of this beloved son is then tested after the manner of Israel's wilderness experience as the Spirit leads Jesus to face the ancient enemy of Adam.[29] Throughout this confrontation the Spirit continually inspires Jesus to interpret his situation with the Scriptures and likewise to submit to the will of God in the face of Satan's seemingly less costly alternatives.[30] Thus, in response to Satan's offer to determine the nature of his sonship (If you are the son . . .), in the Spirit, Jesus chooses instead the way of suffering, he chooses the Father's promised inheritance and he chooses not to pre-empt the Father's promise to save him from death – all 'as it is written'.[31]

The Gospel portrayals of Jesus' commissioning as Messiah round off as the scene changes to the Nazareth synagogue. Again in the power of the Spirit, Jesus announces his commission by using Isaiah 61 to interpret to those gathered that he, as the one especially anointed by God's Spirit, will conduct his ministry in word and deed by the power of God's Spirit to fulfil the salvation of the Lord. As Owen describes it, 'By the Spirit was he *guided, directed, comforted,*

---

29. In contrast to Matthew, Luke slips in his genealogy at this point, linking Jesus with the line running back to Adam.

30. Kimball describes Jesus' use of Scripture as 'a literal application of the OT (i.e. without midrashic techniques) in a debate pattern similar to certain rabbinic disputations in which questions and answers are drawn from Scripture' (Charles A. Kimball, *Jesus' Exposition of the Old Testament in Luke's Gospel*, ed. Stanley E. Porter, JSNTSup 94 [Sheffield: Sheffield Academic Press, 1994], p. 96). Here we are headed towards Vanhoozer's view of Messiah Jesus as 'the pre-eminent performer' in the drama of Scripture. Vanhoozer writes, 'The Son "performs" what God the Father scripted . . . The Son is also the centre of the Spirit's performance in Scripture' (Kevin J. Vanhoozer, *The Drama of Doctrine: A Canonical Linguistic Approach to Christian Theology* [Louisville: Westminster John Knox, 2005], p. 189).

31. The implication is that the narrator is merging Israel's sonship of YHWH with King David's (Matthias Wenk, *Community-Forming Power: The Socio-Ethical Role of the Spirit in Luke-Acts*, JSNTSup 19 [Sheffield: Sheffield Academic Press, 2000], p. 197).

supported, in the whole course of his ministry, temptations, obedience, and sufferings.'[32]

Throughout the rest of the gospel story the evangelists give us insights into how the Spirit enables Jesus to bring to fulfilment the various promises related to salvation. Within this dynamic of Jesus' relating rightly to the Father, his followers and opponents, the Spirit perfects Jesus' humanity by empowering him to entrust himself to the promises of his heavenly Father. This is most noticeable in the light of strong pressure to do otherwise in the forms of various kinds of opposition. The Spirit inspires in Jesus the cognitive gifts of wisdom and discernment promised for the Isaianic Servant, but most of all 'the fear of the LORD' (Isa. 11:2). Apart from this, the accounts are silent on Jesus' emotional state throughout the commissioning episode.

The Spirit and Jesus' feelings?

We know that Jesus, having fasted for forty days, underwent the wilderness temptations in a depleted physical state (Luke 4:2). For Calvin this signified that the Spirit's ministry was primarily to the Messiah's will. On Matthew's account, Calvin noted, 'the Son of God voluntarily endured the temptations, which we are now considering'.[33] The meaning of such enticements in the context of Jesus' human experiences is of particular interest at this point: especially the sense in which it could be said that Christ Jesus was genuinely tempted. Noting the importance of the Spirit's empowering work, Calvin proceeds to explain the phenomenon firstly by pointing to Hebrews 4:15: 'Christ took upon him our infirmity, but without sin' (my tr.). His second defence is quite illuminating in the context of our discussion:

> It detracts no more from his glory, that he was exposed to temptations, than that he was clothed with our flesh: for he was made man on the

---

32. John Owen, *Pneumatologia*, AGES Digital Library John Owen Collection (Edinburgh: Banner of Truth, 1967), 2.4.6, emphases original.

33. John Calvin, 'Harmony of the Gospels', in *Biblical Commentaries* (Albany, Ore.: AGES Software, 1997), p. 187.

condition that, along with our flesh, he should take upon him our feelings.[34]

Calvin here is discussing whether or not Christ Jesus was subject to temptation as a consequence of some kind of weakness, because, 'when temptation falls on men, it must always be owing to sin and weakness'. In terms of our consideration of feelings we might wonder whether Calvin expected the Spirit to act on Jesus' affections as well as his cognitive abilities. The answer appears to be 'yes' to such a question, 'for he was made man on the condition that, along with our flesh, he should take upon him our feelings'.[35] Assuming that some kind of affective response is included in the experience of temptation, Calvin writes:

> Christ was separated from us, in this respect [corruption], by the perfection of his nature; though we must not imagine him to have existed in that intermediate condition, which belonged to Adam, to whom it was only granted, that it was possible for him not to sin. We know, that Christ was fortified by the Spirit with such power, that the darts of Satan could not pierce him.[36]

So the logic appears to be, whatever the exact nature of Messiah Jesus' affective state during his time in the wilderness, it must have been perfected along with his will and his cognitive abilities in order for him to relate rightly to the Father and his people and to overcome the traps of the evil one. The Spirit's work in and for Messiah Jesus was to perfect his humanity.

Having this relational dynamic as the basis of understanding the perfection of Jesus' humanity allows us to read the rest of the gospel events – particularly those that make explicit reference to Jesus' emotional state – as further evidence of the Spirit's work in and for the Son. So whether it is Jesus' anger at the abuses of the temple or the hypocrisy of the Pharisees, whether it is his sadness at the

---

34. Ibid.
35. Ibid.
36. Ibid. p. 188.

death of Lazarus or the failure of Jerusalem, whether it is his terror and stricken lament in the garden of Gethsemane and at the cross, in all of these events the incarnate Son's relations with the Father and others are perfected by the Spirit.

Now concerning what comes from the Spirit . . .

Resurrection and the last days

The climax of the Spirit's perfecting work in and for the Son of God is the resurrection and ascension. With the subsequent out-pouring of the Spirit at Pentecost Jesus is acclaimed and publicly proclaimed to be Lord and Messiah (Acts 2:36).[37] The Spirit has achieved for Jesus far more than any before (whether prophet, priest or king) because the Spirit designates Jesus (in fact, reveals his pre-existent nature) as the Son of God in an absolute sense (Cf. Rom. 1:3–4). Hence when Christ Jesus pours out the promised Spirit on all flesh to mark the season known as the last days, the Father, by his Spirit, is doing far more than endorsing the life and work of Jesus. Rather, he is establishing 'that God was reconciling the world to himself in Christ' (2 Cor. 5:19). Jesus is the one whom YHWH promised he would be when he spoke to Moses from the burning bush, such that Jesus could say to the Pharisees, 'before Abraham was, I am' (John 8:58; cf. Exod. 3:6–8). He is the beloved Son empowered by the Spirit to make purification for sins, and so he sits at the right hand of the Father where he awaits the perfection of God's promise to have his enemies made a footstool (Heb. 1:3; cf. Ps. 110:1). At the same time he mediates God's Spirit to mark the last days (Acts 2:17, 33; cf. Joel 2:28–32) and to continue the Father's work in the Spirit of bringing all things under Him (Eph. 1:9–10).

The Spirit's actions in resurrecting and enthroning the Messiah at the right hand of the Father distinguish Christ Jesus from us even

---

37. Owen saw this work of testimony as 'the head and fountain of the whole office of the Holy Spirit towards the church' (Owen, *Pneumatologia*, p. 136).

as they confirm his ministry for us. Christ Jesus is our everlasting high priest before the throne of God since 'He always lives to intercede for [us]' (Heb. 7:25 HCSB). The resurrected Jesus advocates for us before the Father, offering himself as 'the propitiation for our sins, and not only for ours, but also for the whole world' (1 John 2:2). God's intentions to redeem creation for himself have been achieved in the person of the Lord Jesus and by his Spirit. As I have already explained, the risen Lord Jesus is, in himself, a preview of the new creation. However, the consequences of these actions are yet to be perfected. Hence the glorified royal and eternal Son now awaits the subjugation of his enemies as the 'footstool for [his] feet' (Acts 2:33–36; cf. Ps. 110:1).[38] That is, creation awaits the perfection of God's covenantal promises, the fulfilment of which has been broadcast in the gospel of Christ Jesus. The point of investigating the relationship between Jesus and the Spirit is to understand the perfection of creatureliness in the royal and eternal Son, Christ Jesus. Now we must consider how this description shapes our understanding of God's relationship with the world in the period prior to the return of the King and the coming new creation. What can we apprehend of the perfecting work of the Spirit in anticipation of the universal and everlasting revelation of Christ Jesus as Lord (cf. Phil. 2:9–11)?

The first thing to note is the importance of the framework that has already been established in describing the perfecting work of the Spirit in general. We can summarize this by way of returning to Calvin's comment on Romans 8:14:

> But it is right to observe, that the working of the Spirit is various: for there is that which is universal, by which all creatures are sustained and preserved; there is that also which is peculiar to men, and varying in its character: but what Paul means here is sanctification, with which the Lord favours none but his own elect, and by which he separates them for sons to himself.[39]

---

38. More precisely, the victory over sin, death and evil that God has achieved in the ministry of Christ Jesus awaits perfection in creation.

39. Calvin, 'Romans', pp. 227–228.

Thus far we have considered the Spirit's actions for creation in general and the human creature especially. It is the work most often discussed in describing God's providence towards creation and this was the more obvious focus in Calvin's writings. However, close examination of the career of the Lord Jesus has provided the eschatological direction in the Spirit's work in keeping with Basil's description. The last section of this chapter will consider the particular perfecting actions of the Spirit in the creaturely experience of the elect. For the sake of brevity I shall employ an important Pauline phrase – the mindset of the Spirit – as the means of depicting the experience of the elect awaiting the perfection of God's actions through Christ and in the Spirit.

The mindset of the Spirit

Throughout this chapter we have followed the trinitarian description of God's relationship to the world after the example of Calvin and Basil. In this description the perfecting work of the Spirit is to mediate 'wisdom, counsel, and the ordered disposition of all things' of the Son to all creation. This theological perspective on the 'mindset of the Spirit' will guide our examination of Paul's use of the phrase in Romans 8. In this passage Paul describes life in the last days by way of a contrast between those who live with the mindset of the flesh and those with the mindset of the Spirit (8:6). From a purely lexical perspective, the term 'mindset' (Gk. *to phronēma*) can be variously understood as 'intention, aim, aspiration or striving'.[40] It is their basic disposition that guides and governs the way people express themselves in the network of relations that make up their experience of life. Our examination of the gospel accounts has already provided us with the hermeneutical key for identifying this basic disposition. The mindset of the Spirit is the intentions, aims, aspirations or striving of the royal and eternal Son, Christ Jesus. As we shall see, Paul's mediations support this interpretation.

Calvin, who was sensitive to the way the canonical story eclipses simple lexical or historical judgments, understood mindset to mean as follows:

---

40. BAGD, p. 866.

The same with what Moses calls the imagination (*figmentum* – devising) of the heart, (Gen. 6:5) and that under this word are included all the faculties of the soul – reason, understanding, and affections, it seems to me that minding (*cogitatio* – thinking, imagining, caring) is a more suitable word.[41]

Calvin favoured a predominantly cognitive understanding of the term 'mindset' – thinking, imagining – and it is unfortunate that he sought to expand the idea from the perspective of the negative: 'mind-set of the flesh'.[42] Such a move makes it difficult to distinguish the creaturely faculties involved with the sinful intent that governs those faculties. Paul's only distinction relates to the *direction* of the mindset, namely either towards death or towards life and peace. Thinking, imagining and caring do not, in themselves, lead to death. Rather, it is when these faculties are employed in hostility towards God that the mindset of the flesh reveals itself. This state of affairs is the general and culpable actions of sinful humanity, who receive good gifts from God by his Spirit but fail to use them to the Father's glory as mentioned above. In view of the general nature of the Spirit's perfecting work that mediates 'the wisdom and counsel' of the eternal Son to humanity, and *preserves* truth, beauty and goodness in a world *distorted* by sin, death and evil, it is essential that we differentiate a sense in which the Spirit acts through the royal or incarnate Son to *save* truth beauty and goodness *from* sin, death and evil.

The mindset regenerated by the Spirit

In terms of the Spirit's perfecting work for the elect, Calvin associated the mindset of the Spirit with the doctrine of regeneration.[43] He describes it as 'the secret energy of the Spirit, by which we come to enjoy Christ and all his benefits'.[44] Owen recognizes a great variety

---

41. Calvin, 'Romans', p. 220.
42. Calvin is here contending with Erasmus, who had translated the Greek term as 'affection' (*affectum*), whereas the old translator (Jerome?) had 'prudence' (*prudentiam*), ibid.
43. Ibid., p. 224. Calvin uses the term 'the Spirit of regeneration'.
44. Calvin, *Institutes* 3.1.1.

in 'the application of the outward means which the Holy Spirit is pleased to use and make effectual' regeneration, 'for the Spirit worketh how and when he pleaseth'.[45] Owen portrays the Spirit as working mostly in 'preaching of the word', sometimes without it, as in the case of 'those who are regenerate before they come to the use of reason, or in their infancy',[46] and sometimes by extraordinary means as in the case of the apostle Paul. Yet the great strength of Owen's interpretation of the Spirit's work is his recognition of the interaction between the divine and the mundane:

> Mostly they [the Spirit's acts] are so in and by the use of ordinary means, instituted, blessed, and sanctified of God to that end and purpose. And great variety there is, also, in the perception and understanding of the work itself in them in whom it is wrought, for in itself it is secret and hidden, and is no other ways discoverable but in its causes and effects; for as 'the wind bloweth where it listeth, and thou hearest the sound thereof, but canst not tell whence it cometh, and whither it goeth, so is every one that is born of the Spirit,' John iii. 8.[47]

The Spirit sanctifies the ordinary faculties of individuals by empowering them in many and various ways – both to act and reflect on those actions. Yet the tangible operations of the Spirit are discreet to the point of being as invisible as the wind. The Spirit is the 'secret agent of God's causes',[48] and it is to these causes and effects that we must look in order to see the fruit of regeneration.

Regeneration and the Spirit of sonship

Those with the Spirit's mindset are not simply revived or reanimated in their general temperament towards the world. Their way of being

---

45. Owen, *Pneumatologia*, p. 157.
46. Ibid.
47. Ibid.
48. David A. Höhne, 'The Secret Agent of Natural Causes: Providence, Contingency and the Perfecting Work of the Spirit', in Mark D. Thompson (ed.), *Engaging with Calvin* (Nottingham: Apollos, 2009), pp. 158–178.

in the world is regenerated such that they are reoriented towards their heavenly Father: 'you received the Spirit of sonship in whom we cry *Abba*, Father' (Rom. 8:15). This act of redirection towards the Father is the Spirit's testimony 'together with our spirit that we are God's children' (v. 16 HCSB). *The mindset of the Spirit is to be directed towards the Father.* More than this, the intention of the Spirit is to manifest the disposition of the Son towards the Father in God's children. Paul grasps the essential nature of that disposition by way of reference to the experience of the Lord Jesus in the garden of Gethsemane (cf. esp. Mark 14:36). It was at this point that the royal and eternal Son utters the most fundamental statement of righteous creaturely relations towards God, 'Not my will but yours be done.'[49] In the same way that the Spirit perfected the incarnate Son in self-sacrificial submission towards the Father, so likewise the Spirit of sonship perfects in the sons and daughters of God the disposition of the Son.

The Spirit's act of mediating the disposition of the Son to the children of God aligns their strivings with those of Christ Jesus. Through the perfecting work of the Spirit the children of God join the Son in submitting to the Father, and the importance of the Gethsemane allusion is highlighted with reminder that the Spirit's mindset is revealed when 'we suffer with Him [Christ]' (Rom. 8:17 HCSB). In the flow from chapter 7 to 8 of Romans Paul confronts the chief struggle of the mindset of the flesh, 'For I do not do the good that I want to do, but I practise the evil that I do not want to do' (7:19 HCSB). It is from this mindset which leads to death that Paul desires to be rescued (7:24). The Spirit's mindset enables the children of God to sacrifice self to the will of God and experience the sufferings of Christ Jesus in that event. In fact, the regenerative powers of the Spirit at work in the experience of the children of God distinguish them within a world that is otherwise subjected to the frustration of sin, death and evil (Rom. 8:20). Over and above the providential governance of this world, the Spirit continues to direct the cries of God's children towards the Father in anticipation of their perfection and in the face of their experiences of trial and temptation. As Calvin commented, 'the Spirit takes on himself a

---

49. Matt. 26:39; Mark 14:36; Luke 22:42.

part of the burden, by which our weakness is oppressed; so that he not only helps and succours us, but lifts us up'.[50] The Spirit's mindset is to long for that which has been achieved in the Lord Jesus to be perfected in all creation (Rom. 8:23).

The perfecting work of the Spirit and Christian perfection

At this point we ought to make an important distinction between the ongoing perfecting work of the Spirit for the children of God and the Wesleyan description of the event of perfection in Christian experience. For Wesley, the perfect child of God is one in

> 'whom is the mind which was in Christ,' and who so 'walketh as Christ also walked;' a man 'that hath clean hands and a pure heart,' or that is 'cleansed from all filthiness of flesh and spirit:' one in whom is 'no occasion of stumbling' and who accordingly 'does not commit sin' . . . one in whom God hath fulfilled His faithful word 'From all your filthiness and from all you idols I will cleanse you.'[51]

Wesley was at pains to emphasize that perfection did not imply 'a dispensation from doing good and attending to all the ordinances of God' on the one hand. Neither did perfection imply, on the other hand, 'a freedom from ignorance, mistake, temptation, and a thousand infirmities necessarily connected with flesh and blood'.[52] Nevertheless, he maintained that 'pure love reigning alone in the heart and life'[53] would keep the children of God from voluntarily sinning.[54] Characteristically, Wesley anticipated that this moment of perfection may well come upon the Christian some time after

---

50. Calvin, 'Romans', p. 240.
51. John Wesley, *A Plain Account of Christian Perfection* (London: Epworth, 1960), p. 29.
52. Ibid., p. 28.
53. Ibid., p. 52.
54. Hollenweger maintains that there was some variety in Wesley's description of perfection beyond the *Plain Account*; however, he also admits that Wesley's view of sin was not that of the apostle Paul's (Hollenweger, *Pentecostalism*, p. 156).

justification. Regardless of the actual timespan though, the moment of perfection was the result of a subsequent second blessing of the Spirit: 'None therefore ought to believe that the work is done, til there is added the testimony of the Spirit witnessing his entire sanctification as clearly as his justification.'[55]

There are key theological issues at stake here in distinguishing the perfecting work of the Spirit from this spiritual perfection that Wesley expresses. In Romans 8:11 Paul establishes the connection between the premier act of the Spirit in perfecting Messiah Jesus and the Spirit's subsequent actions in the experience of a Christian: 'the one who raised Christ from the dead [by his Spirit] will bring to life your mortal bodies *via* the indwelling of his Spirit in you'. By the same means as he raised Christ Jesus from the dead, the Father will regenerate our mortal bodies – by his Spirit. As Calvin commented, 'in the person of Christ was exhibited a specimen of the power which belongs to the whole body of the Church'.[56] Yet we must keep in mind that Calvin's language of 'specimen' refers to the quality of the power exercised, not the quantity. In reality the life that is given to our mortal bodies through the Spirit is, in the first instance, a specimen of the everlasting life enjoyed by the resurrected Lord Jesus.[57] Hence Paul writes later that we have the Spirit as 'the first-fruits' not such that we are totally transformed but rather such that we 'groan within ourselves, eagerly waiting for . . . the redemption of our bodies' (Rom. 8:23 HCSB).

The Spirit's regenerating work does produce the new creature 'renewed [in] faculties, with new dispositions, power and ability to perform them. Hence it is called a divine nature. (2 Pet. 1:4).'[58] The

---

55. Wesley, *Perfection*, p. 52. The impact of this teaching as a foundation for western Pentecostalism is well documented by Hollenweger, who makes the significant observation that Wesley's roots lay firmly in Roman semi-Pelagian descriptions of free will as opposed to the Reformed doctrine of predestination.

56. Calvin, 'Romans', p. 225.

57. Hence Paul's portrayal of the Spirit as the 'down-payment of our inheritance' in Eph. 1:14.

58. Owen, *Pneumatologia*, p. 162.

children of God do genuinely call out to the Father in the moment of struggle after the example of Christ in Gethsemane. However, the children of God, still marred by the curse of death, exhibit mortality along with the rest of creation and therefore still succumb to the temptation to choose their own will. Hence the great promise of Romans 8 that the 'Spirit Himself intercedes for us' when 'we do not know what to pray for as we should' (8:26 HCSB). We are not abandoned by God in our failures but rather 'He who searches the hearts knows the Spirit's mind-set' (8:27 HCSB). God considers us his children because the Spirit everlastingly mediates Christ Jesus' disposition to God for his children. The fruit of the Spirit's perfecting work in us is patient endurance in anticipation of the new creation as much, if not more, than 'enthusiastical raptures, ecstacies, voices, or any thing of the like kind'.[59]

Conclusion

We began with the contemporary search for the assurance that God's Spirit is active in the chances and changes of this fleeting world. With the help of Calvin and Owen we have identified a definite means of aligning human experience, which must include our emotional reactions, with the actions of the Holy Spirit in creation. As the perfecting cause of God in the world who mediates the wisdom and disposition of the Son to his creatures, the Spirit guides and governs the creation, moving it towards the perfection of God's intentions for creation in Christ. Though generally invisible, this movement is clearly founded in the life, death and resurrection of Christ Jesus who is the perfection of creatureliness and the one 'in whom all things' subsequently 'hold together'. The particular experience of the elect within this process is the power to call out to God as Father, patiently enduring the trials and temptations of a world that 'groans with the pains of childbirth' in anticipation of the 'glorious freedom of God's children'.

---

59. Ibid., p. 159.

Michael P. Jensen

The surprise of the emotions

In October 2004 my mother-in-law died of breast cancer at the age
of 62, not much more than a year after being diagnosed. Being the
only member of the family experienced at public speaking – and
indeed, at running funerals – I was quite willing to take on the duties
of giving the eulogy at the funeral service when I was asked to by my
father-in-law. In addition, since I was Jackie's son-in-law and not
directly related to her, I could be expected and indeed expected myself
to maintain my composure in the delivery of the task in a suitably
controlled tone, allowing the mourners to grieve in quiet privacy.

The tears, then, took me quite by surprise. I was not far into
retelling Jackie's life story – from her childhood in London to her
arrival in Australia in the 1960s and her conversion to faith in Christ.
At some point in this narrative I was quite overcome by the occasion.
My voice quavered, I could feel myself flushing red, and my face
contorted itself. I could barely continue to read, because I couldn't
see the page in front of me. What words I could get out were
squeezed out through my throat, and I found myself gasping for

breath in between watery sobs. Afterwards my 6-year-old son said to me, 'Your face was all screwed up, Dad.'

I retell this story not because I am hoping to elicit sympathy but rather because of its ordinariness as an episode of the human emotions at work. The strong emotion seemed to come to me in a way that I couldn't predict. It was completely a surprise. I was not feeling anywhere near this level of emotion before the service – not even as I rose to my feet to speak. It was as if there were a force outside of me working on me and causing me to lose self-control of my body in a way that was understandable but still within Anglo-Saxon culture somewhat shameful, especially for men. I am not normally conscious of doing things with my body that I don't directly will. Yet in this moment, normal operations seemed to be suspended and the emotion took control of me.

It is an ordinary episode, but no less complicated for being so. Some of these problems no doubt relate to the difficulty my own culture and gender has with public expressions of emotion. Nevertheless, there is a universal in this particular. It illustrates how troublesome emotions are in thinking cohesively about human being. This trouble pans out in three overlapping ways, to do with agency, the body and reason.

The first difficulty is best explained by asking in what sense I was an agent of my own sobs. Can I really speak in this way, of an emotion controlling me, since the emotion could not be anyone else's? The sobs certainly emanated from my mouth and in my voice. They happened to and in my body. But I was not intending or willing to sob; in fact, I was willing the opposite. Yet I sobbed, and not some demon that had entered me, or some ventriloquist pretending to be me.

Secondly, at the moment of intense emotion, the human being seems to become almost alienated from his own body. Because these emotions are exhibited in such an obviously visceral fashion and yet carry with them unwanted consequences such as the stigma of cultural shame, the human subject may feel that 'I' am other from my physical body. There must be then a purer, non-physical form of 'me' – to which perhaps I can ascend once I am free of the untrustworthiness of my flesh. Even a more honourably perceived emotion like the feeling of loss shares enough in common with the more base desires of our bodies – feelings like hunger, sexual desire, need for sleep – that in experiencing it we still frequently experience this otherness from our bodies. Indeed, if I am to speak of some 'higher' set of emotions, where do I 'feel' them if not in my body?

Thirdly, my perception of myself as a primarily rational creature is disturbed by the experience of strong emotion. But this is because of a hidden assumption that 'reason' and 'emotion' are discrete centres of my person, with reason the more nearly 'spiritual' or more distinctly human of the two. Yet my strong emotion was in fact tied to rational propositions about the occasion. I did not feel at all the same way about the funeral, at which I had ministered, for a woman in her early forties who had committed suicide – even though the circumstances were arguably more tragic. I knew Jackie as my friend and mother-in-law, and as my wife's mother and the granny of my own children. I could calculate what her loss would mean for us. In fact, the more I thought about it, the more I felt about it.

These difficulties are enough to engender a philosophical, psychological and anthropological discussion of the emotions, such as the US philosopher Martha C. Nussbaum provides in her masterful work *Upheavals of Thought: The Intelligence of the Emotions.*[1] The task of a theological anthropology, however, is to begin analysing questions like this in the light of a particular context of human life, namely God. For a Christian anthropology, that context is framed by the themes of the creation of man and woman in the image of God on the one hand, and the presence of sin in human life on the other. These two themes are set in tension with one another, not just in the biblical story but in the existence of every human person. To what degree does this or that feature of my humanity reflect my likeness as a creature made in the divine image of the Creator? Or is it in some way a result of that disorder of personhood that stems from my participation in human fallenness? But Christian anthropology will also speak of a destiny for human beings. The two themes of theological anthropology have their resolution, however, in the person and work of Jesus Christ. Theological anthropology, like all properly Christian theology, must speak an evangelical word, in which the image-of-God humankind is redeemed and perfected.

---

1. Cambridge: Cambridge University Press, 2001.

It has, in the resurrection of Jesus from the dead, a pattern to which human creatures will one day be conformed (Rom. 8:29).

Returning to my troublesome emotions, then, was this event God's will for creatureliness in me? Or was it an instance of sin's distorting effects? If God has no 'body, parts or passions',[2] and yet my emotions are an irreducibly physical component of me, ought I in seeking to be more like him to look to some future beyond or without my body? Or must I think of myself dualistically, as most of the Christian tradition has done, as having a distinct 'soul' for the purer emotions such as joy and hope as well as a body for my appetites such as hunger and thirst? Has 'reason', or the 'rational soul', a more exalted seat in me? What would an account of the human emotions look like in the light of the resurrection of the dead? In what sense can the three problematic aspects of human emotion – to do with agency, body and reason – be addressed from a theological perspective?

The tradition of Christian theological reflection on human emotions has been marked by an understanding of the *imago dei* (image of God) as the capacity for reason, on the one hand, and by a view of the human person as consisting of a separate, even independent, body and soul, on the other. First, I shall show how each of these is a problematic articulation of a scriptural concept. Secondly, I shall revisit both concepts and show how they must not result in either a substance dualism or in a hierarchy of emotions. A theological anthropology that describes the human being as a divinely appointed speech agent offers a description of the place of the emotions in human life without resorting to an unnecessary, unscriptural and unchristological split between body and soul.

Two problems in the traditional theological account of human being

The imago dei
The concept of the *imago dei* is the point through which any genuinely biblical and theological anthropology must surely pass. It is of course

---

2. Article 1 of the *Thirty-Nine Articles of Religion*.

linked closely with the creation of humankind in Genesis 1:26–28 (TNIV):

> Then God said, 'Let us make human beings in our image, in our likeness, so that they may rule over the fish in the sea and the birds in the sky, over the livestock and all the wild animals and over all the creatures that move along the ground.'
>
> So God created human beings in his own image,
> in the image of God he created them;
> male and female he created them.
>
> God blessed them and said to them, 'Be fruitful and increase in number; fill the earth and subdue it. Rule over the fish in the sea and the birds in the sky and over every living creature that moves on the ground.'

Exegetes and theologians are agreed that the phrase 'the image of God' indicates that humankind is to be the reflection of God to the creation. Unlike the other creatures, humans are capable of being the conduit for the divine being in the world he made. The question is, how exactly do human beings reflect the deity? The assumption of many writers has been that the image must refer to a particular capacity or ability given to humankind. That is, there is some capacity or function integral to God that is also fundamental for human beings.

If it is the case that the image of God is found in some capacity that human beings possess, it is not surprising that the *imago dei* has been understood over the course of Christian history as the capacity for rational thought. The argument comes from two directions. On the one hand, it is rational thought that most obviously separates us from the beasts and the birds. Human beings could be said to be unique because of this capacity. As fallen creatures, we lapse when we give ourselves over to our passions and instincts, as the animals do. On the other hand, it would seem that God is distinguished as a being by his supreme capacity for rational thought, in knowledge and in wisdom. Human beings are not by being in his image in any sense equivalent to him in rational capacity, but it would make sense to see them as analogous to him in it.

This position is well attested – even dominant – from the early church onwards. The church's first major theologian Irenaeus, bishop of Lyons (c. 180), wrote of the human being as 'endowed with reason, and in this respect like God'.[3] Gregory of Nyssa (c. 335 – c. 395) wrote of man as the 'rational animal'.[4] The great African bishop Augustine of Hippo (354–430) writes in his commentary on Genesis, 'Man's excellence consists in the fact that God made him to his own image by giving him an intellectual soul, which raises him above the beasts of the field.'[5]

In this way, the image-of-God concept functioned as a kind of mediating principle for an analogy of being between humankind and the divine. The interpretation of the *imago dei* as rationality was then given further impetus by reference to the depiction of Jesus in the New Testament as the logos of God.

The gravest difficulty for the interpretation of the *imago dei* as the capacity for rational thought is a lack of exegetical support. There simply is no obvious biblical connection between the concept of the image of God and any individual faculty belonging to human beings, including rationality. Any drawing of lines between the two notions is necessarily artificial. As Karl Barth wrote, 'it is obvious that their authors merely found the concept in the text and then proceeded to pure invention in accordance with the requirement of contemporary anthropology'.[6] What's more, if the image of God in us is tied to our capacity for reason, then the path to our redemption must surely lie in the refinement of our reason by education and enlightenment. But, perhaps worst of all, the 'image as reason' view is a distorted view of God himself, since his highest virtue, or signal property, must be, on this account, his rationality.

---

3. 'Against the Heretics', in A. Roberts and J. Donaldson (eds.), *The Ante-Nicene Fathers*, vol. 1 (Grand Rapids: Eerdmans, 1975), 4.4.3.

4. 'Of the Making of Man', in P. Schaff and H. Wace (eds.), *The Nicene and Post-Nicene Fathers*, vol. 5 (Edinburgh: T. & T. Clark, 1892), 8.8.

5. 'The Literal Interpretation of Genesis', in *On Genesis*, ed. J. E. Rotelle, tr. E. Hill (Hyde Park, N. Y.: New City, 2002), 6.12.

6. Karl Barth, *Church Dogmatics*, tr. Geoffrey W. Bromiley and Thomas F. Torrance, 2nd ed., 4 vols. (Edinburgh: T. & T. Clark, 1975), 3/1.193.

It would be historically simplistic to claim that the understanding of the *imago dei* as the capacity for rational thought led directly to a denigration of what we now call by the almost impossibly broad term 'the emotions'. Behind this description of the image was an attempt to account for the way in which the Fall had affected the human person such that he or she was often mastered by unruly emotions. But if it is in the area of rationality that we are most like God and most unlike the animals, then it is not a great step to arguing that emotions are what we share with the animals, rather than with God. Or – and this is a more sophisticated concept – the emotions are divided into two distinct kinds: the higher and more pure sort, or the 'affections', which are found in relation to the divine, and the more base 'passions' of our animal nature. The problem is magnified if human nature is held to be a dichotomy between body and soul, as we shall see.

Body and soul

If the *imago dei* hinges on Genesis 1:26–28, then the discussion of human ontology is a commentary on Genesis 2:7: 'Then the LORD God formed a man from the dust of the ground and breathed into his nostrils the breath of life, and the man became a living being.'[7]

How should the 'breathing' and the 'dust' be interpreted? Were they references to the two substances that together form a human person, the body and the soul? The Church Fathers were vigorous in their defence of the psychosomatic unity of the human person against the prevailing Platonic anthropology – which held body and soul to be separable entities, with the person's true identity held in the self-conscious soul. The Fathers did not accept the teaching that the body was merely the prison of the soul (as was taught, for example, in Plato's *Gorgias*), but rather affirmed the goodness of both as created by God. Nevertheless, they did teach that the soul was an independent entity; and despite the desire to maintain the unity of body and soul as necessary to constitute the complete human being, an essentially Hellenistic body–soul dualism became

---

7. Unless stated otherwise, Bible quotations in this chapter are from the NIV.

the norm in patristic Christian anthropology.[8] Tertullian, who wrote an entire work entitled *A Treatise on the Soul*, held body and soul to be separate and indeed separable substances conjoined at conception and torn apart at death.

Regardless, the language of *anima intellectiva*, 'rational soul', came into use to describe what was imparted by God to Adam in Genesis 2:7. It was also equated with the 'spirit' of the human individual. It is there in the Chalcedonian definition in relation to Christology – Jesus is truly human on account of having both a body and a 'rational soul'. The bestowal of rationality on Adam by the Creator in the form of his spirit or soul led inevitably to exaltation of this component as the superior one. The notion of the 'rational soul' was also the parent of the concept of 'the mind', which has subsequently engendered its own debates in the field of philosophy.

The resemblance of the philosophy of René Descartes (1596–1650) to the dominant theological conception of human being is striking; and it is also the case that his influence was to be felt in the theology that followed him. For Descartes, human bodies are ordinary material things that have no mental properties at all. The mind or the soul is a completely non-physical and ultimately independent entity. As he wrote, 'my soul, by virtue of which I am what I am – is entirely and truly distinct from my body and . . . can be or exist without it'.[9]

Once more, we should note the sophistication of the account of human psychology that went alongside this tendency to describe human being in terms of a duality of substance. The 'passions', emanating from the body, were to be distinguished from the 'affections', which were under the command of the rational soul or mind.

The type of dualism bequeathed to the Christian tradition by Greek philosophy and then amplified by Descartes has been widely attacked, however, on a number of philosophical grounds. For example, how does the dualist propose to explain the apparent

---

8. Wolfhart Pannenberg, *Systematic Theology*, tr. Geoffrey W. Bromiley, 3 vols. (Edinburgh: T. & T. Clark, 1991), vol. 2, p. 184.

9. René Descartes, *Meditations on First Philosophy*, tr. Laurence Julien Lafleur, 2nd ed. (New York: Liberal Arts, 1960), p. 132.

dependence of the mind or soul on the brain, which is a physical entity? How can an immaterial entity influence a material one? Increasingly, modern neuroscience is able to explain human consciousness in entirely physical terms. Cartesian dualism then looks metaphysically immodest, and we are compelled to ask whether it is theologically and biblically necessary. We can easily see how it has entered into the bloodstream of Christian orthodoxy from an external source, namely Platonism, even if it has been somewhat modified in the process. Further, the reading of Genesis 2:7 on which dualism is supposedly secured fails to note that animals are also animated by the spirit of life and can be called *nepeš ḥayyâ* (Gen. 1:20; 6:17). Life as a work of the divine breath does not bestow any uniqueness on human beings.[10] The implication for our view of the human emotions is surely this: if Platonic/Cartesian dualism is unsustainable, then the division of the human emotions into discrete 'passions' and 'affections' would seem to be questionable at least.

The human being as a whole being

The Aristotelian dualism of Thomas Aquinas

The story of theological reflection on human nature and the emotions is not, however, one in which an unrestrained Platonism has held complete sway. The turn to Aristotelian psychology by Thomas Aquinas (1225–74) and others after him, including John Owen (1616–83) produced a friendlier account of relations between the body and the soul. Though Aquinas did link rationality to the image, writing that 'intellectual creatures alone, properly speaking, are made to God's image',[11] he was able to account for the rational soul as dependent on the body. The strength of the Aristotelian

---

10. Hans Walter Wolff, *Anthropology of the Old Testament* (London: SCM, 1974), p. 22.

11. *Summa Theologica*, Ia q. 93 a.2, cited in M. Cortez, *Theological Anthropology: A Guide for the Perplexed*, Guides for the Perplexed (London: T. & T. Clark, 2010), p 142.

metaphysical system was its emphasis on particulars. Ideas do not exist apart from their expression. Thus, for Aquinas, the soul is the form of the body. Furthermore, 'a human being is not a soul only, but rather composite of soul and body'.[12]

The strengths of Aquinas's description are, first, that he emphasizes the human person as a whole being, body and soul. The identity of the human person is not reducible to physical materials, but it is not other than that which is encountered in the physical being. Secondly, his description of the 'intellectual soul' as the image of God at least gestures towards the more biblical concept of 'the knowledge of God'. The *anima intellectiva* can then be understood as the human being's capacity for relationship with God and not as an abstract notion such as 'rationality'. It is now my task to follow Aquinas's hunch towards a (brief) reappraisal of human ontology and the *imago*, as we continue in our search for a persuasive theological account of the emotions and their role in human existence.

The imago dei *as the whole being addressed by God*

As US theologian Michael Horton points out, 'For the biblical writers at least, "what is it to be human?" is ultimately a narrative-ethical rather than a metaphysical-ontological question.'[13]

That is to say, it is the commission or task given to human beings at the beginning of the narrative of salvation history that better sums up the meaning of the image of God concept than any speculative attempt to assign it to some inner state or faculty of the human person.[14] This way of addressing the concept allows us to see the

---

12. *Summa Theologica*, Ia q.75 a.4, cited in ibid.

13. Michael Horton, 'Image and Office: Human Personhood and the Covenant', in Richard Lints, Michael S. Horton and Mark R. Talbot (eds.), *Personal Identity in Theological Perspective* (Grand Rapids: Eerdmans, 2006), p. 181.

14. This is the view of both Alistair I. McFadyen, *The Call to Personhood: A Christian Theory of the Individual in Social Relationships* (Cambridge: Cambridge University Press, 1990), and Kevin J. Vanhoozer, 'Human Being: Individual and Social', in Colin E. Gunton (ed.), *The Cambridge Companion to Christian Doctrine* (Cambridge: Cambridge University Press, 1997), pp. 158–188.

Christological references to the image in the New Testament (Col. 1:15; 2 Cor. 3:18) in their proper light. What the image is can be seen nowhere more clearly than in the way in which the second Adam redeems and restores it and indeed fulfils it. Further, as Calvin saw, we are then invited to express this image by putting on Christ, as in Ephesians 4:24: 'and to put on the new self, created to be like God in true righteousness and holiness'.

The task given to human beings at the beginning of Genesis relates to the concept of dominion.[15] It is, of all the creatures, this one whom God addresses as his partner in the project of creation. For the psalmist it is a matter of wonder: 'what is man that you are mindful of him?' (Ps. 8:4 NIV 1984). The human creature is called by God to be his presence in the world; and, as the one addressed by God, is equipped by him for the task. Humans have both the capacity and the responsibility to relate to God – to hear and respond to his call, to speak to him, to enter into covenants with him, to represent him in and to the world. They rule the world, mediate the presence of God to it, and witness to his glory.

It follows from this view of the *imago dei* that it is inclusive of the whole person, and not merely some aspect or faculty. As the Dutch theologian Herman Bavinck writes, 'Nothing in humanity is excluded from God's image; it stretches as far as our humanity does and constitutes our humanness.'[16] It is with her whole being that the human person is to respond with love to God (Deut. 6:5). If, then, we point to certain special capabilities that are given to human beings, it is not to imagine these capabilities as separable from the essential wholeness and unity of being in which she images the divine being. Too often the gifts that go with being created in the image of God have been confused with the essence of the image.

---

15. 'The strongest case has been made for the view that the divine image makes man God's vice-regent on earth' (Gordon J. Wenham, *Genesis 1–15*, WBC 1 [Waco: Word, 1987], p. 31). See also Wolff, *Anthropology of the Old Testament*, pp. 159–161.

16. Herman Bavinck, *Reformed Dogmatics*, 3 vols. (Grand Rapids: Baker Academic, 2003), vol. 2, p. 561.

The human person is equipped by God for the task of mediating his presence to the world, to the glory of God. For the task of naming and ordering and ruling the creation, human beings have been given remarkable capacities in their physical bodies. This includes their remarkable capacity to reason. The human brain, endowed as it is with the faculties of memory, logical deduction, intuition and imagination, is not only able to recognize order in the world as it discovers it; it is also able to bring order to it. With their minds, human beings reveal themselves to be not merely observers of the natural world but able participants in it.

But it is also the case that we are created as feelingful, or affectional beings. It is not enough for us to rule as creatures of sheer will or pure rationality – as if we could. We are called not merely to a dominion over the world, but dominion within in it. Our emotions serve us here in two ways. First, they turn us to our fellow human beings – those for whom we have affections. Our emotions alert us to our mutual dependence on one another for the fulfilling of the divine mandate. Secondly, our dominion is not intended to be a mere assertion of our wills over creation. We quite properly respond to what we encounter in it as it moves us. Even without a theological perspective, philosopher Nussbaum can observe that human emotions involve judgments in which 'we acknowledge our own neediness and incompleteness before parts of the world that we do not fully control'.[17]

Are we different from the animals, then? Indeed, but the difference is not, to use Horton's language, metaphysical-ontological as much as narrative-ethical. We are creatures designed for a particular history – to partner with God in his project of creation. Wolfhart Pannenberg writes:

> when it is a matter of the advantage of humans over all other creatures, the emphasis is not on intellectual ability but on the destiny of fellowship with God and the position of rule associated with closeness to God.[18]

---

17. Nussbaum, *Upheavals of Thought*, p. 19. Interestingly, Wolff summarizes *nepeš* as 'needy man' (*Anthropology of the Old Testament*, p. 10).

18. Pannenberg, *Systematic Theology*, vol. 2, p. 182.

Our capacity for speech is a gift given to us that we might serve the creation and the Creator. This gift has an extraordinary impact on our emotional repertoire. Giving voice to feeling leads to its refinement. As Cambridge theologian Sarah Coakley writes:

> it is surely the case that animals (even higher mammals) and humans experience emotion significantly differently [from each other] as a result of humans having the capacity for language . . . the 'horizons' of emotion and feeling are vastly expanded by linguistic expression.[19]

The presence of 'higher' emotions – ones that cats do not by any measure feel – is not because the image of God has transferred to us some metaphysical property, but because our physical equipment has been moulded for a particular purpose.

Beyond body–soul dualism

In the discussion of human ontology, once again we find Scripture asserting the essential unity of the human person in every aspect. We are not thought of as a soul contained in a body; neither are we composed of two separate substances. It is rather that we can be considered from two angles. Each individual forms a psychosomatic unity, not reducible to the component parts of the body but never less than them either. As Pannnenberg puts it, 'the soul and consciousness are deeply rooted in our corporeality. Conversely, the body is not a corpse. It is an ensouled body in all its expressions in life.'[20]

Though our English Bibles have traditionally translated the Hebrew *nepeš* as 'soul', it is doubtful whether this translation captures the way the word is used in the Old Testament. We have already seen how in Genesis 2:7 the man 'becomes a *nepeš ḥayyâ*', a 'living being'. In this instance, it is not 'soul' that is meant, but rather his whole existence. As Wolff puts it, 'man does not have nephesh, he is

---

19.   Sarah Coakley, 'Postscript: What (if Anything) Can the Sciences Tell Philosophy and Theology About Faith, Rationality and the Passions?', *Modern Theology* 27.2 (2011), p. 358.

20.   Pannenberg, *Systematic Theology*, vol. 2, p. 182.

nephesh, he lives as nephesh'.[21] *Nepeš* is never given the meaning of an indestructible core of being as opposed to the mortal body.[22]

This usage is replicated in the New Testament. For example, Paul's response to the scoffers in 1 Corinthians 15:35–49 offers a theology of new creation built upon the ideas of Genesis 1 and 2, and references Genesis 2:7. As he explains, God has ordered bodies in different ways – the heavenly and earthly bodies differ in glory, for example, but are still parts of the creation order. So it is with the resurrection body and its relationship to the old earthly body. The contrast is made in four ways: perishable versus imperishable, dishonour versus glory, weakness versus power and *psychikon* versus *pneumatikon* (15:42–44). *Psychē* is the word usually translated 'soul' (and was the LXX term for the Hebrew *nepeš*). But quite clearly in the context Paul is meaning to contrast the life force that came with the breath of God in the garden of Eden (Gk. *psychikon*) with the new life of the indwelling Spirit (Gk. *pneumatikon*).

The crucial piece of theological information for human ontology is that Jesus Christ is now in heaven reigning as an embodied person. Heaven is not somewhere, in other words, that only disembodied souls can enter. This is surely the truth that must govern the way we think about the body and the soul. Whatever 'soul' means, it doesn't

---

21. Wolff, *Anthropology of the Old Testament*, p. 10.

22. We ought to notice, too, that in none of the passages usually listed in defence of the distinct 'soul' idea is the word 'soul' (in its Greek or Hebrew form) mentioned. In fact, in the parable of the rich man and Lazarus it seems quite specific that there is a physical afterlife – after all, the rich man asks if Lazarus can cool his tongue with his finger. The word 'body' in Paul's usage need not be contrasted with 'soul', either, since he could easily be speaking of his old, decaying body in contrast to his future embodied existence. Furthermore, it seems a doubtful theological method to sketch a view of the human person on the basis of these references. They do not seem to be teaching us specifically about the composition of the human person, nor about cosmology. In the case of the parable in Luke 16, Jesus is using the pop theology of the day rather than making a concerted case for a particular view of the afterlife. That is not his point.

mean something separable from our bodies as if we have a shadowy other haunting our every move. If we are in Christ when we die, we are 'with him' in the sense that we are with him in heaven now. Paul says to the (living) Colossians our lives are 'hidden with Christ in God' (3:3 TNIV); and there is no sense in which he is saying there is a 'soulish' bit of them in heaven now. Likewise, *post mortem* it is perfectly consistent with the New Testament to say we are 'with Christ' without saying that we have a ghostly other self actually located with him. Our 'with-Christness' consists in his life and the promise it holds for our resurrection on the final day.

Without imagining that I have here resolved the question of human ontology – about which streams of ink continue to flow[23] – we may at least point to the Bible's understanding of the essential cohesion and unity of the human individual. Our capacity for emotion belongs to our whole humanity and, like the whole of our humanity, is both 'very good' and a sign of our limitedness as creatures. The effects of the Fall do not draw a line in us, turning a soul against a body, but cut right through us in every aspect: reason, will and feelings. Our reason and will are as corrupted as our feelings.

On being moved

What does our examination of the human being as a creature called by God, body and soul, for the task of dominion mean for the 'problem' of the emotions with which I began? As in all theological anthropological questions, we are faced with trying to understand what in our humanity is part of our ordinary creaturely being and

---

23. See e.g. the divergent opinions of John W. Cooper, *Body, Soul, and Life Everlasting: Biblical Anthropology and the Monism–Dualism Debate*, updated ed. (Grand Rapids: Eerdmans; Leicester: Apollos, 2000), and Nancey C. Murphy, *Bodies and Souls, or Spirited Bodies?*, Current Issues in Theology (Cambridge: Cambridge University Press, 2006). Cooper's sturdy defence of a holistic dualism in the context of a psychosomatic unity certainly deserves more attention than I have been able to give it here, though I remain unconvinced.

what in us is fallen. From the example of my experience of over-whelming grief, I isolated the three areas of agency, the body and reason as the points at which our emotions seem to complicate our humanity. It is now time to revisit each of these.

'Responsive agency'

We are creatures apt to be moved by our experiences in the world. This seems to cut across our intentionality. We intend to do things, and yet find that our emotions rise up against us, and that we do not what we would, but what we would not. There is no doubt that at times this is evidence of the awful impact of sin on the human indi-vidual – that war within the self which Paul so vividly describes ('I see another law at work in the members of my body', Rom. 7:23). But it is also the case that we can use our will to overrule emotions that are telling us true things about the world and the right way to live in it. If we register revulsion at the sight of evil and this prevents us from doing it even when we intend to, it is an entirely appropriate response. Suppressing disgust, grief or joy may be just as much evidence of the effects of the Fall as evidence of a redeemed self-mastery.

As God's ordained agents for dominion within the created order, we are called to exercise our agency responsively – that is, with due regard to the world we encounter. The world we now inhabit is not what it was, nor what it will be. Just as we are rightly exhilarated by beauty of the world and so recognize its deep goodness, so it is fitting that we groan with longing for it to be redeemed. We observe this of course in the life of Jesus – he is 'deeply moved' (Gk. *embrimōmenos*) by the sight of his friends grieving over Lazarus (John 11:38); and he has compassion (Gk. *esplanchnisthē*) on the crowds (Matt. 9:36) because they were 'harassed and helpless, like sheep without a shepherd'. He is moved by these encounters, and these emotions condition his agency. My response of grief at my mother-in-law's funeral, disturbing and visceral though it was, was entirely and appropriately human. My emotions were in fact telling me a truth about the world and my experience of it.

Bodily feelings

The Christian tradition did in fact always have a positive regard for the body, however much this was compromised. The Bible's insistence on the unity of the human person reminds us that feelings never occur to us somewhere else other than in the body. We know of no human experience that is non-bodily. Christian eschatology points not to a final separation of the soul from the body, but to a renewed and resurrected bodily life – 'the redemption of our bodies' (Rom. 8:23).

As unified beings, then, our emotions are not other than us, or alien to us: they belong to us as an aspect of our whole being – or rather, an experience in our whole being. However exalted or complex these feelings might be, they don't take place in some other non-bodily part of me. My emotions are no less neurological and chemical states than my cat's; my capacity to contemplate my death, to experience ecstasy, to know regret, to feel guilt and shame, to hunger for contact with that which transcends me emerges from my divinely given ability to name and speak about my experiences – a gift that resides in my body.

The combination of the gifts given to humankind in the body is a call in itself to relationship with the divine being. But there isn't within us a specifically non-material bit, including a set of special feelings or affections, with which the non-material divinity may more easily interact. There isn't some centre of non-material experience that is more sanctified or sanctifiable. Paul prays holistically for the Thessalonians: 'May your whole spirit, soul and body be kept blameless at the coming of our Lord Jesus Christ' (1 Thess. 5:23). As part of our embodied experience, our emotions are partly susceptible to our ordering and cultivation of them through discipline and habit. Our incomplete self-mastery in the area of the emotions awaits the liberation and transformation of our bodies, along with the rest of the creation.[24]

---

24. 'Personal bodies' enactments of existential hows expressive of joyous hopefulness involve disciplining their emotions, such as anger, to be appropriate response to the triune God drawing them to eschatological consummation, and that involves learning to discriminate among feelings easily confused with one another' (David H. Kelsey, *Eccentric Existence: A Theological Anthropology*, 2 vols. [Louisville: Westminster John Knox, 2009], vol. 1, p. 522).

Thinking and feeling as components of knowing

Finally, we turn to the often problematic relationship of our emotions to our reason. We feel that the faculty of reason is often clouded by our emotions, somewhat to our embarrassment. We honour the dispassionate perspective of a judge or the cold objectivity of a scientist in a laboratory. We know that a pure emotionalism would be a moral and social disaster. But the older tradition of theologians was on to something when it spoke of the human need for knowledge of God, even though this was often translated as 'reason'. 'Knowledge' is properly a personal category and contains within it not merely our assent to the propositions of some truth but our personal appropriation of it.

The theological understanding of the human person as a whole being helps us a great deal here. Conceptually, we are held back by our tendency to make nouns such as 'reason' and 'emotions' when we are really talking about 'verbs' such as 'thinking' and 'feeling'. Making these concepts into substantives means we tend to go looking for a separate bit of ourselves that corresponds to the two notions. In fact, feeling and thinking are like the two hands with which we grasp the world and that together serve us in gaining knowledge. Just as without good thinking we are prone to inappropriate feelings, so without our feelings we are actually incapable of proper thinking.

What we call our 'subjectivity' is actually vital for us to gain knowledge of the world, of ourselves and of God. The so-called 'objectivity' of the scientist or judge is actually a practice of reorienting and focusing a person's subjectivity to a different end. In fact, losing sight of the role of our feelings in knowing things leads to the hubris of rationalism in that we forget that we know from within the world and its history and not from some perspective only God has. Recognizing the limits of our knowing is vital to our properly and humanly knowing – and is properly part of the scientific method bequeathed to us from the seventeenth century. The knowledge that the distorting effects of sin cut across our thinking as well as our feelings leads us to an appropriate and in fact liberating self-suspicion – reminding us to check and recheck the things we think we know.

PART 4

EMOTIONS IN THE
CHRISTIAN LIFE

8. FROM SAD AND MAD TO GLAD: THE PILGRIM'S PASSIONS

Rhys S. Bezzant

When I first became a Christian, I was taught that my spiritual life operated a lot like a train. The *engine* that pulls the train is powered by the historically verifiable facts of Jesus' life, death and resurrection; he embodies the objective promises of God. The *carriage* that follows next represents our faith, responsive to covenantal promise, and dependent on the certain and validated claims of Christ. Last of all comes the *caboose*, which in this model represents our feelings, or emotional life, which must be relegated to last position behind facts and faith, as they are the least trustworthy feature of human experience, and need guidance from higher-order faculties for their true expression. To seek locomotion or momentum for our Christian life in an order other than this is to court disaster. We are sinners because we neglect to value this divinely ordered sequence, and are prone to give feelings a place of leadership, which they are unable to assume without dethroning Christ. It stands to reason: a caboose cannot pull a train. James Dobson appears to take up this model when he criticizes much contemporary psychology: 'Reason is now *dominated* by feelings, rather than the reverse as God intended . . . emotions must always be accountable to the faculties of reason and will.'[1] We must of course beware the influence of a therapeutic culture in shaping our understanding of anthropology (as Dobson warns), yet nevertheless ask questions afresh to see if such an attenuated account of emotion is theologically justifiable, or indeed pastorally healthy. Is emotion in the Christian life really so dangerous?

This chapter is addressed both to Christians who are seeking to review the part that emotions play in their daily walk with the Lord, and to pastors as they guide those in their care towards greater human maturity and Christian sanctification. I am no expert in pastoral theology, but I do have thirty years' experience in living as a Christian, so I want to be quite intentional in addressing issues most commonly faced by Christian believers from the perspective of a fellow-traveller, and will try to weave together a pastoral approach to emotions drawing on theological and historical debates. The structure given here is quite transparently a tool for us to use in growth towards the fullness of life in Christ. In short, this chapter demonstrates a *model of care* within a *theology of hope*, for we are pilgrims with passions and have not yet reached our awaited destination. It is my basic contention that emotions have great value as maps and resources to help us travel towards the heavenly city, and conversely knowing our destination helps us to prepare our emotions for residence in our new home. Paraphrasing Isaiah, we are the redeemed of the Lord and one day we shall 'come to Zion with singing', 'everlasting joy' shall be upon our heads, and 'sorrow and sighing shall flee away' (see Isa. 51:11).[2] Though life is for us now often saddening or maddening, one day we shall know nothing but gladness for ever.

Recognizing emotions as a created given

Acknowledging our createdness helps us recognize that there are features of our lives that we have had no input to determine: our

---

1. James Dobson, *Emotions: Can You Trust Them?* (Ventura, Calif.: Regal, 1980), pp. 10–11, emphasis original.
2. Unless stated otherwise, Bible quotations in this chapter are from the NRSV.

gender, ethnicity, place in the course of history are all beyond our capacity to choose. As the psalmist has reflected, we are fearfully and wonderfully made, for it was God who knit us together in our mother's womb (Ps. 139:13–14). Our emotional capacities as human beings are understood by God, for just as a father has compassion for his children, so God knows 'how we were made; he remembers that we are dust' (Ps. 103:13–14). Our individual experience as *emotional* creatures is a natural part of our lives as human beings, for the heart (in the language of the Scriptures), where our inner life, emotional states and intellectual capacities cohere, is at the centre of who we were created to be.[3] God has just such a heart too (Gen. 6:6). Consequently, as bearers of the image of God, we reflect to the world something of the qualities of the Creator, who not only deputizes us to rule over the creation in his place (Gen. 1:26–27), but expects us to exercise dominion representing his own character as Ruler as well. We have great dignity as the image and likeness of God, which in Psalm 8 prompts our extravagant praise.

Therefore, it does us no service to ignore our emotions, to pretend that they are not powerful, to relegate them to an optional extra, or to marginalize them as a leisure pursuit. Some of us choose not to look inside that Pandora's box for fear that, once it is open, we shall never be able to fit the emotions back in again. We would rather leave them alone in the hope they will find some equilibrium of their own accord. We fear emotions and their power, but in doing so we take a path that dishonours God. We acquiesce to the view that emotions are more powerful than God, that God is incapable of reshaping them or defanging them, or that God cannot experience emotion himself. We may secretly harbour the opinion that having a particular emotion in the first place is a remnant from a pre-sanctified life that we would prefer to keep hidden. Some see strong emotions as a threat to ongoing sanctification.[4] Despite any of these default reactions, we can't pretend that there will ever be a

---

3. Matthew Elliott, *Faithful Feelings: Emotion in the New Testament* (Leicester: Inter-Varsity Press, 2006), p. 83.

4. Robert C. Roberts, *Spirituality and Human Emotion* (Grand Rapids: Eerdmans, 1982), p. 14.

Christian, a congregation or a church without powerful emotions, and we must not allow ourselves to hold the view that emotions necessarily get in the way of ministry. The most basic lesson for the believer or the Christian pastor is to recognize that *emotions are a given* in human life and Christian experience.[5]

Recognizing emotion in every part of the Christian pilgrimage seems to me to be the most healthy and godly course, even when it makes life and ministry messy or less conducive to the streamlined efficiency of modernist programming. It may appear superficially safer and more attractive to approach life's challenges with a kind of *air war*, dealing principally with higher orders of rationality, and thus avoiding the messiness of 'unconscious processes, because once it dips its foot in that dark and bottomless current, all hope of regularity and predictability is gone',[6] but this is a strategy of easy yet short-lived progress. The danger of inhibiting or denying emotion can be to create an environment in which rationalism rules. Less emotion and more rationality however do not make us more moral.[7] Nor can it be said of the New Testament, or of the Old for that matter, that the goal of our pilgrimage is unalloyed rationality. It is however ultimately more productive to deal with emotions in terms of a *ground war*, where territory is won slowly and steadily,

---

5. Because of the pastoral scope of this chapter, I use the language of emotion, passion and feeling more or less as equivalents, though philosophically they may be distinguished by appeal to the presence of physical sensation, or through the degree of self-awareness they assume. See Robert C. Roberts, 'Feeling One's Emotions and Knowing Oneself', *Philosophical Studies: An International Journal for Philosophy in the Analytic Tradition* 77.2–3 (1995), pp. 319–338. It should also be recognized that the word *emotion* is itself generated by the development within the nineteenth century of psychology as a science. See Thomas Dixon, 'Theology, Anti-Theology and Atheology: From Christian Passions to Secular Emotions', *Modern Theology* 15.3 (1999), pp. 301–305.

6. David Brooks, *The Social Animal: The Hidden Sources of Love, Character, and Achievement* (New York: Random House, 2011), p. 227.

7. The point is often made that psychopaths display no emotion and are overly rational in planning or recounting their crimes.

though significant energy and human resources must be expended to feel and frame them in this kind of combat. If we have learned anything from the postmodern priority of the local over the universal, it is surely an openness to recognize that an individual's emotions are the *sine qua non* of life, as a human being and as a Christian, and that their untidy reality cannot be avoided. Augustine defends the place of emotions in the life of the Christian:

> Among us Christians . . . the citizens of the Holy City of God, as they live by God's standards in the pilgrimage of this present life, feel fear and desire, pain and gladness in conformity with the holy Scriptures and sound doctrine; and because their love is right, all these feelings are right in them.[8]

Many congregational leaders fear the power of emotions and their destabilizing potential. I recently met an acquaintance who told me that he wanted to be a church planter but not one who had responsibility for pastoral tasks. Perhaps formal ministry training has not adequately empowered pastors to face emotions squarely, or hasn't provided them with the skills to draw the sting from emotional crises. Besides, those in pastoral ministry are all too frequently activists, for whom the tedious work of analysing, reframing and tending emotions is too time consuming. We may neither prize nor cultivate the gift of pastoral care at all. In the schema for ministry espoused at Mars Hill Seattle, for example, Mark Driscoll suggests we need more *kings* to set agendas and develop strategies, and more *prophets* or visionary leaders to make the Word of God known.[9] He unfortunately identifies *priests* as pastoral carers, whose task it is to exercise compassion, encourage reconciliation after disagreement and promote grace-centred living.

Unfortunate, because the loaded term 'priest' as a synonym for those engaged in personal ministry is not heard amongst Protestant readers as positive: we are uncomfortable with the term for historical reasons and so antipathy towards the cultivation of this gift mix is further reinforced. Driscoll removes this term from its Old Testament

---

8. Augustine, *Concerning the City of God Against the Pagans*, tr. H. Bettenson (Harmondsworth: Penguin, 1984), 14.9.

9. Mark Driscoll, *On Church Leadership* (Wheaton: Crossway, 2008), pp. 66–68.

context where the priest was not the counsellor but the teacher of the law. Ezra *the priest* didn't comfort his audience but on one particular occasion through his preaching made them cry (Neh. 8:9)! Likewise, the language of priest inadequately serves our pastoral responsibility, for we are not able to imitate Christ as our great high priest when he makes a 'sacrifice of atonement for the sins of the people' (Heb. 2:17), nor are we asked to copy him when he can 'sympathize with our weaknesses' (Heb. 4:15). In the book of Hebrews the only fitting response to Christ as high priest is to approach the throne of grace with boldness. We rightly want to recruit more *kings* and *prophets* for the re-evangelization of the west, but we should recognize that one of them might be sufficient in a congregation, whereas every congregation needs dozens of soul physicians, employed or not, whether we use the term *priest* or not.

Reinterpreting emotions as a Christian gift

Once we have determined to engage with our own emotions or the emotions of members of our congregation, we must take another step, for merely to acknowledge the *presence* of powerful, obscure or complex feelings does not require acknowledgment of their *value*. It is easy to think of emotions as a problem to be solved or dissolved through the use of higher reason, and so fundamentally to denigrate their intrusion into our lives. I want to suggest instead that *emotions are a gift to be received* and not essentially a problem to be solved. Though warped by sin, they are nevertheless a creation good. Emotions are an involuntary, though not morally neutral, reaction to some stimulus, either internal or external, and sometimes leading to physical affect.[10] Of course particular emotional experiences may

---

10. See D. J. Atkinson, 'Emotion', in D. J. Atkinson and D. H. Field (eds.), *New Dictionary of Christian Ethics and Pastoral Theology* (Leicester: Apollos; Downers Grove: IVP Academic, 1995), pp. 341–343. Roberts also holds emotions to be prompted by 'something that happens to us' (Robert C. Roberts, 'Emotions Among the Virtues of the Christian Life', *JRE* 20.1 [1992], p. 43).

not be the kind of gift we want, and we might prefer to remove them from our life, though Paul cautions us against hasty excision. In his estimation even painful experience can be thought of as a gift when consecrated to the cause of Christ: 'he has graciously granted you the privilege not only of believing in Christ, but of suffering for him as well' (Phil. 1:29). John Piper recently described his own experience of cancer in terms of a gift not to be wasted.[11]

While it would be easy to accept the presence of emotions in our lives as Christians as necessary, it does not then necessarily follow that they are noble or valuable. I do not follow the faculty psychology espoused by some seventeenth-century Puritan or Roman Catholic writers, which gave priority to the mind over will and emotions, the emotions being the least praiseworthy or noble aspect of the human constitution. It assumed that there can be nothing rational about emotions, but rather their power to distract from Christian obedience or to undermine godly decision-making is so great that they need both the guardian of the mind and the gaoler of the will to keep them in check. Following recent consideration of the emotions amongst Christian philosophers and psychologists, I rather adopt a less hierarchically defined cognitive understanding of human anthropology, which sees the role of emotions as integrally related to the mind and the will; and so, with the mind and the will, emotions provide us with opportunities to engage in a more nuanced and positive way with our context, relationships or environment.[12] The

---

11. See <http://www.desiringgod.org/resource-library/taste-see-articles/dont-waste-your-cancer>, accessed 5 Mar. 2012.

12. Elliott demonstrates the distinctions between non-cognitive and cognitive theories of emotion, and argues that cognitive theories are presently gaining traction amongst psychologists and philosophers. Cognitive theories make 'thought, appraisal and belief central elements in emotion' (see Elliott, *Faithful Feelings*, p. 31). Roberts defines emotions as 'concern-based construals'; that is, a unified complex of propositional content and felt states (Robert C. Roberts, 'What an Emotion Is: A Sketch', *Philosophical Review* 97.2 [1988], pp. 183–184). Such construals, or ways of seeing things, are shaped by the individual's social significance, relational matrix, character and Christian conviction. See Roberts, 'Feeling One's Emotions', p. 326.

Scriptures simply do not make hermetically sealed distinctions between our responsibility to think and our capacity to emote. Elliott suggests:

> Emotion is not an illogical reflex, unreliable and fickle. Emotions cut through all our talk, all our spin, and take us right to the truth of the matter. That is what God created emotions to do, and that is why . . . God so freely commands emotions all through the Bible.[13]

The Lord Jesus can command love (John 13:34). Paul ends the self-consciously *doctrinal* section of Romans with paeans of *praise* to God's wisdom (Rom. 11:33–36), and begins the *paraenetic* passages with an appeal to transformed *minds* (Rom. 12:1–2). Christian ministry involves *comforting* cheek by jowl with *catechizing* (2 Cor. 1). The Scriptures through the medium of words do engage us rationally, but simultaneously can engage us volitionally and emotionally, dependent on the eloquence of the particular text at hand.[14]

Indeed, emotions and their positive place in human experience and Scriptural testimony are one of the distinctive values with which Christianity stared down rival philosophies in the ancient world, buying into a debate that predated the rise of the Christian movement between Aristotle's and Plato's views of the role of cognition in appraising emotion. Matthew Elliott is surely right to assert the following:

> The idea of extirpating the emotions is an idea unknown in the New Testament . . . The Stoic would not accept or understand either Jesus' or Paul's passionate commitment to the Gospel, to others, or their emotional language. Where the Stoic idea of happiness was a life free from emotion, Paul's joy was an emotional celebration of God and his work of sharing the Gospel.[15]

---

13. Matthew A. Elliott, *Feel: The Power of Listening to Your Heart* (Carol Stream, Ill.: Tyndale House, 2008), p. 52.
14. For the value of Scriptures in forming Christian emotions, see Robert C. Roberts, 'Emotions as Access to Religious Truths', *Faith and Philosophy* 9.1 (1992), p. 90.
15. Elliott, *Faithful Feelings*, p. 241.

Early Christians provided an alternative to magic or immorality by appealing to emotions as a motivator and ethical construct.[16] During the Enlightenment period, Descartes, in ways similar to Plato, presented a case for emotions as a sphere disconnected from rationality. In this non-cognitive framework, emotions are merely physical sensations, sometimes known as passions, which represent animal spirits.

By way of contrast, Jonathan Edwards (1703–58) and his New Light colleagues in the North American Great Awakening rejected such dichotomizing.[17] For Edwards emotions, alongside reason, are constitutive of all human flourishing, and furthermore are not apportioned along gender lines.[18] Edwards provides us with perhaps the most potent theological defence of the cognitive theory of emotions in the modern era. One of his greatest responsibilities in the period of the revivals was to interpret Christian experience both for the revived and for the detractors of the awakening. Edwards takes a mediating position in which emotion is regarded as essential to true religion, so long as emotion is proportionally responsive to an object that has God's blessing, or is God himself.[19] The enthusiasm

---

16. Ibid., pp. 236–268.

17. The recent rediscovery of cognitive factors in the construal of emotional life leads us back to eighteenth-century insights (Dixon, 'From Christian Passions to Secular Emotions', p. 311). Edwards is sometimes assumed to create a wedge between passions and emotions, the former belonging to our animal spirits and the latter to our sanctified self, or even occasionally Edwards is said to espouse a sharp division between body and soul. While at the beginning of the *Religious Affections* he makes some philosophical distinctions to aid clarity, his intent throughout is to defend the unity of the human person against his detractors who splice it up. Extreme passions are dangerous in as far they render the Christian passive, not because they represent an intrusion of a lower self into the higher faculties. See Jonathan Edwards, *Religious Affections*, Works of Jonathan Edwards 2, ed. John E. Smith (New Haven: Yale University Press, 1969), p. 98.

18. Marilyn J. Westerkamp, *Women and Religion in Early America, 1600–1850: The Puritan and Evangelical Traditions* (London: Routledge, 1999), p. 135.

19. Jamie Dow, *Engaging Emotions: The Need for Emotions in the Church*, Grove Renewal Series (Cambridge: Grove, 2005), pp. 10, 22.

of the revivals was not necessarily an experience generated by human instability. Rational opposition to enthusiasm did not necessarily represent God's mind. Edwards reacted to the received model of faculty psychology espoused by some of his Puritan forebears, and instead bundled all the constituent parts of the regenerate believer together, and used the label 'affections' to describe their cumulative impact, suggesting that passions belong with our volition and with our understanding to comprise the human heart.[20] He wrote early in his ministry, 'How the Scriptures are ignorant of the philosophic distinction of the understanding and the will, and how the sense of the heart is there called knowledge and understanding.'[21] Edwards wrote to praise the place of emotion in the human constitution:

> We should realize, to our shame before God, that we are not more affected with the great things of faith. It appears from what we have said that this arises from our having so little true religion . . . When it comes to their worldly interests, their outward delights, their honor and reputation, and their natural relations, they have warm affection and ardent zeal . . . They get deeply depressed at worldly losses, and highly excited at worldly successes. But how insensible and unmoved are most men about the great things of another world! . . . Here their love is cold, their desire languid, their zeal low, and their gratitude small. How can they sit and hear for the infinite height, depth, length, and breadth of the love of God in Christ Jesus . . . and yet be so insensible and regardless! Can we suppose that the wise Creator implanted such a faculty of affections to be occupied in this way?[22]

Affections represent the deepest part of a person. All of me is drawn towards God or is repelled from God. All of me is impacted

---

20. Brad Walton, *Jonathan Edwards, Religious Affections and the Puritan Analysis of True Piety, Spiritual Sensation and Heart Religion* (Lewiston: Edwin Mellen, 2002), p. 220.

21. Jonathan Edwards, 'The Mind', in *Scientific and Philosophical Writings*, Works of Jonathan Edwards 6, ed. W. E. Anderson (New Haven: Yale University Press, 1980), p. 389.

22. Edwards, *Religious Affections*, p. 27.

by sin, including mind, will and feelings, and all of me needs rescue.[23] Edwards's great work *Concerning the Religious Affections* is not simply a handbook on healthy church life but rather a philosophical tool of analysis to determine the roles played by reason, will, emotions and the ministry of the Holy Spirit in the life of the revived. As a work of pastoral theology, it is both dense and daring. He wants to assert that emotions interact with our will and mind, and are not simply dangerous and independent decoys seducing us from the path of truth. In so doing he combines the best of Puritan spiritual insight with revivalist devotion.[24] He asserts that 'True religion, in great part, consists in holy affections ... That religion which God requires, and will accept, does not consist in weak, dull and lifeless wouldings [inclinations], raising us but a little above a state of indifference.'[25] Affections are an expected part, a given, of Christian experience, which have great value in the life of the saint.

If emotions are essential to the nature of affective and true religion, and are to be experienced as a gift from God, like any gift they might involve some unpacking. The twelve certain signs and the twelve uncertain signs of *Religious Affections* are, for example, an aid to the interpretation of experience. This process of reinterpreting emotions may only be achieved slowly because some default reactions are deeply engrained into our patterns of behaviour, which are themselves frequently sinful.[26] Emotions are subject to the effects of the race's fall from grace into sin, along with reason and volition, and are not easy to isolate and unknot. Some Christians may alternatively have such a positive view of emotions and their therapeutic role that no expectation of reinterpretation or provisionality is ever entertained. It may be difficult to reinterpret or retrain emotions

---

23. Mark R. Talbot, 'Godly Emotions (Religious Affections)', in J. Piper and J. Taylor (eds.), *A God Entranced Vision of All Things: The Legacy of Jonathan Edwards* (Wheaton: Crossway, 2004), p. 231, n. 26.

24. Bruce Hindmarsh, *John Newton and the English Evangelical Tradition: Between the Conversions of Wesley and Wilberforce* (Grand Rapids: Eerdmans, 1996), p. 237.

25. Edwards, *Religious Affections*, pp. 95, 99.

26. Dow, *Engaging Emotions*, p. 19.

because we assign the giftlike quality of positive experiences or pleasurable emotions to our own discipline, luck or breeding. In both instances new patterns of response must be encouraged to demonstrate the *reality* along with the *contingency* of our emotional life. Emotions are something we must learn, unlearn or relearn, and this in itself reflects on their cognitive connections.[27] To agree with Edwards's model of affections is to provide space for their malleability and reconstruction. For Edwards, the joy that anchors our experience of Christian discipleship, appealing to 1 Peter 1:8, is itself 'a prelibation of the joy of heaven, that raised their minds to a degree of heavenly blessedness'.[28] The emotion of joy, then, can be seen as a gift of grace generated from our glorious future inheritance, and consequently capable of animating our pilgrim path and encouraging us in a theology of hope. The apostle Paul sets emotions within an eschatological framework as well.[29]

The gift of emotions runs in parallel with the gift of pastoral friendships, which help us in our bleak moments to achieve this task of reinterpretation (Prov. 17:17; 18:24). It may be the friend's or pastor's task to give perspective on a trial or a positive experience. A reminder that other emotions have been transitory, or have

---

27. A recent development within psychology is known as Acceptance and Commitment Therapy (ACT), which recognizes the difficulties of seeing and changing the patterns of emotional response in their immediate context. However, in the medium term this therapy encourages the reinterpretation of unpleasant emotions in line with the value system of the person seeking change and driven by concerted effort to create new patterns. This approach seems to offer a therapeutic structure in parallel with the pastoral and theological framework offered for consideration in this chapter. For a popular exposition of this modification of cognitive behavioural therapy, see Russ Harris, *The Happiness Trap: Stop Struggling, Start Living* (Wollombi, NSW: Exisle, 2007). Conversely, if we were to understand emotions as merely wild and purely physiological reflexes, we would be unlikely ever to domesticate them, even if we saw value in taming them.

28. Edwards, *Religious Affections*, p. 95.

29. Stephen C. Barton, 'Eschatology and the Emotions in Early Christianity', *JBL* 130.3 (2011), p. 588.

required nurture, are health-producing words from a trusted adviser. At other moments, a pastor may have to help a friend facing a debilitating crisis by intervening on her behalf to restore some order or balance. Perhaps at other times the mentor says nothing, in order to show that he or she is not afraid of the power that a particular emotion can unleash. Timely words are of the essence of wisdom, and are tools to reframe the concern. Gifts need to be unwrapped. This can be accomplished not just by individual carers, but by corporate ritualized moments of leverage as well:

> Culture also . . . educates the emotions. It consists of narratives, holidays, symbols, and works of art that contain implicit and often unnoticed messages about how to feel, how to respond, how to divine meaning.[30]

Some emotions do indeed have physiological causes. Neural misfiring has been identified as the cause of some types of depression, which medications can treat. Biochemical aspects of mood disorder must be recognized alongside cognitive contributors, which together constitute treatment guidelines for medical practitioners. A godly response to depressive illness is not merely to encourage positive thinking, or to remind a friend that God disciplines those whom he loves. Nor is it necessarily helpful to set before someone suffering from depression a set of tasks for the week ahead to restore routine and therefore healthy social functioning, without first sitting down with a friend to learn to grieve with those who grieve, and to understand the contours of the sadness. Pastors who once were engineers can be prone to this shortcut. Pastors who were once philosophers can make the mistake of rationalizing the pain away. Melancholy, as the great Puritan physicians of the soul would describe it, is a complicated ailment to diagnose and to treat. But despite these caveats, during my own limited experiences of depression, friends served me well by helping me to reflect upon my environment, my age and stage, and emotional blind spots that otherwise may have remained in the dark. With counselling I was able to learn through the painful experience and allow God to

---

30. Brooks, *Social Animal*, p. 149.

recreate me a little and to be used by him a little more in listening to those who are granted similar afflictions.

Emotions are a gift, so that we may engage more authentically or more comprehensively with the reality in which we live, and to which they are responses. Emotions don't always adequately reflect or convey that reality, of course. Like human conscience, they are an expression of the Creator's design, which may nevertheless require nurture (Rom. 2:14–16), and they too must be educated by the divinely revealed will. Retraining emotions is a complicated task in which we attempt to change the course of an affective river, which has eroded a path through a mental terrain over a long period of time. The river might run through several generations before we are shaped by its course, as is suggested by the study of epigenetics. Plotting a new course may be painful and require much input to achieve, though recent studies in neuroplasticity reflect both the impediments and the possibilities of personal transformation. Being open to the task of retraining emotions has the further helpful concomitant that we disconnect emotion from assurance of salvation, which when coupled too closely leads to pastoral disaster.

Taking the emotional life seriously is an opportunity to receive the gift of spiritual growth. Many psalms begin with lament but end with praise, as does the psalter as a whole, and correspondingly the Christian pilgrim must learn to handle his or her emotions so that the experiences that confront us, and the emotional reactions produced, ultimately contribute to a safe arrival at our spiritual destination. As the psalmist says, 'Weeping may linger for the night, but joy comes with the morning' (Ps. 30:5). We often make the mistake to assume that emotions must be our master on the journey, giving marching orders, and like the sergeant major brooking no response, but we should not remain passive before them upon their arrival, nor smitten by them in their presence. They are not God. They are however great servants, helping us to come to terms with our environment and providing opportunity for recalibration of life on the road.[31] As Dietrich Bonhoeffer wrote to his fiancée, Maria von Wedemeyer, while incarcerated in the Gestapo prison on Prinz-Albrecht-Strasse:

---

31. Talbot, 'Godly Emotions', p. 244.

Stifter once put it very beautifully: 'Pain is the holiest angel, who reveals treasures that would otherwise have remained hidden in the depths for ever. People have become greater through it than through all the world's joys.' It is so, as I keep telling myself in my present predicament: the pain of deprivation, which is often physically perceptible, must exist, and we should not and need not argue it away. But it has to be overcome anew every time, so there is an even holier angel than pain, and that is joy in God.[32]

Bonhoeffer's experience of confinement opened him up to explore the passions of the pilgrim with new insight. He learnt to reinterpret his turbid experience of imprisonment in the light of interactions with other inmates and his jailers and in response to divine reality, and to express it poetically in the haunting piece 'Who Am I?'[33] His own impending end was part of a bigger divine reality. He learnt to be brutally honest with the givens of his situation, to nurture his reactions within them, and ultimately to dedicate them to God. Hope was cultivated in the midst of horror.

Emotions are an integral part of being human, and necessary to Christian identity as we turn our experiences in this world towards the merciful embrace of God, both now and for ever. It is to him that we must ultimately render an account for the way we have appropriated his generosity.

Relating emotions to the glorious giver

Dealing with emotions is a profoundly theological enterprise, for if they are a gift, we find ourselves *answerable to their Giver* for their

32. Dietrich Bonhoeffer and Maria von Wedemeyer, 'Letter, 21 November 1943', in R.-A. von Bismarck and U. Kabitz (eds.), *Love Letters from Cell 92* (London: HarperCollins, 1994), p. 96.

33. Dietrich Bonhoeffer, 'Who Am I?', in J. W. De Gruchy (ed.), *Letters and Papers from Prison*, Dietrich Bonhoeffer Works 8 (Minneapolis: Fortress, 2010), pp. 459–460.

exercise.[34] Emotions are not just theological in the way some Puritans might have conceived them: an opportunity to reconcile in human experience dilemmas (such as divine election and human freedom) that were proving too difficult to reconcile using traditional rational and systematic categories. More profoundly, we are stewards *coram deo* of our emotional life (just as we are stewards of our financial and material life), and we are participants in the life of God, Father, Son and Spirit, whose own emotional life we encounter and whose resources we share. Being the body of Christ, the church shares all the fullness of God (Eph. 1:23) and is central to God's purposes in the world. As Roberts points out, 'there is a necessary connection between the Christian emotions and the Christian story'.[35] We are given *theological permission* to enjoy an emotional connection to God, when we presume human rationality alone is not the bearer of the divine. We are also given a *theological warning* not to expect absorption into the divine, for the mystical must not equal the emotional: there will eternally be a glassy sea between the worshippers and the Lamb (Rev. 4:6). Extravagant worship involves serving our neighbour, but no less waving palm branches in adoration (Rev. 7:9–12). Life's meaning does not consist in the indulgent pursuit of emotion for emotion's sake. Our emotional life must be given back to God the Giver, as indeed all our gifts should be. He is to be praised as the Giver of all good things, for every perfect gift is from above (see Jas 1:17).

All too often our duty towards God displaces our free and emotion-rich devotion to him. We prefer patterns of obedience that make us feel safe, even when they displace the adventure of daily trust in God's guiding hand and surprising provision. Walking in the freedom Christ brings takes energy and emotional engagement that are easy to divert or invest elsewhere. We can offer repeated sacrifice but our heart is far from him. Of course this is a universal human dilemma spoken of by Amos as well as Jesus. The modernist philosophy of Kant (refracted through nineteenth-century Victorian morality) may even encourage us along this path, by which we are

---

34. Brian S. Borgman, *Feelings and Faith: Cultivating Godly Emotions in the Christian Life* (Wheaton: Crossway, 2009), p. 25.

35. Roberts, *Spirituality and Human Emotion*, pp. 21, 25.

encouraged to pursue a deontological ethic that gives an account of human flourishing in terms of *duties for God* rather than a *vision of God* towards which we are moving. A stiff upper lip and 'doing what we must' wrings emotional vibrancy from our experience. As Calvin so succinctly warns:

> Now he who merely performs all the duties of love does not fulfil them, even though he overlooks none; but he, rather, fulfils them who does this from a sincere feeling of love. For it can happen that one who indeed discharges to the full all his obligations as far as outward duties are concerned is still all the while far away from the true way of discharging them.[36]

At another level, recognizing the divinely instituted role that emotions play in our experience, and not categorizing them in some Darwinian fashion as merely physical sensations that are adaptive to our survival needs,[37] introduces an ethical imperative that encourages us all the more to fashion them in godly paths. Rather than excusing emotions, we educate them, and put ourselves in places where they will be seconded by virtues, where *moral muscle memory* is developed.[38] They ought to motivate us towards the good and not the base. Ethical decision-making ought not to be reduced to laws to be obeyed, but to involve the character of the agent as well. Recent ethical inquiry has again seen the need to draw attention to human moral formation in order to complement the categories of either deontological or duty-based ethical deliberation, or consequentialist and utilitarian positions, which have been particularly suited to Enlightenment foundations.[39] Virtue theory is making a

---

36. John Calvin, *The Institutes of the Christian Religion*, LCC 21–22 (Philadelphia: Westminster, 1960), 3.7.7. According to Walton, Calvin can also use the language of the *heart* to represent the entire soul, 'in which reason, will and emotions were all simultaneously operative' (see Walton, *Jonathan Edwards*, p. 177).

37. Elliott, *Faithful Feelings*, pp. 21–22.

38. Brooks, *Social Animal*, p. 290.

39. See Alaisdair McIntyre, *After Virtue? A Study in Moral Theology*, 3rd ed. (Notre Dame: University of Notre Dame Press, 2007).

comeback, for discussion of liminal ethical dilemmas is seen as reductionist and dissatisfying without giving an account of the moral life and the transformed character of the agent facing such dilemmas.[40] To aspire to transformation however requires a vision of what we ought to be. Perhaps connecting our emotions to theological and ethical categories can do more than we imagine to lead us towards God. C. S. Lewis is an advocate for working to embolden our desires in order to steer us along the pilgrim way:

> If there lurks in most modern minds the notion that to desire our own good and earnestly to hope for the enjoyment of it is a bad thing, I submit that this notion has crept in from Kant and the Stoics and is no part of the Christian faith. Indeed, if we consider the unblushing promises of reward and the staggering nature of the rewards promised in the Gospels, it would seem that Our Lord finds our desires not too strong, but too weak. We are half-hearted creatures, fooling about with drink and sex and ambition when infinite joy is offered us, like an ignorant child who wants to go on making mud pies in a slum because he cannot imagine what is meant by the offer of a holiday at the sea. We are far too easily pleased.[41]

We could see ourselves as passive victims before the unassailable power of emotions, which leaves us with the cultural assumption that the only course of action is to emote. A therapeutic world view would encourage their expression. On the other hand, we could agitate to make sure that emotions play an increasingly impotent role in our experience, in which case our pastoral aim is unquestionably self-denial, of either repressive or suppressive variety. In neither instance do we accept any responsibility for moral evaluation or education. If on the other hand emotions are unavoidable, valuable and malleable, then in our own life we have to model a new way of being emotional in a culture where emotion is prized

---

40. Phil C. Zylla, *Virtue as Consent to Being: A Pastoral-Theological Perspective on Jonathan Edwards's Construct of Virtue* (Eugene, Ore.: Pickwick, 2011), p. 2.

41. C. S. Lewis, *The Weight of Glory, and Other Addresses* (New York: Macmillan, 1980), pp. 3–4.

but opportunities for taking a path of expression different from the majority culture are limited. They are experienced as a function of event, perception, belief and biochemistry, but can provide a *provisional and instantaneous insight* into relational dilemmas, which may nevertheless in time give way to other more adequate interpretations. Emotions may not be infallible guides, but they can nevertheless function as *alarms* or *permissions* to orient us to the reality that we inhabit, whether by choice or by imposition, and to 'motivate appropriate reactions to a wide variety of circumstances'.[42] They have a veridical element.[43] According to Roberts's understanding of the Christian vision, 'if the Christian propositions are true . . . emotions are the way in which that truth is perceived, and [are] thus a crucial aspect of the highest quality knowledge of the propositions'.[44] The apostle similarly speaks of the 'eyes of your heart [being] enlightened' (Eph. 1:18).

Emotions are a given, which we do well to acknowledge, even if the sensation is potentially destabilizing, for without owning them, they too easily own us, whether in conscious or subconscious ways. If humans are a bundle of mind, will and emotion, and we are able to recognize the place of each in our lives as part of our creatureliness, indeed as a gift from a Giver, then we shall not resent our emotions, but rather expect that they will provide us as Christians with some useful orientation towards honouring God with all that we are. They can be like an immune system, helping us to identify or fight off invading physical or spiritual threats. They can be like boundary riders, helping us to defend the territory of our dignity as made in God's image. They need to be trained for the task for which God has created them, but this is no less true of our intellect or our volition. Emotions may appear outside our immediate voluntary control, but they are not ultimately impervious to cooperation with

---

42. Graeme M. Griffin, 'Emotion', in J. F. Childress and J. Macquarrie (eds.), *A New Dictionary of Christian Ethics* (London: SCM, 1986), p. 190.

43. Roberts, 'Emotions Among the Virtues', p. 40. This is not to suggest however that any claim to access truth through emotions can be allowed to stand without further critique or contextualizing.

44. Roberts, 'Emotions as Access', p. 90.

mind and will.[45] Indeed, an account of human feeling that is nuanced in this way could actually function as an evangelistic starting point.

Thoughtful expression together with constrained freedom is the most desirable outcome. We must work for a church culture in which there is safety to be honest about our feelings, with encouragement to express a wide range of emotions in ordered ways in the regular meeting of Christians. There needs to be regular opportunities for emotional release, both in public and private settings, so that it feels normal without being required. The conversations, prayers, sermons and liturgical leadership of a minister are a powerful model for our own attitudes. Interestingly, the generation who followed and favoured Edwards in church leadership in New England (known as the New Divinity) believed that the best mechanism for catechism in things rational came through private reading, but it was the task of the public exposition of the Scriptures to inspire passions and develop emotions! Just like a coach of a sporting team, the leader of the emotional community has to work out how to get the most out of each player, when to push and when to let off, what exercises to assign and how to give tips for game day. A great measure of wisdom is required to produce an emotionally functioning, winning fellowship.

I want to put forward this simple model for Christian living as a distillation of larger theological and philosophical themes, a model that has served me well as a pilgrim with passions. At its heart it sets before us the challenge to see our Christian perseverance not merely as a fight in which we beat our bodies, or a race in which we set our mind simply on the unchanging heavenly prize, but to broaden our expectation of growth in *emotional* maturity while we travel the course towards the City of God: we must learn to rejoice, for it is a foretaste of glory. Being transformed from one degree of glory into another, being conformed to the image of Christ, is not achieved without being emotionally reformed according to the arts of affective equilibrium. The Christian life is spiritually dynamic, but the emotional dynamism of the journey is no less to be prized. We should not approach our emotions with disdain, but also nevertheless should

45. Dow, *Engaging Emotions*, p. 12.

not leave them where we found them. We want to be real when we feel sad or mad, and then to coach these very feelings towards the ultimate destination of glad in the City of God. Caring for emotions, whether ours or others', is a theological opportunity to align our lives afresh with what it means to be citizens of the commonwealth of heaven, even if the best illustration of the means of transport for the journey is not a train with an emotional caboose in the last place.

9. TOUCHING THE EMOTIONS: PREACHING THE GOSPELS FOR DIVINE EFFECTS

Peter G. Bolt

The preacher is a boundary rider. He travels along the intersection between the words of Scripture and those who ought to hear those words. God speaks and every human being is called upon to listen. The preacher's task is to help anyone with ears to hear to listen well. The aim of preaching is to help people to listen to the voice of God, who addresses them with his Word by way of the words of Scripture.

In this strange zone in which the preacher travels between text and hearer, emotions play a very significant role in assisting the preacher's fundamental task. Although this is true whatever portion of Scripture is being preached, it is especially true for the four Gospels, which are written in such a way as to convey God's message through engaging the emotions of the readers/hearers.[1] When our

---

1. I have been exploring the intersection between gospel and reader since the 1990s; see esp. Peter G. Bolt, 'The Gospel for Today's Church', in Barry G. Webb (ed.), *Exploring the Missionary Church*, Explorations (Sydney: ANZEA, 1993), pp. 27–59; 'Feeling the Cross: Mark's Message of Atonement', *RTR* 60.1 (2001), pp. 1–17; and *Jesus' Defeat of Death: Persuading Mark's Early Readers*, SNTSMS 125 (Cambridge: Cambridge University Press, 2003).

boundary-riding preacher prepares to preach from a Gospel, that preparation must include exegesis of two kinds: exegesis of the divine message and exegesis of the emotional, affective dimension of the text by which that divine message is conveyed.

Narrative power and emotional engagement

Emotional power of narrative form

It is almost axiomatic amongst literary critics that narrative works powerfully on human beings because of its ability to engage the emotions.

From the other side of the equation, those working on understanding human emotions from the psychological and physiological point of view have also noticed the important connection between narrative and emotions. Despite the difficulties the 'emotional intelligence' movement may have, it can be thanked for alerting us to the fact that intelligence is both cognitive and emotional, and the two should (or even do) work together. Brain science has mapped both cognitive and emotional pathways, which gives rise to the model that we have two kinds of minds, a rational and an emotional mind.[2] The two minds operate in different ways, and narrative is particularly connected to the emotional mind. To quote Daniel Goleman:

> The logic of the emotional mind is *associative*; it takes elements that symbolize a reality, or trigger a memory of it, to be the same as that reality. That is why similes, metaphors, and images speak directly to the

---

2. Daniel Goleman, *Emotional Intelligence: Why It Can Matter More Than IQ* (London: Bloomsbury, 1996), pp. 8–9. Goleman provides a brief description of the emotional systems in the brain, ch. 2. For further detail, and with special focus on empathy, see Simon Baron-Cohen, *Zero Degrees of Empathy: A New Theory of Human Cruelty* (London: Penguin [Allen Lane], 2011), ch. 2. For a fascinating and popular summary of recent brain research in the USA, see Norman Doidge, *The Brain That Changes Itself: Stories of Personal Triumph from the Frontiers of Brain Science* (New York: Viking, 2007).

emotional mind, as do the arts – novels, film, poetry, song, theater, opera. Great spiritual teachers, like Buddha and Jesus, have touched their disciples' hearts by speaking in the language of emotion, teaching in parables, fables, and stories. Indeed, religious symbol and ritual makes little sense from the rational point of view; it is couched in the vernacular of the heart.

This logic of the heart – of the emotional mind – is well-described by Freud in his concept of 'primary process' thought; it is the logic of religion and poetry, psychosis and children, dream and myth.[3]

It may be right to be wary of a kind of emotionalism in preaching that improperly carries the preacher away, or manipulates the congregation.[4] But from what brain science is telling us, it is quite clear that learning is not just cognitive, by way of the rational mind, and it is essential to good learning to engage the emotional mind.[5] Emotional preaching (of a proper kind) is therefore essential if we want our congregation to learn.

Some people are well attuned to their emotional mind. For these people narrative will have the most powerful effect. Goleman again:

> Some of us are naturally more attuned to the emotional mind's special symbolic modes: metaphor and simile, along with poetry, song, and fable, are all cast in the language of the heart. So too are dreams and myths, in which loose associations determine the flow of narrative, abiding by the logic of the emotional mind. Those who have a natural attunement to their own heart's voice – the language of emotion – are sure to be more adept at articulating its messages, whether as a novelist, songwriter, or psychotherapist. This inner attunement should make them more gifted in giving voice to the 'wisdom of the unconscious' – the felt meanings of our dreams and fantasies, the symbols that embody our deepest wishes.[6]

---

3. Goleman, *Emotional Intelligence*, p. 254, emphasis original.

4. Jamie Dow, *Engaging Emotions: The Need for Emotions in the Church*, Grove Renewal Series (Cambridge: Grove, 2005), pp. 3–4.

5. Goleman, *Emotional Intelligence, passim*, but see esp. pp. 10–11, 78–79, 93–95, ch. 16.

6. Ibid., p. 54.

However, that said, not everyone is as well connected to their emotional mind. This will give particular problems to the preacher of the Gospel narratives.

Emotional problems encountered by the preacher

As we preach the Gospel narratives, those narratives do not always meet emotionally healthy people. The narrative meets people with all kinds of difficulties, including emotional difficulties. Congregations are filled with embodied persons, and we know from our *theology* that *all* human beings are damaged human beings, no matter whether the psychological profession might declare them more or less normal than others![7] Narrative arises within a disordered and suffering world and it speaks to a disordered and suffering world. In fact, this is probably part of the explanation for its power!

Who would be a preacher? Think of the emotional mix of the average congregation. Some will have a full and rich range of emotions and have no trouble expressing them, reflecting on them, and telling about them in thoroughly natural ways, if and when the need arises. Others are completely dominated by their emotions and their life is lived in seeming chaos, lurching from one blow-up to another.[8] Some feel, but are not aware of what they feel, and so don't really have an emotional life (if emotion is a rational account of a bodily feeling). Some feel but cannot put their feelings and thoughts about their feelings into words (alexithumics).[9] There are people who are emotionally overclingy in relationships. There are others who are so afraid of emotional intimacy they run as soon as they are 'threatened' by it. Others go beyond mere avoidance of the threatening other, but even fight off such intimacy by engaging

---

7. Christian ministry needs to reckon not only with the sinfulness of human beings, but also with the weaknesses that come along with our fallenness (e.g. Rom. 5:6; Heb. 4:15), which include both the physical and the psychological, both of which have a bearing upon the emotions.

8. Here I draw upon Goleman, *Emotional Intelligence*, p. 48, who lists three styles of attending to emotions: self aware, engulfed, accepting.

9. Ibid., p. 96. Baron-Cohen, *Zero Degrees of Empathy*, pp. 69–70, 88.

in pre-emptive strikes of criticism of others and fault finding, just to keep the distance firm and clear. In religious circles such distancing strategies can even be justified with moralistic judgmentalism, which supposedly provides good reasons why some persons ought to be avoided. Those in the congregation who have suffered abuse or trauma can have diminished emotional responses.[10] Others with more abnormal psychology may not feel, may not dream, and may have little or no awareness of an inner life, and so they find it difficult to live or talk emotionally at all.[11]

This is your congregation as you stand up to preach. And – dare we admit it? – preachers aren't immune from emotional dysfunction either.

Narrative in therapy

But perhaps, rather strangely, even though narrative is best grasped by those who have a healthy emotional life, narrative has also found a place in helping those who have not.

Of course, the narrative has always been a part of psychotherapy, as clients narrate their own story of their present difficulties, their past history, and their perceptions of the future, whether bright or dark. But more recently approaches known as 'narrative therapy' have emerged, to take this a step further. Life has its own basic narrative shape (it has a beginning, a middle, an end) and other narrative-like features as well. We all tell ourselves a story of our lives, complete with our own evaluations, that either help or hinder us from moving forward with ease into our next chapter.

---

10. Actual abnormalities in the emotional systems of the brain can now be demonstrated in various kinds of victims. See Goleman, *Emotional Intelligence*, ch. 13; Doidge, *Brain That Changes Itself, passim*; and Baron-Cohen, *Zero Degrees of Empathy*, pp. 42–43 (Borderline Personality Disorder), pp. 54–59 (Psychopathy), who reports that there has been very little research into Narcissism, however (pp. 62–63).

11. For a recent discussion of the absence of empathy in the abnormal psychology types known as Narcissism, Psychopathy and Borderline Personality Disorder, see Baron-Cohen, *Zero Degrees of Empathy*.

When the self-told story is not a helpful one, the therapist helps clients to tell themselves a new narrative, to reframe, or even 'restory', their past and so restory their present and, most importantly, their future.[12]

The rise of such therapies comes from a recognition that the narrative has power not only to engage the emotions, but also to transform them and bring about a greater level of psychological and emotional health.

Healing through Gospels preaching

These observations from our various scientific circles hold great promise for the preaching of the Gospels in our emotionally challenged congregations. For as the Gospels are proclaimed, their hearers are invited to 'restory' their lives in relationship with Jesus Christ, the Son of God, on a journey from this vale of tears into the glorious kingdom of God.[13]

The four Gospels are well-told, brilliant narratives. The narrative form is particularly appropriate to engage emotionally with the congregation. While the emotionally adept will engage easily, the emotionally challenged will have more trouble. But preachers can proclaim the Gospels, knowing that these narratives in particular hold the key to curing the very emotional problems that make it hard for some to read them properly! The form may help to switch on the inner life, but, more importantly, the gospel message about Jesus Christ helps people to 'wake up', and be renewed from the heart outwards. As Jesus makes all things new,

---

12. See e.g. from the field of Psychology, K. and M. Gergen, 'The Social Construction of Narrative Accounts', in Kenneth J. Gergen and Mary M. Gergen (eds.), *Historical Social Psychology* (Hillsdale, N. J.: L. Erlbaum, 1984), pp. 173–189; and, amongst those exploring biblical narrative in therapy or pastoral care, see John C. Hoffman, *Law, Freedom, and Story: The Role of Narrative in Therapy, Society, and Faith* (Waterloo, Ont., Canada: Wilfrid Laurier University Press, 1986).

13. For one experiment in the use of Gospel stories in pastoral care, see Thomas E. Boomershine, *Story Journey: An Invitation to the Gospel as Storytelling* (Nashville: Abingdon, 1988).

is it too much to expect that the emotional life might also newly spring to life?[14]

The preacher will help here as he continues to model how to perceive the emotional dimensions of the text and to preach so as to make an impact upon the whole person; that is, to engage the congregation emotionally for the maximum impact and learning.

But how do we engage in such 'emotional exegesis'? In what follows I shall first give some theory about how narratives work on readers, before providing an experiment in what I am calling 'emotional exegesis' through explaining Luke's account of the empty tomb (Luke 23:55 – 24:8).

Understanding narratives and their comprehension

When we read a narrative, there are two parts to the transaction: the narrative and the reader. The intersection between text and reader is the boundary in which the preacher has the privilege to operate. It is therefore worth reflecting upon the reading experience, so that the preacher might better facilitate it in the hearers. We can approach the question from both sides of the equation. First, how do narratives make an impact upon their readers? That is, how does the narrative entangle the reader? Secondly, what is the process by which readers come to comprehend and remember a narrative? Or, how does the reader unravel the text?[15]

---

14. Because it is already known that some elements of empathy can be learned, Baron-Cohen is hopeful that those who lack it can acquire a greater empathic facility. He even holds the question open whether those with Zero-degrees of empathy (those previously classified as 'personality disorders') may be able to be helped (Baron-Cohen, *Zero Degrees of Empathy*, p. 120). For those who realize the Gospels' transformative power, these historical narratives about Jesus of Nazareth may well play a part in such inner renewal, as they act as an instrument of the Holy Spirit to bring people face to face with Jesus Christ.

15. I have explored this two-directional model (from Text to Reader; and Reader to Text) further in Bolt, *Jesus' Defeat of Death*.

The narrative entangles

If the narrative is going to make an impact, it will be entangling the reader all the way through.

A basic distinction: story and discourse

Analysis of a narrative is helped by drawing a basic distinction between its 'story' and its 'discourse'.[16] The Story is the *What* of a narrative: what actually happens? Who are the characters? What do they do? Where and when do they do it? Here, basic description is required.

The Discourse is the *How* of the narrative: that is, how does the narrative engage readers and move them towards the narrative outcome? What are the reader-oriented devices that are employed, that reach out and grab readers and seek to bring them through some kind of transformation? It is through paying attention to the Discourse level that we can understand how a narrative works its emotional power.

The relational network

Narratives have their own dynamics, which can be conceived in terms a network of relationships (see figure 9.1 below).[17] Some of those relationships operate within the text (represented as the inner box). But outside the text there is also a transaction between the real

---

16. The distinction is drawn by Seymour Chatman, *Story and Discourse: Narrative Structure in Fiction and Film* (Ithaca, N. Y.: Cornell University Press, 1978), pp. 10, 19. Chatman discusses Story in chs. 2–3 and Discourse in chs. 4–5. Despite a great deal of recent work on the literary nature of the Gospels, few have explored their Discourse level, despite its significance for communication. For two examples of such work, see Robert M. Fowler, *Let the Reader Understand: Reader-Response Criticism and the Gospel of Mark* (Harrisburg, Pa.: Trinity Press International, 2001), and Bolt, *Jesus' Defeat of Death*.

17. This is a modification of Chatman's diagram (Chatman, *Story and Discourse*, p. 151). For an explanation of its use, see Bolt, *Jesus' Defeat of Death*, pp. 4–23.

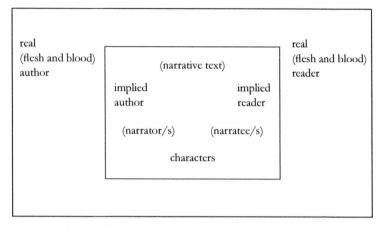

Figure 9.1 Chatman's narrative dynamics

author and the real reader, but this is always mediated through the
interactions within the text. Different aspects of the text will exert
an influence upon different sides of that transaction. Some features,
such as a narrative comment explaining something for the reader,
operate on the side of the author. Other features, such as the chorus
of praise after Jesus' miracles (e.g. Luke 7:16), operate on the
side of the reader. Some characters will echo the voice of the author,
such as, in the Gospels, Jesus, the voice of Old Testament prophecy,
or God's direct voice from heaven, and, perhaps rather surprisingly,
the revelations of the demons also echo the voice of the author and
provide his point of view. On the other hand, much of what happens
in the text will operate on the side of the readers, and certain
characters will be especially helpful in making an impact upon the
readers.[18]

In the sermon the preacher is dealing with the intersection
between text and real reader (top right-hand corner). His task is to
help the text do its work of aligning the implied reader with the real
reader; or, to put it the other way, to assist the real reader to become

18. In Bolt, *Jesus' Defeat of Death*, I argue that the thirteen Suppliants
play a particularly important role in entangling the readers in Mark's
story.

the implied reader. This is the ideal situation in which the text will achieve its maximum impact.

The dynamics of distance

One of the major ways this impact is made is by means of the 'dynamics of distance'. By minimizing distance between the reader and some characters, the narrative aligns the reader with them, and by maximizing distance between the reader and other characters, it misaligns the reader from these others.[19]

One of the major ways of decreasing distance and so producing alignment is through the creation of sympathy for that character.[20] That is, by establishing an emotional connection with the character, and then proceeding to use this emotional connection to move the reader towards the narrative's desired outcome. From the side of the text, therefore, the emotions have a significant role in the reading experience. The narrative entangles through the emotions.

The reader unravels

What about from the side of the reader? How do readers comprehend and remember a story?

Cognitive models: recognition of basic schemata

Earlier empirical studies of the processes involved in comprehending narratives tended to operate on cognitive models, which proposed that comprehension occurred as the reader recognized a 'story grammar', or various *schemata*, in the narrative.[21] So, for example, one cognitive model assigns each statement within a narrative to one of six categories (*schemata*): an event or state, either

---

19. See ibid., pp. 16–22, drawing upon Wayne C. Booth, 'Distance and Point of View: An Essay in Clarification', in P. Stevick (ed.), *Theory of the Novel* (New York: Free, 1967), pp. 87–107.

20. Bolt, *Jesus' Defeat of Death*, p. 19.

21. David S. Miall, 'Beyond the Schema Given: Affective Comprehension of Literary Narratives', *Cognition and Emotion* 3.1 (1989), pp. 2–3.

physical or internal to a character, or a goal, or a style (i.e. how something was done).[22]

A counterpart in the study of the Gospels would be the structuralist approach, in which, for example, the elements of Jesus' parables are understood against the *schemata* of a sender, an object sent, a receiver and a helper.[23]

Such cognitive models, however, are generally more amenable to comparatively simple narratives,[24] but do not even adequately account for something like a short story, let alone the complexities of a novel. The Gospels, too, are far too sophisticated for simple models to account adequately for how these marvellous documents make their impact upon their readers. When analysing the Gospels it is certainly very important to identify macro-level features such as characters, conflict, movement, the use of geography and topography, the manipulation of time, and the broad movements of plot, such as the commissioning of characters, the complication, the turning point, climax, denouement. These broad story features certainly function as *schemata* that, when recognized, assist the reader in comprehending and remembering the narrative.

In recent decades Gospels studies have produced a great deal of good work that analyses the Gospels as narratives according to such features. The tools honed in literary studies have been applied to the Gospels with very good results. Even if it is yet to make much of an appearance in the Gospels commentaries, what is known as 'narrative criticism of the Gospels' has certainly become a force to

---

22. According to Miall, 'Beyond the Schema Given', this is the model of A. C. Graesser, *Prose Comprehension Beyond the Word* (New York: Springer-Verlag, 1981), developing that of J. D. Bransford and M. K. Johnson, 'Contextual Prerequisites for Understanding: Some Investigations of Comprehension and Recall', *Journal of Verbal Learning and Verbal Behavior* 11 (1972), pp. 717–726.

23. For an introduction, see Daniel Patte, *What Is Structural Exegesis?* GBSNTS (Philadelphia: Fortress, 1976). For his discussion of Greimas's actantial model illustrated from the parable of the good Samaritan, see pp. 40–52.

24. Miall, 'Beyond the Schema Given', p. 2.

be reckoned with and it has delivered much of great benefit to the preacher.[25]

But even at this macro level, there is much more to comprehension than simple cognitive recognition of these broad narrative features. This scholarly analysis of the Gospels can often feel like a rush to find the skeletal structure that lies beneath and can leave one feeling as if something important has been lost as the flesh of the narrative and the life it contains is hacked off and left on the scholarly dissecting-room floor.

Amongst other criticisms of the cognitive models of comprehension, one scholar has commented that 'Such models of narrative imply that the emotions that arise in the reader are an after-effect of reading, playing no role in the comprehension process itself.'[26] This is misguided, however, as the psychological process of comprehension is much more complex than the earlier cognitive models allowed.[27]

Affective models
More recent work on the mental processes involved in readers comprehending and remembering narratives has moved away from the cognitive models so amenable to simple stories. Rather than majoring upon the cognitive *schemata* recognized by the rational

---

25. For a brief introduction, see Mark Allan Powell, *What Is Narrative Criticism?*, GBSNTS (Minneapolis: Fortress, 1990).

26. Miall, 'Beyond the Schema Given', p. 13.

27. Ibid., p. 4, summarizes the difficulties of the schema approach as follows: '1. Schema identification is necessary to allow the work of understanding to begin, but the application of schemata is likely to be thwarted or disrupted in a variety of ways by a range of textual features. 2. Providing a causal account of states or events is often problematic, due to uncertainties about how text elements relate or to multiple potential relationships within the text. The status of narrative elements as states or events may itself be indeterminate. 3. A goal-directed account of characters is often inadequate. Goals may be multiple, ambiguous or conflicting, so that their status becomes a focus of narrative interest.'

mind, these studies point to the affective (the emotional) components of a text, which are felt by the emotional mind.[28] Far from being
peripheral embellishment, it is these affective components that bring
comprehension to readers, and that make the narrative meaningful
to them.

Three features of affect assist this comprehension process.
(1) Affect is self-referential. That is, it draws upon the reader's prior
experience to aid comprehension. (2) Affect crosses domains. That
is, an emotion evoked by one textual element can be carried over
into another. (3) Affect is anticipatory. That is, it assists the reader
to make predictions about meaning early in the reading process.[29]

Affective narrative impact
So, whether we approach the reading experience from the way the
narrative entangles the reader or from the way the reader unravels
the narrative, we arrive at the same result. Narratives work by
producing an affective impact; that is, not only do narratives address
the cognitive mind, but a narrative makes its impact through
engaging, evoking and manipulating the feelings of the readers, to
move them forward profoundly.

Clear direction
But what are they moved towards? A narrative moves in a clear
direction, towards some kind of outcome. The Gospels, for example
and generally speaking, each in their own way move readers towards
putting their faith in Jesus as the Son of God, who opens up the
kingdom of God for all who do so.[30]

Open-ended outcomes
Despite this clear direction, however, complex narratives also show
a high degree of indeterminacy that leaves the exact details of the
outcome rather open ended, depending upon the reader. Once again,
this is largely dependent upon the emotions different readers bring

---

28. Miall, 'Beyond the Schema Given', *passim*.
29. Ibid., pp. 2, 4.
30. For Mark, see Bolt, *Jesus' Defeat of Death*, pp. 276–279.

to the narrative, for these colour their response to the narrative, and their responses therefore become more or less unique to them.[31]

When it comes to the Gospels, it is also true that the clear direction towards faith in Christ also moves towards rather open-ended outcomes, for that faith in Christ will take on a different shape depending upon the person responding. Because we are each moved by the text somewhat differently, the preacher cannot really take tight control of what is so often called 'application'. This must to a large degree be left to the Spirit's working through the text on the affections of the hearer.

So, if the affective component of the text is so important, how do we get at it? What is involved in emotional exegesis? Before we turn to our case study, perhaps a basic stance towards emotional exegesis should be outlined.

Emotional exegesis

Embedded emotions
The first step is to realize that the text will have emotions embedded within it. These may be explicitly mentioned, or they can be embedded in the implicit nuances of the vocabulary and details of the characters and their interactions in the story. In fact, every detail in the text will have an affective component of some kind waiting to be discovered.[32]

---

31. Miall, 'Beyond the Schema Given', p. 6: 'Because the self is directly implicated in anticipating the outcome (the meaning which will be attributed to the narrative as a whole), different readers are likely to project different self-related concerns on to the narrative.'

32. The more ordinary broad and simple features of a narrative will also have their affective dimensions. Characters will be characterized either positively or negatively, slanting the reader emotionally for or against them; plot will add tension and resolution, both of which are felt by the reader; things at the beginning evoke the reader to anticipate later complications or turning points or the climax and its resolution; in the rising action towards the climax the tension in the reader increases, only

Meeting our own emotions

The next step is to realize that real readers bring their own emotional repertoire to the reading experience, as damaged and diminished, or healthy and expansive, as it may be. This is what is meant by affect being 'self-referential'. The affective components of the text will strike against the previous emotional experience of the reader. Emotional exegesis will attempt to anticipate the contours of this encounter.

Sympathy to empathy?

Emotional exegesis will also keep an eye on sympathy and/or empathy. The words 'sympathy' (feeling with) and 'empathy' (feeling for) are both important to narrative impact, but the relationship between the two is not exactly clear. Literary critics tend to speak of the creation of sympathy between the reader and certain characters within the narrative. Psychology speaks of empathy, the ability to feel for others, as being at the higher end of emotional aptitude. It consists of (at least) two stages: the *recognition* of the thoughts and emotions of another person, and an appropriate emotional *response* of one's own.[33] Those who lack empathy will probably not have the emotional wherewithal to apprehend the narrative fully.

---

to be resolved by the climax one way or the other, towards tragedy or comedy; in the denouement there is the opportunity to relax after this heightened moment of tension, and to gain some satisfaction from the unravelling of loose ends.

  Other common devices will also have affective components, such as anticipation–retrospection; time manipulation; the distinctions between scene and summary, telling and showing; the relative degrees of intrusiveness of the narrator's voice; the levels of narration. All these elements work towards producing the impact of the narrative and this is largely through affective, not cognitive, means. The process of touching upon and engaging, evoking and changing, the readers' feelings is primary to the narrative's facilitating their proper comprehension of its message.

33. Baron-Cohen, *Zero Degrees of Empathy*, p. 11.

It would be worthwhile to explore further how these two things work together, but for present purposes suffice it to say that if the narrative works its power, then perhaps the sympathy it creates in the reader is a step towards greater emotional health. Perhaps by creating sympathy the narrative moves the reader towards greater facility in empathy? This would then be part of the Gospels' power to transform readers into better human beings: by bringing them face to face with Jesus and helping his humanity to rub off on theirs.

Emotional transformation

Narratives work this emotional transformation by a process of familiarization and defamiliarization. For the Gospels I think we should also add the third step of refamiliarization, which I shall explain later in the case study.

So, for example, the affective components at the beginning of a passage may tend to familiarize the readers, to align them with the world they already know. But once this familiarization has taken place, the text will then move to defamiliarization. What readers are led to anticipate at the beginning may not turn out that way by the end. This creates a disturbance in readers as a step towards bringing about their transformation.[34]

With an eye on this process, emotional exegesis will watch how the affective components change the reading of the text as the

---

34. Miall, 'Beyond the Schema Given', p. 4: 'The outcome of a literary narrative, therefore, may include the following: Causes are not what the reader might have believed (a cause may be more complex, profound, or obscure); goals may be ineffective or turn out to have been inappropriate, so that the story becomes a critique of the goals as such. Thus, the reader's effort after meaning is directed towards developing a schema for the narrative that transcends the more simple schemata with which he started. The aim of comprehension can be described as the creation of schemata, rather than their application.' For more on this defamiliarization, see Wolfgang Iser, 'The Reading Process: A Phenomenological Approach', in Jane P. Tompkins (ed.), *Reader-Response Criticism: From Formalism to Post-Structuralism* (Baltimore: Johns Hopkins University Press, 1986), pp. 50–69.

reading process moves on. There is an essential attention to the text being read in time, from point A to point B, or 'from left to right'. Emotional exegesis won't read the text as a flat book, but as a dynamic movement from beginning to end.[35]

Hear, see, turn, be healed

The ultimate aim of emotional exegesis is the healing of the congregation. Jesus often used the language of the senses to talk about faith in him. As he explained the parable of the sower he quoted Isaiah 6:

> For this people's heart has grown dull,
>   and with their ears they can barely hear,
>   and their eyes they have closed,
> lest they should see with their eyes
>   and hear with their ears
> and understand with their heart
>   and turn, and I would heal them.
> (Matt. 13:15 ESV)

Although he puts it in the negative, here Jesus outlines the way of finding healing. Through hearing, the people see; and through seeing they understand with their heart; and through understanding, they turn; and as they turn they are healed.

Jesus uses this sensory, affective, language to speak of the clear movement towards faith and healing. If preaching the Gospels is to make its proper impact, it needs to help people hear, so they can see. This is the language of inner vision and imagination, the language of apocalyptic – the language of the emotional mind. And

---

35. This requires certain other 'formal features', such as concentric patterns for example, to be domesticated within an overall movement forward through the narrative. For reading as a temporal experience, see Wolfgang Iser, 'Interaction Between Text and Reader', in Susan R. Suleiman and Inge Crosman (eds.), *The Reader in the Text: Essays on Audience and Interpretation* (Princeton: Princeton University Press, 1980), pp. 106–119.

as they hear and see, they will understand. This is the language of the rational mind. And as they understand, they turn and are healed. This is the language of transformation of life by reception of Christ's salvation.

If this is what the preaching of the Gospels ought to aim at, then this is also what emotional exegesis ought to bear in mind as its aim.

To illustrate the application of some of this theory, my next task is to provide a case study in emotional exegesis, by examining Luke's empty tomb scene (Luke 23:55 – 24:8).

Emotionally coming alive: a case study in emotional exegesis (Luke 23:55 – 24:8)

Explicit emotions

The Gospels often mention the emotions explicitly (see table 9.1 overleaf for emotions mentioned in Luke 24, my tr.). In our passage this occurs twice: in verse 4 the women were perplexed (Gk. *en tō aporeisthai*) at what they found; in verse 5 they became frightened (Gk. *emphobōn de genomenōn autōn*).

What is the effect on readers when emotions are mentioned? I have already stated that a major part of affect is that it is self-reflective. In addition, the affective component crosses domains. To put these two things together, emotions are readily generalizable. Although the text places the emotion in a certain domain, the readers will readily transfer that emotion to a domain in which they themselves have experienced, or will experience, that emotion.

And so, for our two examples, you may never have discovered an empty tomb, and so experienced the exact kind of perplexity this sent the women into. But you have experienced perplexity, and given that bodies don't usually disappear from tombs, you can easily enter into this emotion. This is the kind of situation in which I imagine I would certainly be perplexed!

Or, again, you may never have met an angel, and therefore never have felt the women's specific angel-in-a-tomb-induced fear. But you have been afraid, and will be afraid again. Your previous experience of fear helps you enter into the women's experience here. And

Table 9.1 Emotional terms in Luke 24

24:4	While perplexed	*en tō aporeisthai*
24:5	Becoming frightened	*emphobōn de genomenōn*
24:11	As if nonsense	*hōsei lēros*
24:11	And they were not believing them	*kai ēpistoun autais*
24:12	Marvelling	*thaumazōn*
24:21	We hoped	*ēlpizomen*
24:22	Amazed	*exestēsan*
24:32	Our hearts burned	*hē kardia hēmōn kaiomenē*
24:37	Becoming startled and frightened	*ptoēthentes de kai emphoboi genomenoi*
24:38	Why are you troubled, and why are doubts rising up in your heart?	*ti tetaragmenoi este kai dia ti dialogismoi anabainousin en tē kardia hymōn?*
24:41	While they still disbelieved and marvelled from joy	*eti de apistountōn autōn apo tēs charas kai thaumazontōn*
24:52	With great joy	*meta charas megalēs*
24:52	Worshipping	*proskynēsantes*
24:53	Blessing God	*eulogountes ton theon*

it is probably even more specific than this. It may also be that you have been at a graveside and felt the fear of its gaping jaws, and so the fear-in-a-graveyard speaks even more powerfully to you. But even if you haven't, you readily feel this kind of fear because of the fear of death that lies deep within every human soul (Heb. 2:14–15). Because we, the readers, know what it is to be afraid, and we especially know what it is to be afraid of death, we are drawn into the women's experience and this aligns us with their experience in the narrative. We bring our fears into their fears, and we are with them, waiting for the next thing to happen.

When the angels speak, we hear it from the women's point of view, in the exact historical circumstance being recounted, but because our feelings are already aroused, we also hear the words of the angels somehow addressing us in the midst of our fears as well. The fears of the women thus function to enable our own self-reflection and as that self-reflection on fear crosses to other domains, so the remarkable statement made to the women is heard into those new domains: 'He is not here, but has risen' (v. 6).

Overtones, undertones, nuances and gut feelings

However, and as usual, there is more affective material in this passage than simply that conveyed by the explicit mention of two emotional states. Practically every item evokes its overtones, undertones, emotional nuances or gut feelings.

Studies have shown, in fact, that a narrative can have a greater affective impact if the explicit mention of emotions is kept to a minimum, allowing the emotional power to be generated by more implicit means.[36]

This is probably because emotions beneath the surface of the text correlate with the powerful emotions that sit beneath our own surface. 'Emotions that simmer beneath the threshold of awareness can have a powerful impact on how we perceive and react, even though we have no idea they are at work.'[37] Although emotions can be aroused *after* our thoughts, there is a 'down deep and dirty' kind of emotional response that is visceral, or as the evolutionary psychologists put it, *reptilian*.[38] Even if we aren't thinking about it, these

---

36. See e.g. the analysis of Virginia Woolf's story *Together and Apart* (1944), in Miall, 'Beyond the Schema Given', who concludes, 'the power of a literary text such as this lies beyond the sentences of the text itself, in activating vectors of concern within the reader that are likely to continue resonating for some time to come. In this sense the overall schema which is being created by the story constitutes a part of the reader's continual creation of the self through the work of the emotions' (p. 13).

37. Goleman, *Emotional Intelligence*, p. 55.

38. See e.g. David M. Schnarch, *Passionate Marriage: Love, Sex, and Intimacy in Emotionally Committed Relationships* (New York: H. Holt, 1998), pp. 135–136, who argues the brain has three parts with 'increasing evolutionary sophistication: the *reptilian* brain, the *mammalian* brain, and the *neocortex*' (emphases original); see also pp. 147, 259, 281, 299, 331, 342, 344, 351. Schnarch uses this notion to humorous effect: e.g. David M. Schnarch, *Resurrecting Sex: Resolving Sexual Problems and Rejuvenating Your Relationship* (New York: HarperCollins, 2002): 'People become

reptilian responses will be evoked as the text washes over us to engage us.

For example, even the presence of women in the account imports affective undertones, for, rhetorically speaking, women are emotional softeners.[39] Or again, action correlates with emotion. When the passage reports action, it automatically evokes emotion for those readers properly emotionally attuned. When a group of women go to the graveyard with a bunch of spices (v. 1), the readers' previous experience indicates that this would be a journey filled with grief. When we recall that their friend and relative in this instance was brutally crucified, the end of this journey would be nothing short of overwhelming. When the women press their faces to the ground (v. 5), even if we were not told that they were afraid, this action itself already speaks loudly of such an emotion.[40]

But there are even more affective dimensions in this text.

Sensual (or, at least, sensory) arousal
Narratives use the language of the senses to tap into sensual memories, and this is also a way of creating the affective impact. We

---

reptiles when they get really anxious. The reptilian part of our brain takes over and the worst in us comes forward, lashing out to protect ourselves and snapping at whatever we deem threatening. And when we're "reptilian", everything looks threatening. There's nothing wrong with being a reptile, and reptiles do have sex. However, they don't make love. If we want to make love, we need *human* sexuality. To have that, we must soothe our anxiety so the thinking part of our brain (our neocortex) can run the show' (pp. 142–143). Although Schnarch is clearly addressing a specific aspect of human life, it can also be argued that the Gospels, through the presentation of Jesus, the one who defeats death, actually deal with the deepest of all anxieties (the fear of death, Heb. 2:15), which also makes people more 'reptilian' than human. The Gospels utilize the 'reptilian' emotions in order to bring about their greater humanization.

39. Bolt, *Jesus' Defeat of Death*, p. 19, n. 87.
40. Such clues will be difficult to pick up for those with a diminished capacity for empathy.

have already noted Jesus' use of the language of the senses of sight and hearing as metaphors for access to the inner world of mind and heart to convey the notion of faith.[41]

The account of the burial in Luke begins with a group of sympathetically portrayed women preparing spices and ointments (Luke 23:56). This becomes something of a focus of this introductory portion of the scene, since the spices appear again as the women go to the tomb (24:1).

These sweet-smelling perfumes evoke the bitter reality of tombs and graves. In modern western society where we are hermetically sealed from the realities of corpses, our sensory memories may be inactive here. But in many cultures throughout history and still today the events and rituals around burial are very real. When someone dies, someone else has to lay the body out, closing the orifices, tying the jaw closed. Somebody has to touch the cold skin of the one who used to be warm to the touch. And here, from everything they knew about the normal processes of death and decay, they assumed someone had to use perfume and spices to keep the stench of death at bay.

The women had followed Jesus' body to the tomb (23:55), and saw where he was laid. They assumed the body would soon begin to decompose. So they went home and prepared spices to complete the burial (23:56). This wasn't embalming, just stench minimization.[42] Part of a proper burial, it was a token way of showing respect for their loved one.

The Sabbath was a problem (23:56b). The women's piety prevented them from taking the spices to the tomb. As far as they

---

41. According to John, Jesus also used the sensory language of taste, and he expressed his call to believe by asking people to eat and drink his flesh and blood. He called upon people to come to him as a thirsty person to water, a hungry person to bread. This is where his miracles are not operating upon a physical–spiritual dichotomy, but, given that our reality is bodily, his miracles convey something real about our access to his new reality. We are healed as we hear and see and understand and turn.

42. R. N. Jones, 'Embalming', in *ABD* 2, p. 495.

knew,[43] Jesus' body was busily decomposing in the tomb for that
entire day, and by the time the Sabbath was over, he was one quarter
of the way towards the stench Lazarus' sisters expected on that
famous day in Bethany (John 11:39). Actions correlate with emotions
and so reports of actions evoke feelings in the reader, and the
women's rush to the tomb at the first opportunity to do so not only
arouses a sense of their devotion to Jesus, but also evokes the
sensory memory of the stench of death. For anyone familiar with
the way these things usually went would imagine that, by this stage,
this was probably already getting out of hand.

The perfumes mentioned before and after (Luke 23:56; 24:1), so
lovingly prepared, speak of the solution to this problem. But they
evoke a sensory memory of their own. The spices used for burial,
if smelled previously in the readers' experience, once smelled again,
evoke their correlation with burial and so they stand for, symbolize,
remind and evoke all the things associated with death and burial,
grief and loss.

And so for those readers who had that smell in their nostrils
and the smell memory in their minds, the mention of these death-
covering spices has an affective impact. As the spices are prepared
(23:56), their sweet smell fills the house during the long Sabbath,
reminding everyone that the death of Jesus, with all its overtones,
has occurred; and on the first day after that long Sabbath day the
women take the solution to deal with the problem. By the use of
these perfumes, as the women go to the tomb, the stench of death
is in the air. And even in this world of ours, the hearers know and
feel that stench far too well.

Familiar feelings
The scene has begun with familiarization. The affective dimensions
of a narrative draw the reader in, because their connection with
common bodily experience connects the world of the reader
with that of the text. The affective component has a large role in the

---

43. These Galilean women were evidently unaware that two powerful
    Jerusalemites, Joseph and Nicodemus, had already cared for Jesus'
    body; see John 19:38–42.

process of familiarization, in which the narrative engages us by its very familiarity with our own world.

The opening verses of Luke's scene (23:55 – 24:1) familiarize the readers with the tragic reality of death and burial, experiences of life we all know so well, but wish we didn't know at all. By arousing the stench of death, the scene evokes the shadow of death under which we all labour. Jesus' need for proper burial to cover death's stench arouses all the feelings of a world gone wrong, a world in which the shroud of death covers the nations (Isa. 25:7–8). Sadly and tragically, this is the world with which we are all familiar. We wish we weren't but we are.

The mention of the Sabbath day is also part of the process of familiarization. The day of rest looked forwards to the great day of rest at the end of time, the day of resurrection. This future prospect clashed severely with the scene at the tomb, as the hope of resurrection inbuilt into the Sabbath is a stark reminder of the horror of the grave for which it is the solution.

But the affective components of the narrative have a larger purpose than simply familiarization. Making contact and drawing the reader in, showing the readers that the world of the text is a slice of life through their own world, is simply the first step towards creating the impact the narrative is driving towards. In order to move towards this goal, familiarization issues in defamiliarization. The world we know so well is about to change for ever.

Unfamiliar dissonance

The defamiliarization begins with what the women discovered on arrival. Luke's account is structured by what they found (v. 2) and what they did not find (v. 3). Nothing in all their experience (nor in our experience) prepared them (or us) for what they found.[44] The familiarity of death and graves is shattered by the women's

---

44. Whereas Matthew and John provide ways of familiarization, namely grave robbery and the moving of the body, Luke provides no alternative theory. The absence of explanation leads us to wonder at the puzzle, and so the defamiliarization process begins with a kick-start.

discoveries: in verse 2 they find the stone rolled away, and in verse 3 they do not find the body of Jesus.

At this point Luke adds explicit mention of feelings (v. 4) but does so in passing, by means of a subordinate clause (Gk. *en tō aporeisthai autas peri toutou*). But this is enough for our own perplexity to be acknowledged and we are drawn into the account and aligned with the women, ready to see the next event through their eyes and ears, and our sensory experiences are combined with theirs.

In passing, it is worth noticing that perplexity is more than just a simple feeling: perplexity has a cognitive component to it. So we are in search of a rational solution to allow the mind to domesticate the bodily state. This word anticipates the possibility that our emotional and rational minds will work together towards a more settled disposition regarding what occurred on that morning so long ago.

The defamiliarization continues with another reference to sensory data, in what they saw next. Notice the language of vision: introduced with the attention-grabbing command to see (v. 4b, 'and behold'; Gk. *kai idou*), which irresistibly calls the reader to see what they saw. This is followed immediately by a report of what they saw: not just two men, but 'two men in lightning-like clothing' (my tr.). This unusual language evokes Luke's previous usage of the word for 'lightning' (10:18; 11:36; 17:24). This is heavenly apparel, apocalyptic clothing.

This illustrates the way affect crosses domains. In 10:18 Jesus said he saw Satan fall from heaven like lightning. In 11:36 he said he had come like a lamp casting its lightning rays into the darkness of our souls. In 17:24 he said the kingdom of God will arrive as lightning flashes from one end of the sky to another. Now, as the mention of lightning-like clothes evokes these previous references, it is as if this moment is the fall of Satan from heaven, the arrival of the kingdom of God, and the penetration of Christ's light into our souls.

The appearance of these men in dazzling clothing is not familiar to normal human experience, although it is familiar to Bible readers as a vehicle for divine communication. It is thus at one and the same time, defamiliarizing and refamiliarizing – more of which I shall explain below. Especially in the apocalyptic book of Daniel, heavenly visitors provided guidance as to the meaning of Daniel's extra-ordinary heavenly visions. And it is clearly not unimportant that these allusions to Daniel also evoke his prophecy of the resurrection of the dead (Dan. 12:1–3).

Once again this massive defamiliarization of the appearance of these heavenly visitors is followed by an account of the women's explicit emotions, this time 'fear' (24:5; Gk. *emphobōn de genomenōn autōn*). Here the emotion is reinforced by its correlation with action: they press their faces to the ground. This brings us back from our drift through previous apocalyptic associations of the word 'lightning' to the women, and so to the historical account. But it is not just them in this graveyard. Because explicit emotions reach out and grab our own situations of fear, we are sympathetic and so are drawn to them. We are with them, faces pressed to the ground, ready to experience the next event from their point of view.

The third part of this defamiliarization process comes with a question asked by the men (v. 5). This is a weird question, whichever way you read it and its very weirdness brings further dissonance, continuing the defamiliarization now moving us towards the final impact of the account.

The question clashes with what we know of these women. 'Why do you seek the living among the dead?' (Luke 24:5 ESV). This is not what they were doing. For the whole story so far, they have been focused on the body of Jesus (they saw where it was laid, 23:55; they prepared spices, 23:56; they went to the tomb with the spices, 24:1; they found the stone rolled away, 24:2; but they did not find the body, 24:3). This focus on the dead body of Jesus is familiar to them and to us. All they expected was to complete the burial and be done with Jesus for ever, except in sad and tragic memory (cf. 24:21). They had come to the tomb seeking the *dead*, not the living, among the dead. This is the world they knew so tragically well. This is the world we know so tragically well. But the men's weird question clashes with this sad familiarity.

The question is, of course, put to the women in the light of the situation they weren't expecting, but which the men knew now prevailed and was about to be revealed.

The fearful women then hear a strong declaration of the new state of affairs of which they were unaware and of which we were unaware: 'He is not here, but has risen.' This is the climax: total defamiliarization. What could possibly have happened?

Refamiliarizing reflection

At this point a refamiliarization takes place. This step is not always spoken about in narrative theory but is necessary in the Gospels. The Gospels are apocalyptic narratives of theologically significant historical events. They speak of God's events in human history on our behalf. And God has been working towards these events for a very long time.

The men in the apocalyptic clothing call upon the women to 'remember' (v. 6b). To remember is to exercise the inner recall of the mind; that is, both cognitive and emotional minds. This is a call for the settled inner life to be invoked to bring the present dissonant events into a more settled state and so enable the women to move towards a more settled disposition towards these events.

The men give the women specific items to remember (vv. 6b–7). It is a call to remember Jesus' own words, back in Galilee, before the distress and turmoil of these last days. He had predicted that the events of this strange morning would occur. Behind his predictions also lay further predictions of Old Testament pattern and prophecy.

As participants in these events, the women were called upon to reach into their 'raw memory', but as readers of the account, we can also remember by recalling Jesus' words that we read earlier in Luke's account and which are now embedded in our 'reading memory'. However, although the vehicle by which this memory comes is different, the experience of remembering is precisely the same, and so once again we are closely aligned with the women. They are called upon to remember and so we are called upon to remember, and with this memory the defamiliarization of the empty tomb will be refamiliarized. This refamiliarization, however, will not take us back exactly to where we began – that will not happen. It will not simply take us back to our tragic experience of death in the midst of life, but now we bring into that tragic experi- ence the event of this first Easter morning, in connection with Jesus' predictions and Old Testament prophecy before that.

The scene closes by reporting that the women remembered (v. 8), and, as they remembered, so do we. This memory – with all its deep emotional resonances – now becomes the abiding disposition to which the scene has moved us.[45]

Impact and outcome

The affective elements of this scene have helped to move us cognitively towards a very different world than that with which we were familiar at its outset. We readers still live under the shadow of death. But now we remember something different that has changed life in this world.

What God said would occur, has occurred. What Jesus said would occur has occurred. Into the familiar world of death and tombs and the stench of death has come a man, and exactly according to what he said he would do and what Old Testament prophecy expected, 'He is not here, but has risen.' This is the sentence that now stands over life under the shadow of death.

We have felt the impact of the narrative through its engagement with our grief, our perplexity, our fears, in this world in which we live with the stench of death in our nostrils. The outcome of the narrative has a clear direction: to see this world so firmly under the shadow of death, as the same world in which a man has risen from the dead, all according to plan. This is the settled disposition to which the scene moves us. Although each of us may respond in a variety of different ways, all of these responses will reflect this posture of faith.

Emotional exegesis: a preacher's checklist

Having looked at our case study on emotional exegesis, perhaps there might be some value in presenting, but without elaboration, a brief checklist to help the preacher engage in it. Emotional exegesis will involve answering (at least) such questions as:

- Who are the characters and How are they related?
- What emotions are explicitly mentioned?

---

45. Memory is closely associated with the emotional limbic system; see Goleman, *Emotional Intelligence*, pp. 10–11, 20–22, 85–86.

- What emotional nuances lie behind the words?
- How does the text use the language of the senses?
- What is the direction the passage moves its reader towards?
- Can the stages of this movement be mapped from familiarization, to defamiliarization, to refamiliarization?
- How does the transaction between Jesus and the characters prepare us for the kingdom of God?
- What outcomes might be provoked, but not prescribed, for the reader?

Preaching the Gospels for divine effects

The Gospels are well-told narratives that bring God's message to a lost and dying world, about his Son, Jesus Christ, who is risen from the dead. The Gospels communicate powerfully through touching our God-given emotions, engaging them and transforming us through this process to live by faith in Jesus Christ, to find salvation in him, and, thereby to become better human beings, set on a new journey towards the kingdom of God.

Those who have the privilege of preaching the Gospels ought to preach the divine message in the same way it comes to us. They ought to preach the emotion embedded in the text so as to touch the God-given emotions embedded in the congregation, in order to achieve divine effects, in the very midst of all our weakness.

10. TOGETHER, WITH FEELING: CORPORATE WORSHIP AND THE EMOTIONS

David G. Peterson

By way of introduction, consider with me the implication of two complementary texts, one from the Old Testament and one from the New Testament. Psalm 111:1 speaks of praise being offered to God *wholeheartedly*, and suggests that there is a special significance to praising God in the company of his people:

> Praise the LORD!
> I will give thanks to the LORD with my whole heart,
>   in the company of the upright, in the congregation.[1]

God's people are to love him with all their heart and with all their soul and with all their might (Deut. 6:5), and praise is clearly meant to be an expression of such love. Genuine praise will not simply be a formal confession of truths about God, but an expression of gratitude and love from the *heart*. Praising God in the congregation of his people will therefore be a way of uniting and strengthening

---

1. Bible quotations in this chapter are from the ESV.

believers in their relationship with him. As the rest of the psalm shows, such praise should move us to fear God and live before him with wisdom.

Hebrews 10:24–25 indicates that Christian gatherings are meant to be *provocative*, having a transforming effect on those who participate:

> And let us consider how to *stir up* one another to love and good
> works, not neglecting to meet together, as is the habit of some, but
> encouraging one another, and all the more as you see the Day drawing
> near. (My emphasis.)

The call to 'consider' one another (Gk. *katanoōmen*) implies thoughtful reflection on the needs of other believers and recalls the challenge of 3:12 to 'take care' (Gk. *blepete*) with respect to the spiritual health of the congregation. With a clear understanding of local needs, we are in a better position to 'stir up one another to love and good works'. The extraordinary expression used here (Gk. *eis paroxysmon*) literally means *for provocation*. Sometimes this terminology conveys 'intense emotion, often of a negative kind, such as anger (Deut. 29:28 [LXX 29:27]) or strong disagreement (Acts 15:39). Here it communicates positive stimulation or motivation.'[2]

Church is meant to be a stirring experience, moving believers to serve God with a love that is expressed in good deeds. Some form of mutual exhortation is the means highlighted in 3:13 and 10:25. 'Exhorting' is a better translation than 'encouraging' here (Gk. *parakalountes*), because the writer's own example in his 'word of exhortation' (13:22; Gk. *logos tēs paraklēseōs*) is to blend teaching with warning and every motivation to serve God faithfully.

Putting these texts together, we can see how important praise and exhortation are for the edification of the church and the glorification of God. Praise and exhortation are meant to be vigorous and provocative, involving the intellect, will and emotions. Biblical

---

2. P. T. O'Brien, *The Letter to the Hebrews*, PNTC (Grand Rapids: Eerdmans; Nottingham: Apollos, 2010), p. 370. The expression *agapēs kai kalōn ergōn* is probably a hendiadys, indicating that love is expressed in good deeds.

psychology will not allow us to appeal to one aspect of the human person in isolation from the rest.

Gospel-focused gatherings

The concluding verses of Hebrews 12 link acceptable worship with gratitude to God for the gift of salvation, expressed in terms of 'a kingdom that cannot be shaken' (12:28; cf. 10:34; 13:14). Such worship is literally *service* to God (Gk. *latreuein*, as in 9:14; cf. Rom. 12:1 [*latreia*]). Hebrews 13 makes it clear that this service is to be rendered in every sphere of life. Along with gratitude, acceptable worship is to be expressed with reverence and awe, and we are to remember the holiness of God and his imminent judgment (cf. Deut. 4:24).[3] 'Reverence' (Gk. *eulabeia*) means 'circumspection' or 'respect' for God and his will (cf. 5:7; 11:7), while 'awe' (Gk. *deos*) introduces the more sombre note of fear before God as judge.

By implication, Christians need to be regularly reminded about the character of God and his gracious work of salvation in Christ, to move them to faithful service. From Hebrews 13:15–16 it is clear that *words and actions flowing from gratitude to God* are the worship that please him:

> Through [Jesus] then let us continually offer up a sacrifice of praise to God, that is, the fruit of lips that acknowledge his name. Do not neglect to do good and to share what you have, for such sacrifices are pleasing to God.

In language borrowed from Hosea 14:2 (LXX), our 'sacrifice of praise' consists of lips that acknowledge the name or character of God. The 'name' to be confessed could be specifically that of Jesus, since the focus of Christian confession in 3:1, 4:14 and 10:23 is Jesus as Son

---

3. H. Strathmann, '*latreuō, latreia*', *TDNT* 4, p. 64, writes that the essence of this service is 'a manner of life which is pleasing to God and which is sustained both by gratitude and by a serious sense of responsibility'. The certainty of God's grace must not obscure the truth that a terrible judgment awaits the apostate (cf. 2:2–3; 6:4–8; 10:26–31; 12:14–17).

of God and high priest. Confession of Christ *in personal or corporate acts of praise* could thus be on view in 13:15. The immediate context, however, is concerned with believers acknowledging Christ *in the world*, in the face of opposition and suffering. In its widest sense, then, this sacrifice of praise will be rendered by those who confess Jesus 'outside the camp', in various forms of public testimony or evangelism. Offering praise to God in a congregational context ought to be a stimulus for effective confession elsewhere.

Hebrews 13:16 employs transformed cultic language in another way, to show how doing good and sharing what you have can be pleasing to God. Such 'sacrifices' cannot be regarded as cultivating God's favour, since Christian worship is meant to be an expression of gratitude for the care that he first showed us. Indeed, as 13:21 makes clear, God himself must 'equip you with everything good that you may do his will, working in us that which is pleasing in his sight, through Jesus Christ'. So doing good and sharing what you have indicates a love for others that is God-given (cf. 6:10; 10:34; 13:1–4).

Hebrews makes it clear that exhortation, prayer and praise should be focused on the promises of God and the encouragement the gospel can bring for godly living. Preaching and teaching should combine a thoughtful restatement of biblical truths with an application to the needs of those present – their struggles and temptations, but also the opportunities they have to speak and act for God in everyday life. Corporate worship ought to be thoughtful and provocative, motivating and inspiring, appealing to our minds, emotions and wills.

As we come together to serve one another in love, we are serving God and glorifying him together. As we pray together and praise God, he makes it possible for us to encourage one another and pursue his goals for the church. We should hold the vertical and the horizontal together when we consider what is happening when Christians engage in corporate worship and edification.[4]

---

4. Cf. D. G. Peterson, *Engaging with God: A Biblical Theology of Worship* (Leicester: Apollos; Downers Grove: IVP Academic, 1992), pp. 194–221.

Exhortation for change

We have already noted the way Hebrews highlights the importance of gospel-based exhortation: negatively, it is the antidote to apostasy (3:13); positively, it is a means of provoking one another to love expressed in good deeds (10:24–25). It is with this ministry in view that the writer also says, 'by this time you ought to be teachers' (5:12). Hebrews offers a model of life-changing exhortation in the way the argument is presented and applied to the situation of those addressed (13:22).[5]

Similar terminology is used elsewhere in the New Testament in association with the ministry of prophets and teachers (e.g. Acts 15:32; 20:2, 7–12; Rom. 12:6–8; 1 Cor. 14:31; 1 Thess. 2:12; 3:2; 1 Tim. 4:13). The apostle Paul uses the terminology extensively, in a way that suggests it involves an *appeal* on the basis of instruction, either previously given or outlined in the immediate context (e.g. Rom. 12:1; 1 Cor. 1:10; 2 Cor. 10:1; Phil. 4:2; 1 Thess. 2:3–4; 4:1).[6]

What we describe as 'congregational preaching' may involve some combination of proclamation, teaching and exhortation, varying according to the nature of the topic and the needs of the situation. However, it is easy for exhortation to be loosed from instruction. It is also common enough for proclamation or teaching to be given without the sort of appeal found in the New Testament, where the writers clearly seek to inform minds, challenge emotions and move the wills of those addressed.

So, for example, it is helpful to observe how Paul makes his appeals by using expressions such as 'by the mercies of God' (Rom. 12:1), or 'by our Lord Jesus Christ and by the love of the Spirit'

---

5. O'Brien, *Hebrews*, pp. 20–36, has much to say about this, especially in relation to the structure and flow of the argument, and the rhetorical devices used by the writer to motivate the readers.

6. A quick survey of texts in the same English version will reveal various ways in which the verb *parakalein* and the noun *paraklēsis* are translated in different contexts. These include 'exhort', 'encourage', 'urge', 'entreat', 'appeal', 'comfort' and 'console'. Cf. G. Braumann, *'parakaleō'*, in *NIDNTT* 1, pp. 569–571.

(Rom. 15:30), or 'by the meekness and gentleness of Christ' (2 Cor. 10:1). Such references to the character of God and the way he has engaged with us through his Son and his Spirit highlight the fact that Christian exhortation arises out of a relationship with God already established by his grace. It is a call to live faithfully and productively within that relationship.

Nevertheless, Paul uses many rhetorical devices to persuade his readers, and structures his argument so that they will respond in the way he outlines. For example, in 1 Thessalonians 1 – 3 he gives thanks at some length for the faith, hope and love of his converts, and speaks in detail about the affectionate relationship he has with them and the efforts he has made to see them again and supply what is lacking in their faith. When he turns to exhortation in 1 Thessalonians 4 – 5, he blends personal appeal with instruction, warning and encouragement, sometimes picking up the positive things said about the Thessalonians in the earlier chapters and urging them to 'do so more and more' (4:1).

Emotional engagement

As Paul expresses his own wholehearted commitment to Christ and the welfare of his converts, he often urges them to respond with affection, zeal, fervency, joy, compassion and care. Consider the practical implications of these injunctions in Romans 12:

> Love one another with brotherly affection. Outdo one another in showing honour. Do not be slothful in zeal, be fervent in spirit, serve the Lord. Rejoice in hope, be patient in tribulation, be constant in prayer. Contribute to the needs of the saints and seek to show hospitality.
>
> Bless those who persecute you; bless and do not curse them. Rejoice with those who rejoice, weep with those who weep. (Rom. 12:10–15)

Several of these imperatives have an emotional dimension. Most could be applied to times of congregational ministry, as well as to everyday encounters with other believers.

The command to 'love one another with brotherly affection' reflects 'the early Christian understanding of the church as an extended family, whose members, bound together in intimate fellow-ship, should exhibit toward one another a heartfelt and consistent concern'.[7] Meeting together provides particular opportunities for expressing such love in practical ways.

Instead of flagging in zeal, Christians are to be 'fervent in spirit'. The verb *zeōn* means 'boiling' or 'burning' and was used figuratively with reference to emotions and desires.[8] Although the apostle could be urging Christians to maintain a strong emotional commitment to the Lord in their own spirits (cf. Acts 18:25), *tō pneumati* should probably be taken instrumentally in Romans 12:11 to give the meaning 'be set on fire by the Spirit'.[9]

The following expression is 'serving the Lord' (Gk. *tō kyriō douleuontes*), recalling the challenge of 12:1 about presenting ourselves to God as 'a living sacrifice', which is your 'understanding worship' (Gk. *tēn logikēn latreian*).[10] The Spirit of God makes such service possible as he influences and moves our spirits (cf. Rom. 8:9–10, 12–16).

A link could be made with the warning in 1 Thessalonians 5:19 not to 'quench the Spirit'. This is followed by the exhortation not to 'despise prophecies, but test everything' and 'hold fast what is good' (5:20–21). Spirit-directed congregational prophecy or preaching will be one of the ways that believers are stirred or 'set on fire' to serve the Lord.[11] But the Spirit may also minister to us as

---

7. D. J. Moo, *The Epistle to the Romans*, NICNT (Grand Rapids: Eerdmans, 1996), p. 777. The terms are *philadelphia* (brotherly love) and *philostorgoi* (loving dearly).

8. BAGD, p. 338.

9. Moo, *Romans*, p. 778. Moo goes on to say that this means being directed by 'the enthusiasm of humble service of the Master who bought us'. Cf. G. D. Fee, *God's Empowering Presence: The Holy Spirit in the Letters of Paul* (Peabody, Mass.: Hendrickson, 1994), pp. 611–612.

10. Cf. Peterson, *Engaging with God*, pp. 174–176, for an argument in favour of this translation.

11. For a discussion about what such prophesying in 1 Corinthians means, see D. G. Peterson, '"Enriched in Every Way": Gifts and Ministries in 1 Corinthians', in B. S. Rosner (ed.), *The Wisdom of the Cross: Exploring 1 Corinthians* (Nottingham: Apollos, 2011), pp. 134–163.

we sing together (Eph. 5:18–19) or pray together (1 Cor. 14:15; Eph. 6:18).

A simple pair of exhortations in Romans 12:15 covers the highs and lows of daily existence: 'Rejoice with those who rejoice, weep with those who weep' (cf. 1 Cor. 12:26). Here the apostle draws out the practical implications of loving one another 'with brotherly affection'. We are encouraged to be empathetic, acknowledging what others are going through and seeking to identify with them in those experiences. As Douglas Moo rightly observes:

> Love that is genuine will not respond to a fellow believer's joy with envy or bitterness, but will enter wholeheartedly into that same joy. Similarly, love that is genuine will bring us to identify so intimately with our brothers and sisters in Christ that their sorrows will become ours.[12]

It is worth asking whether our congregational life makes it difficult for us to follow these apostolic injunctions. How well do people in our church know one another and how much do they care for one another? Is our ecclesial culture so intellectualized that we seek to avoid displays of emotion in church? Does our style of gathering have space for testimony, mutual exhortation, the sharing of personal grief or joy? How pastorally relevant is our preaching? To what extent do our prayers relate to the real-life struggles of those who gather?

Unavoidable public grief or joy

There are times in the life of a congregation when it is almost impossible to avoid some public expression of grief or joy. Announcement of accidents, sickness or the death of a much-loved congregational member may cause such grief. Care must be taken about the way these things are made known and opportunity should be provided for people to grasp the bad news and pray about it together.

---

12. Moo, *Romans*, p. 782. Although Rom. 12:14 clearly talks about attitudes towards unbelieving outsiders, Moo rightly argues that Paul returns to relationships amongst Christians in 12:15.

My most memorable experience of this was having to announce to a chapel full of theological students that one of their number had died suddenly the night before. We made sure that faculty and student leaders were informed beforehand, so that they would be ready to comfort and pray with those who were suddenly confronted with the shocking news. The service was radically changed at the last minute to account for this announcement and people were encouraged to stay behind at the end to pray together in small groups or one to one.

A congregational funeral or memorial service may be an expression of shared grief or a time of rejoicing and giving thanks together. Much depends on the circumstances of the person's death and the sort of relationship that members of the congregation had with the deceased. Leading such events in an appropriate manner can be difficult, because it is easy for a minister to be overwhelmed by strong emotions when they are being expressed by others. There is nothing wrong with leaders being emotional in public, though there can come a point when this is difficult for the majority to handle.

One such event in my experience was a farewell sermon preached by someone who wept almost continuously during the delivery, for 20 minutes or more. At first, it was very touching and others were moved to tears. After a while, it became awkward because most had adequately expressed their grief and the preacher had not. The message was hard to understand and probably did not make the desired impact because the congregation became too worried about the minister and how he was coping with the grief of leaving.

Public joy and excitement may be expressed with the announcement of births, engagements, special birthdays or the appointment of a new minister for the congregation. A testimony about someone's conversion or experience of answered prayer may bring unexpected tears of joy.

Planned public grief or joy

Is it legitimate to move people to express grief or joy? Is it manipulative? Is it necessary? What about sermons or entire services

designed to move people to repentance? Paul talks about a godly
grief that leads to repentance:

> For even if I made you grieve with my letter, I do not regret it – though
> I did regret it, for I see that that letter grieved you, though only for a
> while. As it is, I rejoice, not because you were grieved, but because you
> were grieved into repenting. For you felt a godly grief, so that you
> suffered no loss through us. For godly grief produces a repentance that
> leads to salvation without regret, whereas worldly grief produces death.
> (2 Cor. 7:8–10)

Worldly grief will not bring about a change of behaviour, but godly
grief leads to repentance and salvation (cf. Pss 34:18; 51:17).[13] Even
godly grief may last only a short time, because it is not an end in
itself. A sermon or letter designed to move people to repentance
may stimulate various expressions of grief in a congregation. Some
will be more overt than others in grieving over sin, but the critical
issue is practical repentance.

Sermons and services may also seek to move people to anger
concerning some injustice and promote a godly desire to set things
right. Other occasions may be designed to elicit joy in God and in
his salvation. Christmas and Easter services may be particular
examples of this. Paul's exhortation to 'rejoice in hope' (Rom. 12:12)
is a reminder that gospel promises are the basis for such rejoicing,
not the enthusiastic pleading of ministers or musicians for people
to 'get happy'!

Paul's teaching about joy and rejoicing in the Lord shows that
Christian joy is more than a mood or an emotion. Surveying everything that the apostle says about this in Philippians, Peter O'Brien
concludes:

> Joy is an understanding of existence that encompasses both elation and
> depression, that can accept with creative submission events which bring

---

13. P. Barnett, *The Second Epistle to the Corinthians*, NICNT (Grand Rapids:
    Eerdmans, 1997), p. 374, defines 'godly' grief (*kata theon*) as 'God
    intended' or 'godlike' grief.

delight or dismay because joy allows one to see beyond any particular event to the sovereign Lord who stands above all events and ultimately has control over them.[14]

Nevertheless, it would be strange if Christian joy had no emotional expression, given the fact that we are emotional beings and God's command is to love him 'with all your heart and with all your soul and with all your might' (Deut. 6:5).

Words and music

Robert Smith addresses the subject of music and the emotions in chapter 10 and so I don't want to steal his thunder. But this quote from contemporary musician and pastor Bob Kauflin makes an important point:

> Some Christians repress their emotions as they sing. They fear feeling everything too strongly and think maturity means holding back. But the problem is *emotionalism*, not *emotions*. Emotionalism pursues feelings as an end in themselves. It's wanting to feel something with no regard for how that feeling is produced or its ultimate purpose. Emotionalism can also view heightened emotions as the infallible sign that God is present. In contrast, the emotions that singing is meant to invoke are a response to who God is and what he's done. Vibrant singing enables us to combine truth *about* God seamlessly with passion *for* God.[15]

The distinction between emotions and emotionalism is helpful. Biblical teaching would suggest that emotion is an important aspect of our personalities and therefore part of our response to God. However, emotions give no clear indication of the genuineness of the heart's commitment or of the Holy Spirit's power and presence. Our physiological and psychological individuality will mean that

---

14. P. T. O'Brien, *Philippians*, WBC 43 (Waco: Word, 1983), p. 18.
15. B. Kauflin, *Worship Matters: Leading Others to Encounter the Greatness of God* (Wheaton: Crossway, 2008), p. 99, emphases original.

emotions are excited and expressed differently, even when confronted by the same stimuli in a given context. Emotionalism, as defined by Kauflin, clearly goes beyond biblical teaching by making the pursuit of feelings an end in itself and by identifying heightened emotions with the presence of God.

Most of us from a conservative evangelical background would be fearful of encouraging emotionalism and steer away from anything that could potentially lead people in that direction. But do we overcorrect to the point that our services in general and our singing in particular are fairly lifeless and uninspiring? I suggest that the problem is not simply the music but the words we say or sing, the way we pray and give thanks, the way we preach and the way we lead services.

In 1746 Jonathan Edwards wrote about words and music in this way:

> The duty of singing praises to God seems to be appointed wholly to excite and express religious affections. No other reason can be assigned why we should express ourselves to God in verse, rather than in prose, and do it with music but only, that such is our nature and frame, that these things have a tendency to move our affections.[16]

It is important to notice that Edwards stressed the value of poetry or verse as well as music in moving our affections. Only words can teach biblical truth to us, and only God's words reflected back to him in prayer, praise and thanksgiving can adequately express what needs to be said or sung to him. Text without music does not necessarily have less emotional significance, despite what our culture says.

Expressing biblical truth together

In this volume Peter Bolt draws attention to the way narrative works powerfully on us because of its ability to engage the

---

16. J. Edwards, *A Treatise Concerning Religious Affections in Three Parts* (Edinburgh: Banner of Truth, 1961), pt. 1, §2, p. 9.

emotions.[17] I have already drawn attention to the way the epistle writers appeal to the whole person in the way they present their arguments. Consider also the way that biblical poetry affects us.

There is emotive power in the praises, laments and prayers of the Bible, such as the Song of Moses in Exodus 15 celebrating the exodus deliverance and God's relationship with his people, David's lament over Saul and Jonathan in 2 Samuel 1, and Daniel's prayer of confession in Daniel 9. There are New Testament models in Luke 1 – 2 and in the Revelation to John. These are vigorous, searching, convicting and compelling texts. How well do the words of contemporary Christian songs compare with these biblical examples? To what extent do our corporate prayers employ such powerful language?

An extensive range of real-life situations is addressed in the Psalms with various expressions of emotion. Why do many churches today read psalms only as lessons for instruction and not recite them or express their content together as prayer, praise or lament? Why can't we use the words God has given us to address him any longer? It may be necessary to use only selected portions of psalms with congregations unfamiliar with their content. Some explanation of context and meaning may also help people to use them more effectively. But why abandon the practice completely?

We are impoverished in our gatherings when we rely so much on the words of contemporary songs to teach us biblical truth and to express faith, hope, love and repentance to God. Singing has almost completely replaced the reciting of biblical texts together, rejecting a practice that has been at the heart of Christian gatherings from the earliest times.

As well as providing for the reciting of biblical texts, our Reformation liturgies were deeply infused with biblical language, in content and in style. For example, compare the wording of this familiar prayer from *The Book of Common Prayer* (1662) with Daniel's confession in Daniel 9:

---

17. He notes that the emotionally challenged will have more trouble perceiving the emotional dimensions of a text. Preachers need to model how to perceive those dimensions and emotionally engage the congregation for the maximum impact and learning.

Almighty and most merciful Father, we have erred and strayed from thy
ways like lost sheep. We have followed too much the devices and desires
of our own hearts. We have offended against thy holy laws. We have left
undone those things which we ought to have done, and we have done
those things which we ought not to have done, and there is no health in
us. But thou, O Lord, have mercy upon us, miserable offenders. Spare
thou them, O God, which confess their faults. Restore thou them that are
penitent, according to thy promises declared unto mankind in Christ Jesu
our Lord. And grant, O most merciful Father, for his sake, that we may
hereafter live a godly, righteous, and sober life, to the glory of thy holy
name. Amen.

Note the powerful effect of words coupled together ('Almighty and
most merciful', 'erred and strayed', 'devices and desires'). Note the
variety of ways in which sin is expressed and the need for God's
deliverance is articulated. Observe that the length of the prayer gives
you time to consider carefully what you are doing and to be impacted
by the language to the point where you feel you want to repent and
seek God's mercy again.

Many contemporary churches seem to have given up confessing
sins together and being assured of God's forgiveness. Objections
to the practice are sometimes voiced in terms of a supposed conflict
with the doctrine of justification by faith, without considering the
meaning of passages such as Hebrews 4:14–16 or 1 John 1:8–10.
Even when prayers of confession are included in services, they are
often short and lack the power of biblical confessions and traditional
liturgies to move the heart and convict people of the need to do
business with God.

However, what might be called 'gospel-inspired praying' involves
more than confessing our sins together and being assured of God's
forgiveness. It involves praying for a greater impact of the gospel
on our own lives, as Paul does for his converts in many of his letters
(e.g. Eph. 1:15–22; 3:14–19; Phil. 1:3–11; Col. 1:3–14). The apostle
asks for a deeper knowledge of God's will, wisdom for fruitful living,
greater certainty about the hope to which God has called us, and a
profound experience of God's love and power.

The *affective* dimension of such requests can be seen when Paul
prays that his Christian brothers and sisters might be 'rooted and

grounded in love', that they might 'know the love of Christ that surpasses knowledge', and that their love might abound 'more and more with knowledge and discernment'.[18] Many of the collects in *The Book of Common Prayer* reflect such concerns.

Puritan prayers from the sixteenth and seventeenth centuries pick up many biblical themes and express a longing for godliness in a way that is very moving. Some of the language may be strange to us, but the desires should be those of every genuine believer. Powerful words are used, with some repetition and parallelism, to move us to share the sentiments and say a vigorous 'Amen'. Here is one example:

> O Lord God, thou art our Preserver, Governor, Saviour, and coming Judge. Quieten our souls to call upon thy name; detach us from the influence of the flesh and the sense; impress us with the power of faith; promote in us spirituality of mind that will render our services acceptable to thee, and delightful and profitable to ourselves. Bring us into that state which attracts thine eye, and prepare us to receive the proofs of thy love. Show us our danger, that we may fly to thee for refuge. Make us sensible of our sin's disease, that we may value the good Physician. Placard to us the cross, that it may slay the enmity of our hearts. Help us to be watchful over our ways, jealous over our tempers, diligent over our hearts. When we droop, revive us. When we loiter, quicken us. When we go astray, restore us. Possess us with more of that faith which is the principle of all vital godliness. May we be rich in faith, be strong in faith, live by faith, walk by faith, experience the joy of faith, do the work of faith, hope through faith. Perceiving nothing in ourselves, may we find in the Saviour wisdom, righteousness, sanctification, redemption.[19]

Gospel-inspired praying also asks God to open doors for the gospel and give his servants boldness to proclaim it (Eph. 6:19–20;

---

18. D. A. Carson, *A Call to Spiritual Reformation: Priorities from Paul and his Prayers* (Grand Rapids: Baker; Leicester: Inter-Varsity Press, 1992), examines prayer passages and themes in detail and applies them to contemporary Christian life.

19. A. Bennett, *The Valley of Vision: A Collection of Puritan Prayers and Devotions* (Edinburgh: Banner of Truth, 1975), pp. 396–397.

Col. 4:3–4). Gospel-inspired praying asks for gospel workers to be delivered from opposition and danger (Rom. 15:30–32; 2 Thess. 3:1–2) and to have opportunities to strengthen new converts (Rom. 1:9–13; 1 Thess. 3:10). There is a passion in Paul's prayers and a kingdom focus that is not often heard in the intercessions I experience in church.

We live in a very prosaic culture, where speech has to be plain, matter of fact, mostly lacking feeling or imagination. Poetry is shunned and rhetoric is regarded as artificial and theatrical. We have largely capitulated to this culture, abandoning biblical patterns of prayer and biblical language in a desire to be relevant. As well as losing biblical *content* from our services, we have lost the animation and persuasive power of much biblical *speech*. Public prayer is so often bland and predictable, relying too much on the *ex tempore* capabilities of those rostered to lead in prayer each week.

Many churches seem to think that songs will do the work that biblical words were designed to do. But Harold Best provides this salutary challenge:

> In a culture of addiction (and music can be a form of addiction), we must dissociate ourselves from music as the primary social glue in the secular world and spiritual glue in the ecclesiastical world. We must realize that, if we are to be a biblical church, not simply a culturally relevant church, we must discount such heavy dependence on our limited and provincialized inventory of works and get down to the business of depending on the power of the Word and the force of the unleashed gospel. We must look to the Spirit, not to our humanly contrived proxies, as the only Paraclete.[20]

Experiencing God's Spirit together

In Romans 5:5 Paul proclaims that 'God's love has been poured into our hearts through the Holy Spirit who has been given to us.' 'Poured out' suggests a generous abundance. Sometimes, this verb

---

20. H. M. Best, *Unceasing Worship: Biblical Perspectives on Worship and the Arts* (Downers Grove: InterVarsity Press, 2003), p. 151. For many years Best was the dean of the Conservatory of Music at Wheaton College.

is used with reference to the Spirit (Acts 2:17–18; 2:33; 10:45; Titus 3:6), but the subject here is 'God's love' and the Spirit is the agent (Gk. *dia pneumatos hagiou*). Since 5:6–11 goes on to explain how God has shown his love for us *historically* in the death of his Son, 5:5 must mean that this objective reality is 'actually brought home to our hearts (so that we have recognised it and rejoice in it) by the Holy Spirit who has been given to us'.[21]

The Holy Spirit makes possible an experience of God's love that changes hearts and lives, sustaining hope in the midst of sufferings. Since the heart in Paul's thought embraces mind, will and emotions,[22] the implication is that the Spirit works in each area of our personalities. Most commentators rightly take 'the love of God' to refer to God's love for us, but it is also true that God's love moves us to love him in return, and love for others is kindled by love for God (cf. 1 John 4:19–21).

This vivid, experiential description of the Holy Spirit's work suggests the fulfilment of Deuteronomy 30:6. God circumcises the heart of his people so that they can love him with all their heart and soul, and love their neighbours as themselves. Elsewhere, Paul makes it clear that love for others is a fruit of the Spirit's presence in our lives (Gal. 5:22).

Romans 5:6 clearly applies to the Spirit's work in conversion, enabling us to believe the gospel and experience personally the love of God shown in the death of Jesus for us 'while we were still weak'. May it not also be true that the Spirit helps us to rejoice in God's love and be moved by it afresh every time we are confronted by gospel truths in reading, sermon, testimony, prayer and praise?

Paul's teaching in 1 Corinthians 12 – 14 is that the Holy Spirit provides gifts and ministries 'for the common good' (12:7). When these gifts and ministries are exercised in love, the church is built up

---

21. C. E. B. Cranfield, *A Critical and Exegetical Commentary on the Epistle to the Romans*, 2 vols., ICC (Edinburgh: T. & T. Clark, 1975), vol. 1, p. 263. The passive implies that God the Father has poured out his love through the ministry of his Spirit.

22. Cf. J. D. G. Dunn, *The Theology of Paul the Apostle* (Edinburgh: T. & T. Clark, 1998), pp. 73–75.

and matured. Even visiting unbelievers may be convicted of sin and converted by experiencing congregational prophecy (14:23–25). So the general sense of these chapters is that God continues to meet with us and change us through Spirit-directed ministries in the body of Christ. In this way he continues to deal with us individually and corporately.

The Spirit is given 'that we might understand the things freely given us by God' (1 Cor. 2:12; cf. Eph. 1:17; Phil. 3:15). We can engage in ministry to one another with 'words not taught by human wisdom but taught by the Spirit, interpreting spiritual truths to those who are spiritual' (2:13). However, the Spirit's ministry to the heart is not simply intellectual, but influences the whole personality, mind, will and emotion. We may enjoy this influence on ourselves as we take time to read the Scriptures and pray privately, but the New Testament suggests that there is a greater potential for being impacted by the Spirit when gathered with other believers to give and receive in ministry.

Conclusion

A faithful application of the Scriptures in congregational gatherings, through teaching, singing, praying and other ministries, will continue to move our hearts in love towards God and towards one another. The Holy Spirit works in us individually and corporately through such ministries to continue God's transforming work. God engages with us in a personal way through his Spirit, influencing mind, will and emotion.

Expressions of emotion vary according to personality and context. Emotional intensity is not necessarily a sign of the Spirit's presence or of greater spiritual commitment. Renewed minds will discern 'what is the will of God, what is good and acceptable and perfect' (Rom. 12:2) and seek to do God's will in every area of life (12:3–21). But generosity, zeal, cheerfulness, brotherly affection, fervency, rejoicing and weeping are just some of the words used in connection with the will of God for us. These suggest the need for a whole-hearted engagement with God and with one another, involving our emotions.

The Christian gathering should be the place where believers are provoked and stirred to respond in this way, and where practical opportunities are provided for expressing godly affections. Although we should avoid manipulating emotions, worship without emotion, either corporately or individually, is likely to be mechanical and sterile, not the offering of our whole selves to God in Christ that the New Testament enjoins.

11. MUSIC, SINGING AND THE EMOTIONS: EXPLORING THE CONNECTIONS

Robert S. Smith

Introduction

Music, singing and emotions: what are the connections? The question is by no means new, but it's certainly one that has received renewed attention in recent times. Of particular interest is the power of music to foster emotional health and psychosocial well-being. For example, in his *Musicophilia: Tales of Music and the Brain*, neurologist Oliver Sacks not only explores the pathologies of musical response from a clinical point of view, but also provides a deeply personal and moving account of the role music played in lifting him out of depression after the death of his mother. Sacks writes:

> For weeks I would get up, dress, drive to work, see my patients, try to
> present a normal appearance. But inside I was dead, as lifeless as a
> zombie. Then one day as I was walking down Bronx Park East, I felt
> a sudden lightening, a quickening of mood, a sudden whisper or
> intimation of life, of joy. Only then did I realize that I was hearing music,
> though so faintly it might have been no more than an image or memory.
> As I continued to walk, the music grew louder, until finally I came to its

source, a radio pouring Schubert out of an open basement window. The
music pierced me, releasing a cascade of images and feelings – memories
of childhood, of summer holidays together and of my mother's
fondness for Schubert . . . I found myself not only smiling for the first
time in weeks, but laughing aloud – and alive once again.[1]

The fact that music and singing have a profound ability both to
impact and express human emotions will not come as a surprise
to many. Common experience confirms the connection, as does the
biblical witness. 'Is anyone cheerful?', writes James. 'Let him sing
songs of praise' (Jas 5:13).[2]

However, when one starts to probe into the precise connections
between music, singing and the emotions and asks a seemingly
innocent question such as, How can a piece of music be both expressive of emotion and also generate emotion in human beings?, we
suddenly find we have entered a realm where a number of distinct
disciplines intersect. For example, musicology, psychology, neurology,
biology, anthropology, philosophy and theology all have an interest
in such questions and (on their better days) provide complementary
accounts and partial answers. But (on their worse days) they provide
competing accounts that simply increase the level of crosstalk and
confusion.

So how should we proceed in trying to understand the connections
between music, singing and emotion? My approach in this chapter is
threefold. First, I wish to offer some reflections on the world that
God has made, drawing on some of the less controversial findings
of various musicological, psychological and neurobiological studies.
Secondly, I shall offer some reflections on the word that God has
spoken, exploring some of the links we find between music, singing
and emotions in the Old and New Testaments. Thirdly, I want to
offer some reflections on the history of Christian thought, drawing
on the insights of a number of theologians who have wrestled with
these matters – despite coming to differing conclusions.

---

1. O. Sacks, *Musicophilia: Tales of Music and the Brain* (London: Picador,
   2007), p. 298.
2. Unless stated otherwise, Bible quotations in this chapter are from the ESV.

Definitions

But before going further, I need to define how I am using the three terms 'music', 'singing' and 'emotion'.

Music

Music can be variously defined from a range of different perspectives. For example, it can be defined *phenomenologically*; that is, in terms of its being an organized arrangement of sounds and silences. Or it can be defined *functionally*; that is, in terms of its being a communicative activity that conveys moods to the listener. Or it can be defined *culturally*; that is, by taking account of the fact that the line between what is regarded as music and what is regarded as noise changes over time and varies from culture to culture. Without disputing the value of any and all of these definitions, in this chapter I am simply using it to refer to music that has no lyrical content; that is, by 'music' I mean 'instrumental music'.

Singing

My definition of singing follows from this. By 'singing' I mean more than the activity of making musical sounds with the human voice. That is an entirely legitimate activity and a valid way of defining 'singing'. It is not, however, how I am using the term. By singing I mean the musical communication of words that have meaning at least to the person singing them, if not to the person or persons hearing them as well. It is in that sense that I am distinguishing music from song.

Emotion

Here again there are many possible definitions (depending on whether one thinks of emotions as primarily cognitive or primarily non-cognitive or as some combination of the two).[3] I am using the word in a fairly unsophisticated way to cover a broad range of perceptions, expressions of feeling (such as joy or grief) and the related

---

3. For a useful and informed discussion of the debate between cognitive and non-cognitive theories of emotion, see M. Elliott, *Faithful Feelings: Emotion in the New Testament* (Leicester: Inter-Varsity Press, 2005), pp. 18–42.

bodily changes that normally accompany such feelings (like smiling or crying). The question I am pursuing, then, may be expressed thus: How do music and song influence and express such perceptions and reactions?

Limitations

Before we turn to the first part of our study, let me briefly mention some of things this chapter will not attempt do. First, I shall not attempt to identify (let alone discuss) the many functions of music and singing in general human experience – such as their ability to help us remember events and words – or the many purposes music and singing serve in the gatherings of God's people – such as their ability to unite people and express fellowship. Secondly, I shall not attempt to provide a survey of everything the Bible has to say about music and singing – as valuable as that would be.[4] Thirdly, I shall make no reference to the many different types of music and song that have arisen and been utilized in church history, nor make any assessment of which types of music or styles of singing are best suited to Christian use.[5]

Soundings from the world that God has made

With these things understood, let us embark on an exercise in sanctified natural theology (or, more accurately, natural anthropology) to see what we can learn from the world that God has made.

Music and emotions

How do we begin to account for the fact that music can both express and arouse emotion? Stephen Davies, a philosopher at the University

---

4. For those interested, a detailed survey can be found in D. A. Foxvog and A. D. Kilmer, 'Music', in *ISBE* 3, pp. 436–449.

5. To my mind, the most accessible treatment of the history of Christian music can be found in A. Wilson-Dickson, *The Story of Christian Music: From Gregorian Chant to Black Gospel, an Authoritative Illustrated Guide to All the Major Traditions of Music for Worship* (Oxford: Lion, 1992).

of Auckland with an interest in the aesthetics of art, suggests that the connection lies in what he calls 'Appearance emotionalism'.[6] That is, music appears to be sad (for example) in the same way a weeping willow looks sad. Because the tree is bent over, it appears to resemble a person racked with grief. Davies puts it like this: 'The resemblance that counts most for music's expressiveness . . . is between music's temporally unfolding dynamic structure and configurations of human behaviour associated with the expression of emotion.'[7]

So, to continue the example above, music can recall an appearance of sadness by a gradual downward movement, or by utilizing underlying patterns of unresolved tension, or by employing dark timbres, or thick harmonic bass textures.[8] Clearly, Davies is onto something here. Indeed, it is well known that minor keys and slow tempos tend to express and evoke sadness, just as major keys and fast tempos tend to express and evoke happiness. However, I have deliberately said 'tend to' because the 'expressiveness' of a piece of music is largely 'response dependent' – that is, it is realized in the listener's response. And not all listeners have the same response. For perceptions of similarity are not always shared. One person may see them and so be deeply moved by a piece of music, while another may miss them altogether and be quite unaffected.

Nevertheless, the fact that many listeners have a similar response to the same piece of music, suggests that there must be some objective component to its emotional expressiveness, even though the same emotions are not always subjectively experienced by all listeners in the same way. The reason for the variation is simple: not only is each listener unique, but music is never heard in a vacuum. Jeremy Begbie from Duke Divinity School (who, as well as being a systematic theologian, is a trained musician with a particular interest in the interface between theology and the arts) explains why:

---

6. S. Davies, 'Artistic Expression and the Hard Case of Pure Music', in M. Kieren (ed.), *Contemporary Debates in Aesthetics and the Philosophy of Art* (Oxford: Blackwell, 2006), pp. 179–191.

7. Ibid., p. 181.

8. Ibid., p. 182.

music is never heard on its own but as part of a perceptual complex that includes a range of non-musical phenomena: for example, the physical setting in which we hear the music, memories of people associated with it, artificial images (as in the case of film and video), words (the lyrics of a song, program notes, the title of a piece, what someone said about the piece on the radio), and so on . . . Music is perceived in a manifold environment. And this generates a fund of material for us to be emotional 'about'.[9]

But alongside these associations, there is now a growing body of literature stemming from a range of neurobiological studies showing how emotional responses to music have a direct effect on our hormone levels. For example, some music can increase levels of melatonin (which can help to induce sleep) and likewise decrease levels of cortisol (the hormone associated with stress).[10]

In addition to this, a number of neuroimaging studies have mapped the effects of music on the paralimbic regions of the brain, regions that are associated with our capacity to process and express emotion. As these regions are stimulated by music, the net effect is a highly therapeutic one for both mind and body. Dr Randall McClellan explains why:

Emotions that are not expressed when they are felt may be turned inward where they can add stress to weakened parts of the body. When the stress is prolonged our natural ability to resist disease is impaired and illness may ensue . . . When used regularly, music is an effective vehicle for the dissipation of normal day-to-day emotional stress. But in times of intense emotional crisis, music can focus and guide emotional release by bringing the emotion to catharsis and providing it with the means of expression.[11]

---

9. J. S. Begbie, 'Faithful Feelings', in J. S. Begbie and S. R. Guthrie (eds.), *Resonant Witness: Conversations Between Music and Theology* (Grand Rapids: Eerdmans, 2011), p. 339.

10. L. Heslet, 'Our Musical Brain', p. 5, available online at <http://www.saludart.com/sys/upload/Heslet.pdf>, accessed 12 Sept. 2011.

11. R. McClellan, *The Healing Forces of Music: History, Theory, and Practice* (Lincoln, Nebr.: iUniverse.com, 2000), p. 146.

Singing and emotions

So clearly there is much to be said for the healing effects of music. But what happens when we bring the human voice into the picture? How does singing both express and evoke emotion? Here again theories abound, and various insights can be gleaned from a number of disciplines.

What is incontrovertible is that voice is 'an essential aspect of human identity: of who we are, how we feel, how we communicate, and how other people experience us'.[12] It is also clear that the human voice has the capacity to convey emotion in a range of different ways – through changes in pitch, contour, volume, and so on. It is also significant that the six primary human emotions – fear, anger, joy, sadness, surprise and disgust – are all usually expressed vocally,[13] and are likewise differentiated by strong vocal acoustic variation.[14] As Dr Graham Welch from the University of London puts it, 'Each of these basic emotions has a characteristic vocal acoustic signature and an acoustic profile that is associated with a strong characteristic emotional state.'[15] In other words, even if we do not understand the words someone is saying or singing, it is usually fairly obvious what emotion is being conveyed.

Added to all this, and this is the main point I want to highlight, is the fact that when we sing, we usually sing words with meanings, and those words not only facilitate the communication of the *cognitive content* of the song, but the singing of them helps communicate the *emotional content* of the song as well. More than that, the fact that we are singing these words (or hearing them sung) also helps us to feel an emotion appropriate to the words we are singing (or hearing).

12. G. F. Welch, 'Singing as Communication', in D. Miell, R. A. R. MacDonald and D. J. Hargreaves (eds.), *Musical Communication* (Oxford: Oxford University Press, 2005), p. 245.

13. I. Titze, *Principles of Voice Production* (Englewood Cliffs: Prentice-Hall, 1994).

14. K. R. Scherer, 'Expression of Emotion in Voice and Music', *Journal of Voice* 9.3 (1995), pp. 235–248.

15. G. F. Welch, 'Singing as Communication', p. 247.

This truth was captured beautifully and succinctly by the late Yip Harburg – the man who wrote the lyrics for all the songs in *The Wizard of Oz*, including the hauntingly evocative classic 'Over the Rainbow'. What Harburg famously said was this: 'Words make you think a thought; music makes you feel a feeling; a song makes you feel a thought.' The physiological reality behind this observation, as a number of neuroimaging studies have now shown, is that whilst the majority of sensorimotor processes for singing and speaking are the same, singing engages parts of our brain (particularly in the right hemisphere) that speaking alone does not.[16] This is why singing is a unique activity not only for expressing and conveying emotion, but also for processing the emotional dimensions of cognitive thought.

It is not surprising, then, that people who have experienced great trauma can sometimes find it very difficult to sing – for singing threatens to awaken their emotional processes, which they have deliberately shut down in order to protect themselves from the full horror of what they have experienced. But it is also why singing can function as a very effective means of gently releasing suppressed emotions and of helping people to process the truth and reality behind their inner pain.

My positive point here, however, is simply that *singing* not only helps us to engage the emotional dimensions of our humanity, but that singing *truth* helps us to engage with the emotional dimensions of reality, thus helping to bridge the gap between cognitive knowledge and experiential knowledge. This is a point we shall return to below.

Soundings from the word that God has spoken

Moving now from the world that God has made (and what can be observed by various natural anthropological means), we turn to the word that God has spoken. What can we learn from God's special revelation in Scripture about the connections between music, singing

---

16. E. Özdemir, A. Norton and G. Schlaug, 'Shared and Distinct Neural Correlates of Singing and Speaking', *Neuroimage* 33 (2006), p. 633.

and our emotions? We begin with some soundings from the Old
Testament.

The Old Testament

The first thing the Old Testament reveals is a profound link between
the joy that results from experiencing God's salvation and the making
of music and the singing of songs. We see this first in Exodus 15
where, after the Lord has rescued the people of Israel from the
Egyptian army, Miriam takes a tambourine in hand (v. 20) and as all
the women follow her with tambourines and dancing, she sings to
them, saying:

> Sing to the Lord, for he has triumphed gloriously;
> the horse and his rider he has thrown into the sea.
> (Exod. 15:21b)

And so the beginning of the chapter tells us that Moses and the
people of Israel followed suit, singing to the Lord, saying:

> I will sing to the Lord, for he has triumphed gloriously;
>   the horse and his rider he has thrown into the sea.
> The Lord is my strength and my song,
>   and he has become my salvation;
> this is my God, and I will praise him,
>   my father's God, and I will exalt him.
> (Exod. 15:1b–2)

As John Durham points out, this celebration of 'Yahweh present
with his people and doing *for* them as no other god anywhere and
at any time *can* be present to do . . . is a kind of summary of the
theological base of the whole Book of Exodus.'[17] For that reason,
'it is more than merely a hymn of Yahweh's victory over Pharaoh
and his Egyptians in the sea'.[18] Indeed, its primary focus is on

---

17. John I. Durham, *Exodus*, WBC 3 (Waco: Word, 1987), p. 210, emphases
    original.
18. Ibid., p. 210.

the kind of God the Lord is, and the kinds of things he does, and the kind of response this creates. In that sense it is paradigmatic. Not surprisingly, then, other Scriptures pick up these very same themes and forge the same connections – most notably Isaiah 12:

> You will say in that day:
> 'I will give thanks to you, O Lord,
>   for though you were angry with me,
> your anger turned away,
>   that you might comfort me.
> Behold, God is my salvation;
>   I will trust, and will not be afraid;
> for the Lord God is my strength and my song,
>   and he has become my salvation.'
> With joy you will draw water from the wells of salvation.
> And you will say in that day:
> 'Give thanks to the Lord,
>   call upon his name,
> make known his deeds among the peoples,
>   proclaim that his name is exalted.
> Sing praises to the Lord, for he has done gloriously;
>   let this be made known in all the earth.
> Shout, and sing for joy, O inhabitant of Zion,
>   for great in your midst is the Holy One of Israel.'
> (Isa. 12:1–6)

As Barry Webb points out in his exposition of this chapter, 'The singing in this chapter follows in the same way that the song of Exodus 15 followed the original exodus.'[19] In fact, the words in Isaiah 12:2 – 'for the Lord God is my strength and my song, and he has become my salvation' – are almost an exact quotation of Exodus 15:2. And the beginning of verse 5 – 'Sing praises to the Lord, for he has done gloriously' – clearly echoes Exodus 15:21.

---

19. Barry G. Webb, *The Message of Isaiah* (Leicester: Inter-Varsity Press, 1996), p. 77.

The simple message here is this: *where there is salvation there is joy, and where there is joy there is singing.* They follow one another as night follows day and day follows night. For as people are taken from an experience of slavery to an experience of redemption, from an experience of God's anger to an experience of his comfort, from a place of fear to a place of trust, they have every reason to rejoice. And out of their joy they sing and make music.[20]

Precisely the same connections are seen in the book of Psalms. The opening verses of Psalm 98 are just one of many similar examples:

Oh sing to the LORD a new song,
    for he has done marvellous things!
His right hand and his holy arm
    have worked salvation for him.
The LORD has made known his salvation;
    he has revealed his righteousness in the sight of the nations.
He has remembered his steadfast love and faithfulness
    to the house of Israel.
All the ends of the earth have seen
    the salvation of our God.
Make a joyful noise to the LORD, all the earth;
    break forth into joyous song and sing praises!
Sing praises to the LORD with the lyre,
    with the lyre and the sound of melody!
With trumpets and the sound of the horn
    make a joyful noise before the King, the LORD!
(Ps. 98:1–6)

However, it is not just joy and gladness that can be expressed in music and song, but grief and anguish as well. This is seen particularly in the book of Psalms where almost half of the psalter is made up of psalms that are laments – either in whole or in part. The value

---

20. J. A. Motyer, in his commentary on these verses, helpfully speaks of the phenomenon of song as 'an inner welling up of joy'. See J. A. Motyer, *The Prophecy of Isaiah* (Leicester: Inter-Varsity Press, 1993), p. 129.

of such laments, as Walter Brueggemann points out, is that they are completely honest about the fact that 'our common experience is not one of well-being and equilibrium, but a churning disruptive experience of dislocation and relocation'.[21] And the relevance of these psalms to this study is that they, like the rest of the psalter, were all intended to be sung – either by the congregation or by the Levitical choir.[22]

So, for example, Psalm 5 – which begins, 'Give ear to my words, O LORD; / consider my groaning. / Give attention to the sound of my cry' – is addressed to the Choirmaster and contains the instruction 'For the flutes'. Psalm 6 – which begins, 'O LORD, rebuke me not in your anger, / nor discipline me in your wrath. / Be gracious to me, O LORD, for I am languishing' – is likewise addressed to the choirmaster with an instruction that it be played with stringed instruments. In fact, most of the better-known lament psalms – such as Psalms 13, 22, 42, 51, 69 and 88 – are all addressed 'to the choirmaster'.

However, the members of the temple congregation were far from passive spectators. They were not simply sung to by the choir. As John Kleinig in his study of the place of choral music in Chronicles points out:

> The choir addressed them directly and invited them to join in its praise (1 Chron. 16:8–13). The congregation did so by responding with certain stereotyped words and refrains (1 Chron. 16:36b). It thereby became an active partner in praise.[23]

The obvious point to be made from this is that the people of Israel were encouraged and instructed to sing not only in their times of joy, but also in their times of grief. And the importance of lament (of vocalizing grief in song) is that it helps to facilitate the transition from

21. W. Brueggemann, *Praying the Psalms: Engaging Scripture and the Life of the Spirit*, 2nd ed. (Eugene, Ore.: Wipf & Stock, 2007), p. 7.

22. B. W. Anderson, *Out of the Depths: The Psalms Speak for Us Today* (Philadelphia: Westminster, 1983), p. 32.

23. J. W. Kleinig, *The Lord's Song: The Basis, Function, and Significance of Choral Music in Chronicles* (Sheffield: JSOT Press, 1993), p. 95.

disorientation to reorientation (or 'dislocation' to 'relocation', to use Brueggeman's terms). In other words, lament is productive – or, at least, it ought to be. The purpose of expressing our fears and failures, our darkness and distress, and particularly doing so in song, is to help us process our emotional pain and so bring us to a point of praise. This is clear not only from the shape of numerous individual psalms which begin with lament and end with praise (e.g. Pss 3 – 7), but from the shape of the entire psalter – with the laments dominating the earlier books and the praises dominating more and more in the latter books, particularly in the final five psalms (Pss 146 – 150).[24]

So there is much for us to learn here. Karl Kuhn focuses the chief lesson when he says, 'As paradigms of faith and piety, the Psalms champion the affective dimension of devotion to and trust in God as elicited by the story of God's care for Israel.'[25] And my point is that this 'affective dimension' to authentic faith is, quite intentionally and by divine design, linked to music and song.

The New Testament

When we come to the New Testament, the first thing to note is the emotional dimension of the Spirit's fruit, and the Spirit's role, therefore, in bringing us to emotional maturity. That is, most (if not all) of the aspects of the fruit of the Spirit listed by Paul in Galatians 5, whilst clearly not being exclusively emotional in nature, and profoundly practical and relational in their outworking, none-theless have an irreducible emotional component.[26] Furthermore,

---

24. W. McConnell, 'Worship', in T. Longman III and P. Enns (eds.), *Dictionary of the Old Testament: Wisdom, Poetry and Writings* (Downers Grove: InterVarsity Press, 2008), p. 931.

25. K. A. Kuhn, *The Heart of Biblical Narrative: Rediscovering Biblical Appeal to the Emotions* (Minneapolis: Fortress, 2009), p. 9.

26. R. C. Roberts, *Spirituality and Human Emotions* (Grand Rapids: Eerdmans), 1982, p. 12. Matthew Elliott makes this point strongly in his study of joy in the New Testament. Indeed, he laments the either–or approach of those who see joy as either essentially cognitive or essentially emotional, speaking of its 'essential cognitive emotional nature' (M. Elliott, *Faithful Feelings*, p. 181).

learning to bear such a fruit is part and parcel of the process of being transformed into the likeness of Christ (2 Cor. 3:18) or growing up into Christ (Eph. 4:15). And this clearly involves growing up emotionally as part of the package.[27] Jeremy Begbie puts the point well: 'Through the Spirit, we are given the priceless opportunity of – to put it simply – growing up emotionally: having our emotions purged of sin and stretched, shaped, and reshaped.'[28]

But does this have anything to do with music and song? Begbie certainly thinks so. In fact, he immediately follows the preceding statement with this one: 'It is perhaps in worship and prayer, when we engage with God directly and consciously, that this will be (or ought to be) most evident.'[29] In a more recent chapter he makes his thought even more explicit: 'music is particularly well suited to being a vehicle of emotional renewal in worship, a potent instrument through which the Holy Spirit can begin to remake and transform us in the likeness of Christ, the one true worshipper'.[30]

But the question for many is, Does the New Testament ever make this connection? I believe so. And the place where it does is Ephesians 5:18–21:

> And do not get drunk with wine, for that is debauchery, but be filled with the Spirit, addressing one another in psalms and hymns and spiritual songs, singing and making melody to the Lord with your heart, giving thanks always and for everything to God the Father in the name of our Lord Jesus Christ, submitting to one another out of reverence for Christ. (Eph. 5:18–21)

Now a detailed exegesis of these verses will not be attempted here. For our purposes, the key issue turns on the relationship between

---

27. Begbie, 'Faithful Feelings', p. 353.
28. J. S. Begbie, *Resounding Truth: Christian Wisdom in the World of Music* (London: SPCK, 2008), p. 303.
29. Ibid, p. 303.
30. Begbie, 'Faithful Feelings', p. 353.

the command in verse 18 ('be filled with or by the Spirit')[31] and the
five participles in verses 19–21 ('addressing', 'singing', 'making
melody', 'giving thanks' and 'submitting'). It is commonly argued
that these five participles are best understood as 'result participles'.[32] That is, when a church is filled by the Spirit these will be
the results. This reading is certainly possible, both grammatically
and theologically, and its implication – that singing is one of the
key indicators of a Spirit-filled church – has considerable historical
support.[33]

However, I believe there is a stronger case to be made for understanding the participles of verses 19–21 as 'means participles'; that
is, Paul is here identifying the means by which he expects his readers
to carry out his exhortation to be filled by the Spirit. What I am
suggesting, then, is that, like the commands to 'walk by the Spirit'
(Gal. 5:16) or to 'let the word of Christ dwell in your richly', being
filled by the Spirit is not a matter of 'letting go and letting God', but
(as Eph. 5:17 says) a matter of understanding the will of the Lord

---

31. Paul's language suggests that the Spirit is the *instrument* of filling rather
    than being the *content* of the filling. For the grammatical arguments that
    lead to this conclusion, see H. W. Hoehner, *Ephesians: An Exegetical
    Commentary* (Grand Rapids: Baker, 2002), p. 703; P. T. O'Brien, *The
    Letter to the Ephesians* (Leicester: Apollos, 1999), pp. 391–393.

32. See e.g. the arguments listed by O'Brien, *Ephesians*, p. 387, n. 107.

33. Grammatically, either a 'means' reading or a 'result' reading is
    possible. Interestingly, Daniel Wallace rejects the 'means' reading on
    theological grounds. He believes 'it would be almost inconceivable to
    see this text suggesting that the way in which one is to be Spirit-filled
    is by a five-step, partially mechanical formula!' (D. B. Wallace, *Greek
    Grammar Beyond the Basics* [Grand Rapids: Zondervan, 1996], p. 639).
    However, this is not only a caricature of the 'means' reading (for the
    participles are neither a formula nor are they mechanical) but also
    begs the question as to why such a reading is more inconceivable
    than his own suggestion that the participles provide 'the way in
    which one measures his/her success in fulfilling the command of
    5:18' (p. 639).

and then doing that will.[34] So Paul does not leave his readers to guess
how his command is to be carried out. He spells it out in detail: we
are to address one another in psalms and hymns and spiritual songs,
we are to sing and make melody to the Lord with our hearts,[35] we
are to give thanks always and for everything to God the Father in
the name of our Lord Jesus Christ and we are to submit to one
another out of reverence for Christ. These are the means (according
to this passage at least) by which the Spirit fills the church with the
fullness of God in Christ (Eph. 3:19; 4:13).[36]

So to draw the obvious conclusion, singing and making music
are vital means not only of addressing one another with the word

---

34. Indeed, the means reading of Eph. 5:18–21 is strengthened by a
comparison with Col. 3:16, where singing is clearly the means by which
the word of Christ richly indwells the church (see P. T. O'Brien,
Colossians, Philemon, WBC 44 [Waco: Word, 1982], p. 208). For to be
indwelt by the word of Christ (both personally and corporately) is not
a different experience from being 'filled by the Spirit'; Christ's person is
not separate from his word, nor is he separate from his Spirit. It is by
the Spirit that Christ himself dwells in our hearts through faith (Eph.
3:17). Therefore, as we sing the word of Christ to one another, 'with
thankfulness in our hearts to God', we are not only instructed and
made wise, but we have a greater experience as a community of what it
means to be filled full in Christ, in whom 'the whole fullness of deity
dwells bodily' (Col. 2:9–10).

35. As Andrew Lincoln rightly points out, the 'heart' refers to the believer's
'innermost being . . . where the Spirit himself resides (cf. 3:16, 17,
where the Spirit in the inner person is equivalent to Christ in the heart)'
(A. T. Lincoln, *Ephesians*, WBC 42 [Waco: Word, 1990], p. 346).

36. As Timothy Gombis puts it, 'The church is to be the temple of God,
the fullness of Christ by the Spirit *by* being the community that speaks
God's word to one another, sings praises to the Lord, renders
thanksgiving to God for all things in the name of the Lord Jesus Christ,
and lives in relationships characterized by mutual submission' (T. G.
Gombis, 'Being the Fullness of God in Christ by the Spirit: Ephesians
5:18 in Its Epistolary Setting', *TynB* 53.2 [2002], p. 271, emphasis
original).

of God (thereby edifying the church) and making melody to the Lord (thereby praising our Saviour), but of being filled with or by the Spirit and so growing up into Christ.[37] And that (as I have suggested) includes coming to emotional maturity in Christ. As Jeremy Begbie expresses it, 'To grow up into Christ is to grow up emotionally as much as anything else, and carefully chosen music in worship may have a larger part to play than we have yet imagined.'[38]

Soundings from the history of Christian reflection

We now turn, finally, to take some quick soundings from the history of Christian reflection on these matters.

Cautious concern
First, let me give you two examples of 'great ones' who have expressed a 'cautious concern' about the power of music and song.

Augustine
In his famous *Confessions*, Augustine is not short of things to say about music and singing – and most of it is extremely positive. Indeed, he claims that when sacred words are combined with pleasant music, then 'our souls (*animos*) are moved and are more religiously and with a warmer devotion kindled to piety than if they are not so sung'.[39] In other words, Augustine recognized and appreciated that when our emotions are moved by a song, the effect is not only felt in a warmer heart, but also expressed in an enhanced desire to please God. He continues:

> When I remember the tears which I poured out at the time when I was first recovering my faith, and that now I am moved not by the chant but

---

37. See further, R. Smith, 'Psalms, Hymns and Spiritual Songs: What Are They and Why Sing Them?', *CASE* 23 (2010), pp. 26–29.
38. Begbie, 'Faithful Feelings', p. 353.
39. Augustine, *Confessions*, tr. Henry Chadwick (Oxford: Oxford University Press, 1991), 10.33.49.

by the words being sung, when they are sung with a clear voice and entirely appropriate modulation, then again I recognize the great utility of music in worship.[40]

At the same time Augustine was reluctant to give singing his unqualified blessing. Indeed, he claimed to 'fluctuate between the danger of pleasure and the experience of the beneficent effect' of singing.[41] He was particularly concerned about the danger of being so carried along by the music of the song that he would become impervious to the words being sung. Here is what he says: 'Yet when it happens to me that the music moves me more than the subject of the song, I confess myself to commit a sin deserving of punishment, and then I would prefer not to have heard the singer.'[42]

John Calvin

The same kind of ambivalence appears in John Calvin. On the one hand, Calvin readily acknowledged the value of singing the psalms (and also some of the Bible's other songs), for the reason that they 'stimulate us to raise our hearts to God and arouse us to an ardour in invoking as well as in exalting with praises, the glory of his name'.[43] Indeed, in his 1537 *Articles Concerning the Organisation of the Church* he makes the singing of psalms obligatory![44] On the other hand, he too was qualified in his endorsement of singing. His reason for caution is that 'music has a secret and incredible power to move our hearts. When evil words are accompanied by music, they

────────────────

40. Ibid. 10.33.50.

41. Ibid.

42. Ibid.

43. J. Calvin, *Articles Concerning the Organisation of the Church* (1537), cited in Charles Garside, Jr., 'The Origins of Calvin's Theology of Music: 1536–1543', *Transactions of the American Philosophical Society* 69.4 (1979), p. 10.

44. R. W. Holder, *John Calvin and the Grounding of Interpretation: Calvin's First Commentaries* (Leiden: Brill, 2006), p. 256.

penetrate more deeply and the poison enters as wine through a funnel into a vat'.[45]

Admittedly, Calvin's primary concern here is with 'evil words' – that is, untruth – and so presumably he would not object to hearts being moved by the truth. But even when the words are good we are not out of danger. For, like Augustine, Calvin warns, 'We should be very careful that our ears be not more attentive to the melody than our minds to the spiritual meaning of the words.'[46] For this reason, Calvin also has a concern about the intentions and purposes of both those who write songs and those who choose them, and likewise how and why they are sung. It is this concern that lies behind his comment that the singing of songs is a 'most holy and salutary practice' when it is done properly, but 'such songs as have been composed only for sweetness and delight of the ear are unbecoming to the majesty of the church and cannot but displease God in the highest degree'.[47]

Enthusiastic embrace
Others, however, have been considerably more enthusiastic about the benefits of music and singing, and significantly less nervous about its dangers.

Martin Luther
Luther, an accomplished musician, was a great lover of music. He was also greatly appreciative of music's capacity to produce a variety of emotional dispositions. As he says:

> Next to the Word of God, music deserves the highest praise. She is a mistress and governess of those human emotions . . . which control men or more often overwhelm them . . . Whether you wish to comfort the sad, to subdue frivolity, to encourage the despairing, to humble the

45. Cited in H. R. Van Til, *The Calvinist Concept of Culture* (Phillipsburg: Presbyterian & Reformed, 1972), p. 110.

46. J. Calvin, *Institutes of the Christian Religion*, ed. John T. McNeill, tr. Ford Lewis Battles (Philadelphia: Westminster, 1960), 3.20.32.

47. Calvin, *Institutes* 3.20.32.

proud, to calm the passionate or to appease those full of hate . . . what more effective means than music could you find.[48]

However, it was not music in itself that was Luther's primary interest, but music as a vehicle for praising God and proclaiming his word. In other words, in Luther's estimation singing is 'word ministry', and although not a substitute for the preached word, it is a complement to the preached word and a form of word ministry with added emotional power:

> Music is a vehicle for proclaiming the Word of God . . . [T]he gift of language combined with the gift of song was only given to man to let him know that he should praise God with both word and music, namely, by proclaiming [God's word] through music and by providing sweet melodies with words.[49]

In fact, in Luther's estimation, music was so important to life in general and to ministry in particular that he did not believe that one should become a teacher or a preacher without some musical skill. To quote:

> I always love music; who so has skill in this art, is of a good temperament, fitted for all things. We must teach music in schools; a schoolmaster ought to have skill in music, or I would not regard him. Neither should we ordain young men as preachers, unless they have been well exercised in music.[50]

Jonathan Edwards

As is well known Edwards had a very high regard for singing, believing that "Tis plain from the Scripture that it is the tendency

---

48. M. Luther, 'Preface to Georg Rhau's Symphonoiae iucundae' (1538), in J. Pelikan and H. T. Lehmann (eds.), *Luther's Works*, tr. C. M. Jacobs, rev. E. W. Gritsch, 55 vols. (Saint Louis: Concordia; Philadelphia: Fortress, 1955–86), vol. 53, p. 323.

49. Luther, 'Preface', pp. 321, 323–324.

50. M. Luther, *The Table Talk of Martin Luther*, tr. and ed. William Hazlitt (London: H. G. Bohn, 1857), p. 340.

of true grace to cause persons very much to delight in such religious exercises.'[51] Not surprisingly, Edwards often preached on singing, and in a sermon on Colossians 3:16 argued that 'the ends of it are two: to excite religious and holy affection, and secondly to manifest it'.[52] In his *A Treatise Concerning Religious Affections*, Edwards expands on these points as follows:

> the duty of *singing* praises to God, seems to be appointed wholly to excite and express religious affections. No other reason can be assigned, why we should express ourselves to God in verse, rather than in prose, and do it with music, but only, that such is our nature and frame, that these things have a tendency to move our affections.[53]

Now it must be said (and has already been pointed out in this volume) that Edwards's idea of affections should not be equated with modern concepts of emotions (particularly the non-cognitive variety). However, it is a mistake to think that Edwards's understanding of the affections excludes an emotional dimension. To the contrary, true affection, for Edwards, has a necessary emotional component. On this point Edwards is crystal clear:

> There is a distinction to be made between a mere *notional understanding*, wherein the mind only beholds things in the exercise of a speculative

---

51. J. Edwards, 'A Treatise Concerning Religious Affections', in E. Hickman (ed.), *Works of Jonathan Edwards*, 3rd ed., 2 vols. (Edinburgh: Banner of Truth, 1974), vol. 1, p. 255.

52. J. Edwards, '398. Col. 3:16', in *Sermons, Series II, 1736*, in *Works of Jonathan Edwards Online Vol. 51*, Jonathan Edwards Center at Yale University, available online at <http://edwards.yale.edu/archive?path= aHRocDovL2Vkd2FyZHMueWFsZS5lZHUvY2dpLWJpbi9uZXdwa Glsby9nZXRvYmplY3QucGw/Yy40oOToyNS53amVv>, accessed 12 Sept. 2011.

53. Edwards, 'Religious Affections', p. 242. Edwards defines 'affections' as 'the more vigorous and *sensible exercises of the inclination and will* of the soul' (p. 237, emphasis original).

faculty; and the *sense of the heart*, wherein the mind don't [*sic*] only *speculate* and *behold*, but *relishes* and *feels*.[54]

So to return to the key point: the purpose of singing, in Edwards's estimation, is to excite and express such affections.

Conclusions

What conclusions should be drawn from this study? I am tempted simply to say, 'those who have ears to hear, let them hear'. But I should probably say a little more about the implications of all this for personal growth and for church life.

Implications for personal growth

On the personal front, let me say this: if music and singing are important to you (particularly singing to and of the Lord) and if you find they not only bring you joy but also great comfort, then you are not alone. In fact, you stand in a long line of saints who share the same sense of gratitude for such gifts and abilities and have experienced the same sense of release and reorientation that comes through singing the word of God. This is normal. This is healthy. This is scriptural. This is good.

Now, of course, we are not all the same. We have different bodies, different brains, different personalities and differing emotional responses to most things. What is more, we have different musical tastes. But my encouragement to one and all (but particularly to those who see themselves as 'musically challenged') is to make the best use you can of the gifts of music that God has either given to you, or placed around you. And, in particular, learn to use the voice that God has given you, to sing to him and of him. Luther's encouragement on this score is worth heeding:

> Music is one of the best arts; the notes give life to the text; it expels
> melancholy, as we see in king Saul. Kings and princes ought to maintain

---

54. Ibid., p. 283, emphases original.

music, for great potentates and rulers should protect good and liberal arts and laws; though private people have desire thereunto and love it, yet their ability is not adequate. We read in the Bible, that the good and godly kings maintained and paid singers. Music is the best solace for a sad and sorrowful mind; by it the heart is refreshed and settled again in peace.[55]

In short, we should recognize the good gift that God has given us to nourish our emotional health, and be open to Jeremy Begbie's thought that music and singing may need to play a larger part in our Christian growth than we have hitherto allowed or imagined. It is one of the means that God has provided and that the Holy Spirit uses to help make us people who feel and respond in ways that please him.[56]

Implications for church life

In terms of the implications for church life, it should be clear that music and singing, whilst not of the *esse* (essence or being) of the church, are vital for the *bene esse* (the health or well-being) of the church. So we would be foolish to neglect them – particularly when Scripture commends them so strongly. At the same time we must also be careful to protect them – for there is always the possibility of misusing music and song. As Jeremy Begbie astutely observes, 'If the orientation is askew, or the emotion inappropriate, then manipulation, sentimentality, and emotional self-indulgence are among the ever-present dangers.'[57]

But these dangers can be avoided and, indeed, must be avoided so that as we sing the living and life-giving word of God, music and song can fulfil their divinely appointed office of reintegrating and reorienting us both personally and corporately, binding us together in prayer and praise to God and drawing us out of ourselves and towards each other in genuine love and sympathy.[58]

---

55. Luther, *Table Talk*, pp. 340–341.
56. S. Guthrie, 'Singing in the Body and in the Spirit', *JETS* 46.4 (Dec. 2003), p. 643.
57. Begbie, 'Faithful Feelings', p. 353.
58. Stephen Guthrie puts it like this: 'Music, of course, does not remake us; the Holy Spirit does. But it seems possible that music may be one

Voltaire supposedly once made a remark along the lines that 'if it's too silly to be said it can always be sung' – and no doubt examples could be multiplied to illustrate the validity of this observation. But if the thrust of my argument in this chapter is correct, then I think we can and must say this: if it is important enough to be said, then it *could* (and in the right manner, time and place *should*) also be sung. Why? Because singing helps us to process and express not only the cognitive dimensions of truth but also the emotive dimensions as well. Such are the God-ordained connections between music, singing and the emotions.

---

means by which the Holy Spirit makes us people who feel and respond. We are brought to our senses. We are drawn out of the darkness of self-absorption and become aware of the world around us, our place within and responsibility to it. In song we move in a dance of sympathy with the others who are singing, and by the body are drawn out of ourselves and into the Body' (Guthrie, 'Singing', p. 643).

INDEX OF SCRIPTURE REFERENCES

OLD TESTAMENT

Genesis
1 *178*
1:20 *173*
1:26–27 *102, 187*
1:26–28 *169, 171*
2 *178*
2:7 *171, 172, 173, 177, 178*
4:6 *128*
6:5 *159*
6:6 *124, 187*
6:17 *173*
22:1–18 *99*
31:30 *60*
49:6 *60*

Exodus
3:6–8 *156*
7:3 *123*
7:13 *123*
7:22 *123*
8:15 *123*
15 *247*
15:1–2 *262*

15:2 *263*
15:20 *262*
15:21 *262, 263*
17:1–7 *124*

Numbers
11:4 *52, 133*
11:8 *46, 64*
11:34–35 *60*

Deuteronomy
1:27 *97*
4:24 *237*
6:5 *175, 235, 245*
12:15 *60*
12:20–21 *60*
29:28 *236*
30:6 *251*
32:11 *135*

Joshua
9:6 *120*

Judges
10:16 *123*

1 Samuel
6:13 *152*

2 Samuel
1 *247*
7:12 *152*
18:31 – 19:7 *99*

1 Kings
19:11–12 *148*

2 Kings
13:23 *97*

1 Chronicles
16:8–13 *265*
16:36 *265*

2 Chronicles
8:6 *60*
36:15 *97*

Nehemiah
8:9 *190*

Psalms

2:7 *152*
3 – 7 *266*
5 *265*
6 *265*
8 *187*
8:4 *175*
10:3 *60*
10:17 *60*
13 *265*
21:2 *61*
22 *265*
22:1 *106*
30:5 *198*
33:6 *147*
34:8 *91*
34:18 *244*
36:7–10 *55*
42 *265*
51 *265*
51:17 *244*
69 *265*
78:23–31 *60*
78:38 *97*
86:15 *97*
88 *55, 265*
89:26–27 *152*
90:4 *135*
95:9 *124*
98:1–6 *264*
103:5 *61*
103:13–14 *187*
104:30 *145*
106:14 *60, 133*
110:1 *156, 157*
111:1 *235*
111:4 *97*
112:4 *97*
112:10 *60*
127:5 *61*
139:13–14 *187*
140:8 *60*
145:8 *97*
146 – 150 *266*

Proverbs

10:24 *63*
13:12 *61*
17:1 *46, 64*
17:17 *196*
18:24 *196*

Isaiah

1:5 *128*
3:13–15 *124*
11:2 *152, 154*
12:1–6 *263*
12:2 *263*
12:5 *263*
25:7–8 *229*
42:1 *152*
51:11 *186*
60:4 *120*

Jeremiah

8:10–12 *124*
8:18–22 *124*
8:21–22 *136*
9:1 *136*
9:10 *136*
12:15 *97*
32:31–32 *124*

Lamentations

2:6 *124*
3:32 *97*

Ezekiel

16:43 *124*

Daniel

9 *247*
12:1–3 *231*

Hosea

4:4–6 *124*
9:15 *97*
14:2 *237*

Joel

2:28–32 *156*

Micah

7:19 *97*

Malachi

1:3 *97*

NEW TESTAMENT

Matthew

3:17 *152*
5:28 *61*
6:13 *64*
8:15 *98*
9:20 *98*
9:36 *25, 180*
13:15 *222*
13:17 *62*
14:14 *25*
15:32 *25*
18:27 *25, 26*
20:34 *25, 98*
23:37–39 *136*
26:39 *130*
26:41 *64*
27:46 *106*

Mark

1:11 *152*
1:14–45 *119*
1:22 *119*
1:23 *119*
1:32–33 *119*
1:40–45 *116, 118, 123, 126*
1:41 *117, 118*
1:43 *117, 118*
2:1 *119*
3:1–6 *116, 126*
3:5 *117, 119, 123, 124, 151*
3:6 *119*
3:7 – 6:6 *119*

3:35 *120*
4:19 *61, 63, 133*
4:20 *120*
4:40 *120*
5:34 *120*
5:36 *120*
6:1–6 *116, 119, 126*
6:6 *117, 118, 120, 125*
6:6 – 8:21 *120*
6:8 *120*
6:30–44 *116, 126*
6:34 *117, 120, 124*
6:37 *120*
6:38 *120*
6:41 *120*
6:44 *120*
6:52 *120*
7:1–5 *117*
7:2 *120*
7:5 *120*
7:27–29 *120*
8:1–10 *116, 126*
8:2 *117, 120, 124*
8:2–3 *117*
8:3 *120*
8:4 *120*
8:5 *120*
8:6 *120*
8:11–12 *117*
8:11–13 *116, 126*
8:12 *124*
8:14 *120*
8:14–21 *120*
8:16 *120*
8:17 *120*
8:19 *120*
10:13–16 *116, 126*
10:14 *117*
10:17–31 *116, 126*
10:21 *117, 118*
14:32–42 *116, 117, 126*
14:33 *117*
14:33–34 *117, 123*
14:36 *161*

14:38 *64*
15:34 *106*

Luke
1:1–4 *137*
1:3 *138*
1:78 *25, 134*
1 – 2 *247*
3:22 *152*
4:2 *154*
4:10–11 *135*
4:13 *64*
4:16–30 *126*
4:25–27 *135*
4:28 *125*
5:12–16 *126*
5:13 *133*
6:6–11 *125, 126*
6:36 *30, 135*
7:1–10 *132*
7:9 *133*
7:11–17 *132, 134*
7:13 *133*
7:16 *214*
8:13 *64*
8:14 *46, 64*
9:10–17 *126*
10:18 *230*
10:21 *134*
10:21–22 *152*
10:21–24 *132*
10:33 *26, 134*
11:4 *64*
11:36 *230*
12:49–50 *133*
12:49–53 *132*
12:50 *133*
13 *135*
13:24 *131*
13:31 *135*
13:31–35 *132*
13:34 *133, 135, 136*
15:16 *62*
15:20 *26, 134, 135*

16 *178*
16:21 *62*
17:22 *62*
17:24 *230*
18:15–17 *126*
18:18–30 *126*
19:41 *133, 136*
19:41–44 *132*
22:14–23 *132*
22:15 *52, 62, 63, 133*
22:28 *64*
22:39–46 *126*
22:40 *64*
22:43–44 *126, 128, 130*
22:45 *125*
22:46 *64*
23:55 *227, 231*
23:55 – 24:1 *229*
23:55 – 24:8 *212, 223*
23:56 *227, 228, 231*
24:1 *226, 227, 228, 231*
24:2 *229, 230, 231*
24:3 *229, 230, 231*
24:4 *223, 224, 230*
24:5 *223, 224, 226, 231*
24:6 *225*
24:6–7 *232*
24:8 *232*
24:11 *224*
24:12 *224*
24:21 *224, 231*
24:22 *224*
24:32 *224*
24:37 *224*
24:38 *224*
24:41 *224*
24:52 *224*
24:53 *224*

John
8:44 *61, 133*
8:58 *156*
11:35 *101*
11:38 *180*

John (*cont.*)
11:39 *228*
13:34 *192*
17:4–5 *100*
18:36 *131*

Acts
1:18 *25*
2:17 *156*
2:17–18 *251*
2:33 *142, 156, 251*
2:33–36 *157*
2:36 *156*
2:39 *120*
10:45 *251*
15:32 *239*
15:39 *236*
18:5 *133*
18:25 *241*
20:2 *239*
20:7–12 *239*
20:19 *64*
20:33 *61*

Romans
1:3–4 *156*
1:9–13 *250*
1:24 *61*
1:26 *64*
2:14–16 *198*
3:4 *112*
5:5 *55, 250, 251*
5:6 *251*
5:6–11 *251*
5:8 *55*
6:12 *61*
7:5 *64*
7:7 *61*
7:7–8 *61*
7:19 *161*
7:23 *180*
7:24 *161*
8:1 *87*
8:6 *158*

8:9–10 *241*
8:11 *163*
8:12–16 *241*
8:14 *145, 157*
8:15 *161*
8:16 *161*
8:17 *161*
8:18 *64*
8:20 *161*
8:23 *162, 163, 181*
8:26 *164*
8:27 *164*
8:29 *168*
9:1 *28*
9:1–5 *28*
9:2 *28*
9:3 *28*
9:15 *30*
11:33–36 *192*
12:1 *30, 237, 239, 241*
12:1–2 *192*
12:2 *252*
12:3–21 *252*
12:6–8 *239*
12:10–15 *240*
12:11 *241*
12:12 *244*
12:14 *242*
12:15 *242*
13:9 *61*
13:14 *62*
15:30 *55, 240*
15:30–32 *250*

1 Corinthians
1:10 *239*
2:12 *252*
2:13 *252*
4:16 *29*
9:25 *131*
10:6 *60*
10:13 *64*
11:1 *29*
12:7 *251*

12:26 *242*
12 – 14 *251*
14:15 *242*
14:23–25 *252*
14:31 *239*
15:35–49 *178*
15:42–44 *178*

2 Corinthians
1 *192*
1:3 *30*
1:5 *64*
1:7 *64*
1:23 *27*
1:23 – 2:11 *27*
1:24 *28*
2:1–2 *28*
2:3 *28*
2:4 *28*
2:7 *28*
2:11 *27*
3:14–15 *90*
3:18 *175, 267*
4:2 *25*
4:8–9 *33*
4:10–11 *33*
4:12 *33*
4:17 *57*
5:2 *24*
5:19 *156*
6:12 *25*
7:8–10 *244*
7:15 *25*
10:1 *239, 240*
11:2 *26*
11:28–29 *28*

Galatians
4:14 *64*
5:16 *62, 268*
5:17 *62*
5:19–22 *48*
5:22 *55, 251*
5:24 *61, 64*

Ephesians
1:9–10 *150, 156*
1:15–22 *248*
1:17 *252*
1:18 *203*
1:23 *200*
2:3 *62*
2:13 *120*
3:14–19 *248*
3:17 *269*
3:19 *269*
4:13 *269*
4:15 *267*
4:22 *62*
4:24 *175*
4:32 – 5:1 *30*
5:17 *268*
5:18 *268*
5:18–19 *242*
5:18–21 *267, 269*
5:19–21 *268*
6:18 *242*
6:19–20 *249*

Philippians
1:3–11 *248*
1:8 *23, 25, 30, 33, 230*
1:23 *62, 63*
1:29 *191*
1:30 *131*
2:1 *25*
2:1–2 *30*
2:3 *30*
2:5–11 *30, 101*
2:8 *30*
2:9–11 *157*
3:10 *64*
3:15 *252*
4:2 *239*
4:9 *29*

Colossians
1:3–14 *248*
1:8 *55*

1:15 *175*
1:16–17 *150*
1:24 *64*
1:29 *131*
2:1 *131*
2:9–10 *269*
3:3 *179*
3:5 *62, 64*
3:12 *25, 30*
3:16 *269, 274*
3:17 *269*
4:3–4 *250*

1 Thessalonians
1:6 *29*
1 – 3 *240*
2:2 *131*
2:3–4 *239*
2:12 *239*
2:17 *62, 63*
2:17 – 3:9 *27*
3:2 *239*
3:10 *250*
4:1 *239, 240*
4:5 *62, 64*
4 – 5 *240*
5:19 *241*
5:20–21 *241*
5:23 *181*

2 Thessalonians
3:1–2 *250*

1 Timothy
1:13 *26*
1:14 *26*
3:1 *62*
4:13 *239*
6:9 *61, 63, 64*
6:12 *131*

2 Timothy
1:4 *24*
1:7 *55*

2:22 *62*
3:6 *61*
3:11 *64*
4:3 *61*

Titus
2:12 *62*
3:3 *46, 62, 64*
3:6 *251*

Philemon
7 *25*
12 *25*
20 *25*

Hebrews
1:3 *114, 156*
2:9–10 *64*
2:14–15 *224*
2:15 *226*
2:17 *190*
3:1 *237*
3:9 *64*
3:12 *236*
3:13 *236, 239*
4:14 *237*
4:14–16 *248*
4:15 *98, 114, 154, 190*
5:7 *237*
5:12 *239*
6:10 *238*
6:11 *62*
7:25 *157*
9:14 *237*
10:23 *237*
10:24–25 *236, 239*
10:25 *236*
10:32 *64*
10:34 *237, 238*
11:7 *237*
12:28 *237*
13:1–4 *238*
13:14 *237*

Hebrews (*cont.*)
13:15 *238*
13:15–16 *237*
13:16 *238*
13:21 *238*
13:22 *236, 239*

James
1:2 *64*
1:12 *64*
1:14–15 *63*
1:17 *200*
3:13 – 4:12 *46*
3:14 *46*
3:16 – 4:1 *46*
4:1 *46, 64*
4:1–2 *63*
4:3 *46, 64*
5:13 *255*

1 Peter
1:6 *64*
1:8 *196*
1:11 *64*
1:12 *62*
1:14 *61*
2:2 *24*
2:11 *43, 61*
3:8 *30*
4:3 *61*

4:12 *64*
4:13 *64*
5:1 *64*
5:9 *64*

2 Peter
1:4 *62, 163*
2:9 *64*
2:10 *62*
2:13 *46, 64*
2:18 *62*
3:3 *61*

1 John
1:8–10 *248*
2:2 *157*
2:16–17 *63*
3:17 *25, 30*
4:19–21 *251*

Jude
16 *61*
18 *62*

Revelation
3:10 *64*
7:9–12 *200*
9:6 *62*
18:14 *61, 63*
21:4 *112*

APOCRYPHA

1 Esdras
1.22 *124*

2 Maccabees
2.26 *129*
3.14 *131*
3.16 *131*
15.19 *131*

4 Maccabees
1.20 *46*
1.24 *46*
1.28 *46*
1.33 *46*
5.23 *46*
6.35 *46*
7.8 *129*
9.31 *46*

Sirach
30.21 *128*
30.23 *128*
38.18 *128*

Wisdom
7.2 *46, 64*
16.20 *46, 64*

Faithful Feelings
*Emotion in the
New Testament*
Matthew Elliott

ISBN: 9781844740796
320 pages, paperback

Everything we do, say and think is, in some sense, emotional.
We describe ourselves and our experiences in terms of how
we feel.

In this significant new study, Matthew Elliott asks, 'What is an
emotion?', and applies recent studies of emotion to the New
Testament. While he discusses the vocabulary of emotion
– love, joy, hope, jealousy, fear, sorrow, anger – his primary
concern is with emotion itself, how it was perceived by the
New Testament writers in their cultural context, and what role
they thought it should play in the lives of Christian believers.
He argues that our feelings play an essential role in Christian
faith, theology and ethics.

*'This book shows originality in its choice of subject, in the
application of current research in psychology to ancient texts,
in the comprehensiveness of its scope, and to some extent in
the interpretation of individual texts. There is no other book
that covers the same ground, and the topic is an important
one.'* I. Howard Marshall

discover more great Christian books at www.ivpbooks.com

Full details of all the books from Inter-Varsity Press – including reader reviews, author information, videos and free downloads – are available on our website at **www.ivpbooks.com**.

IVP publishes a wide range of books on various subjects including:

Biography

Christian Living

Bible Studies

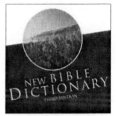
Reference

Commentaries

Theology

On the website you can also sign up for regular email newsletters, tell others what you think about books you have read by posting reviews, and locate your nearest Christian bookshop using the *Find a Store* feature.

IVP publishes Christian books that are **true to the Bible** and that **communicate the gospel, develop discipleship** and **strengthen the church** for its mission in the world.